Our Encounters with Stalking

Edited by

*Sam Taylor, Alec Grant and
Helen Leigh-Phippard*

PCCS BOOKS
Monmouth

First published 2017

PCCS Books Ltd
Wyastone Business Park
Wyastone Leys
MONMOUTH
NP25 3SR
UK
Tel +44 (0)1600 891 509
www.pccs-books.co.uk

Our Encounters with Stalking

A CIP catalogue record for this book is available from the British Library

ISBN 978 1 910919 24 8

Cover designed in the UK by Nick Podd
Printed in the UK by Imprint Digital, Exeter

Contents

Conclusions and reflections

Acknowledgements

We would like to thank the following people and organisations who contributed to this book and without whom this publication would not have been possible:

- all the writers who contributed to this book, who have given their time to share their personal and professional experiences of stalking with the passion to make a difference to people affected by it
- Catherine Jackson and colleagues at PCCS Books for their professional, patient and kind support throughout the sometimes challenging process of producing this book
- Alec Grant, who originally came up with the idea to publish collections of narratives by 'experts by experience' in 2011 – brilliant!

All royalties from the sale of this book will go to Veritas-Justice, a local stalking advocacy service based in Sussex, which also continues to support people affected by stalking through Writing for Recovery and peer support groups.

Editors and contributors

Editors

Dr Alec Grant is now an independent scholar, having retired from his position as Reader in Narrative Mental Health in the School of Health Sciences at the University of Brighton in May 2017. He qualified as a mental health nurse in the mid-1970s, and went on to study psychology, social science and psychotherapy. He is widely published in the fields of ethnography, autoethnography, narrative inquiry, clinical supervision, cognitive behavioural psychotherapy, and communication and interpersonal skills. He originated the *Our Encounters...* PCCS book series with the late Professor Fran Biley of Bournemouth University, and was lead editor of the first two books in this series, *Our Encounters with Madness* (2011) and *Our Encounters with Suicide* (2013).

Helen Leigh-Phippard has a PhD in international relations and was a university lecturer until she developed mental health problems in the late 1990s and was diagnosed with psychotic depression. In late 2004, she joined Brighton & Hove Mind's LiVE (Listening to the Voice of Experience) project and, since then, has been actively engaged in local service user participation. She contributes to the development and delivery of training to local mental health service providers, to the training of nurses and paramedics at Brighton University and psychologists at the University of Sussex and to the development of research within Sussex Partnership Trust as a member of the trust's Lived Experience Advisory Forum (LEAF). She contributed to the first book in this series, *Our Encounters with Madness* (2011).

Sam Taylor is co-founder and Director of Veritas-Justice, an independent stalking advocacy service. In 2011 Sam gave evidence and was instrumental in the stalking law reform campaign, having experienced four years of stalking by her former partner. This landmark campaign led, on 25 November 2012, to stalking becoming a criminal offence in England and Wales. Sam is an accredited independent stalking advocate and a lecturer/trainer, developing and delivering sessions on stalking to multi-agency professionals. She has a Masters in creative writing and personal development and runs Writing for Recovery courses for people who have been affected by stalking and mental health problems.

Contributors

After her daughter Clare's murder in September 2005, **Tricia Bernal** began to campaign and, with two other mothers, set up the Clare, Rana and Tania Trust, speaking at conferences about their daughters' cases, and raising awareness of stalking and the need for early intervention. Tricia went on to co-found the charity PAS (Protection Against Stalking). She travels the country talking of the danger signs of stalking, and assists in the training of police officers, judges, magistrates, independent domestic violence advocates and other relevant agencies. In 2010, along with Suzy Lamplugh Trust and Network for Surviving Stalking, PAS helped to instigate the first national helpline for stalking victims. In 2012, PAS received the Dod's Charity of the Year award and Campaigning Charity of the Year for leading a parliamentary evidence-gathering campaign to highlight the need for a specific stalking law. This was passed in the record time of 10 months. Tricia is also a family support worker for the charity Advocacy after Fatal Domestic Abuse, supporting and giving advocacy to families through the review process, inquests and hearings. She sits on the Home Office QA Panel assessing domestic homicide reviews and also on the Association of Chief Police Officers stalking and harassment working group.

Hetti Barkworth-Nanton is an experienced business leader with over 25 years in commercial programme and finance leadership, gained in leading organisations such as Vodafone, BT, Centrica and British Airways. Hetti is also committed to broader change in society, developing up-and-coming leaders through facilitation at Windsor Leadership, a cross-sector leadership development trust. She is an active campaigner for the elimination of domestic abuse after her best friend, Jo, became a victim of domestic homicide in 2010, which inspired her to set up, with Jo's mother Diana Parkes, the Joanna Simpson Foundation, which focuses on the needs of children affected by domestic abuse and homicide. The Foundation has worked with senior policy makers across the public sector, resulting in the first ever legal guidance to prosecutors in domestic homicide trials, including a specific set of requirements on the handling of child witnesses. The Foundation's first investment has introduced ground-breaking early intervention therapy for children bereaved through domestic homicide. She is also a Pioneer for Safelives, was instrumental in encouraging the Duchess of Cornwall to speak out about domestic abuse in 2016, and recently established the Centre for Generational Reform.

Professor Jim Barnes is a chartered psychologist and an Associate Fellow of the British Psychological Society (BPS). His personal research interests focus on the neuropsychological aspect of cognition, particularly psychosis and hallucinations in clinical patients and the general population. He did his PhD at the Institute of Psychiatry in London under the supervision of Professor Tony David, before moving to Birkbeck and then Oxford Brookes University. Jim has been involved in a variety of projects with individuals with Parkinson's disease, exploring their visual hallucinations and the ways in which they deal with their symptoms. His interest in coaching psychology and its use with clinical patients led him to be a founder member of the BPS Special Ggroup in Coaching Psychology.

Richard Bates began his policing career in 1998, having graduated from the University of Oxford. Serving first with Thames Valley Police, Richard undertook a broad range of both uniform and strategic roles before transferring to Sussex in 2010 as a uniformed sergeant. Promoted to Detective Inspector in 2011, Richard developed an interest in dealing with serious and complex investigations, leading teams of detectives in both Eastbourne and Uckfield. Following his promotion to Chief Inspector in 2014, Richard served as Head of the Local Policing Branch before moving into the Public Protection command and back into the detective field. As head of Brighton's Safeguarding Investigation Unit, Richard leads a team of specialist police officers and police staff, responding to and investigating reports of child abuse, sexual violence and abuse, domestic abuse and other offences committed against vulnerable adults. As a member of the Public Protection command team, Richard holds the portfolio lead for adult safeguarding.

Liz Godfrey has stood witness to the battles fought to promote safety for women and children. From the cries of Erin Pizzey in 1971, through to stalking law legislation in 2012, Liz has both seen and experienced the injustices of the social and judicial systems of this country over many decades. Her strengths and motivations are inspired by the humbling stories of heroism and sacrifice made by women, with women and for women, which provide the backdrop for much of Liz's history.

Rachel Griffin joined Suzy Lamplugh Trust from Victim Support, where she managed projects and policy relating to domestic violence, police and crime commissioners and partnership working. Previously she was at Voice for the Child in Care, where she established the Alliance for Child-centred Care. Before going into policy and development, Rachel was a fundraiser for five years, first at the National Deaf Children's Society and then at The Prince's Trust. She was a trustee of the Prisoners' Education Trust from 2003 until 2011 and she began her career as Vice-President (women) at Oxford University Student Union, after graduating in Modern Languages.

Peter James is one of the UK's most treasured crime and thriller novelists. His Roy Grace detective novels have sold more than 18 million copies worldwide in total. The series is now published in 37 territories. Educated at Charterhouse, and then at film school, Peter is an established film producer. He has produced numerous films, including *The Merchant of Venice*, starring Al Pacino. He has an Honorary Doctorate from the University of Brighton in recognition of his services to literature and the community, is patron of Neighbourhood Watch nationwide, patron of Crimestoppers in Sussex, patron of Brighton & Hove Samaritans, and patron of Relate, among many other charitable posts. He has twice been Chair of the Crime Writers' Association and has won many literary awards, including the publicly voted ITV3 Crime Thriller Awards People's Bestseller Dagger, and he was shortlisted for the Wellcome Trust Book Prize. He won the US Barry Award for Best British Crime Novel in 2012 and in 2015 was voted by WH Smith readers as The Best Crime Author of All Time. Born and brought up in Brighton, Peter divides his time between his homes in London and Sussex. Find out more about Peter James at www.panmacmillan.com and Peter's website www.peterjames.com

Claudia Miles is a qualified solicitor with a Masters in human rights and gender studies. Her specific interest in research and practice incorporates the issues of stalking particularly in the context of the family court process and how they are addressed and responded to by our legal system. Claudia has worked extensively in both private practice and the academic sector, and through that time she has gained varied and valuable experience on the many legal and personal challenges faced by women and their children going through legal proceedings in the Family Court. Claudia is an accredited Independent Stalking Advocate and facilitates training and support for individuals and organisations in safeguarding, stalking, DASH and litigant-in-person workshops.

Anna Stanley is 22. After surviving the difficult years with her mother's abusive partner, she obtained a degree in philosophy. She now works with people who have mental health problems. She is interested in forging a career with people who suffer with anxiety and post-traumatic stress disorder after having to process the issues which arose after she and her mother became safe again.

Naomi Stanley was born in Canada and lives in Sussex, England. She has three adult daughters. Naomi is a former photographer and nurse, and has now retired. At the same time as coping with being stalked by her ex-partner, she was a whistleblower on Jimmy Savile and Broadmoor. Currently, she is in remission from cancer and writing her autobiography. She likes walking on the beach, gardening, photography, cats and writing.

Dr Emma Short is based at the University of Bedfordshire. She is a chartered psychologist, Associate Fellow of the British Psychological Society (BPS) and a registered psychologist with the Health and Care Professions Council. As Director of the National Centre for Cyberstalking Research, she is a researcher in online behaviour. Emma's research has identified that the impact of sustained online threat that characterises cyberstalking poses significant risk, with many victims reporting clinical levels of post-traumatic stress disorder.

On 19 August 2011, **Rachel Williams** became a survivor of an attempted murder through domestic abuse. Her estranged husband shot her with a sawn-off shot gun, and then pummelled her. Six weeks later her 16-year-old son Jack took his life. Rachel has turned her mess into her message, and has vowed to see change with domestic violence in her lifetime. She highlights the need to engage with survivors of domestic abuse and the need to listen to them/us. Rachel hated the 'Victim' label and soon shook it off; she is now a Victor, who is campaigning and working with the Welsh Government, the police, Welsh Women's Aid and Llanelli Women's Aid to find a cure for this epidemic called domestic abuse. She is an Ambassador for Children Matter (Welsh Women's Aid) and also an Ambassador for Llanelli Women's Aid. She is keen to work with those who are on the same mission.

Kristiana Wrixon managed the set-up and launch of the National Stalking Helpline at Suzy Lamplugh Trust between 2010 and 2015. In that time, she provided advice and support to thousands of people affected by stalking. Further to this, Kristiana led on stalking policy for Suzy Lamplugh Trust between 2010 and 2016. She was involved in the successful campaign for the introduction of a specific law against stalking in England and Wales, and advocated for the needs of stalking victims as part of the Home Office Violence Against Women and Girls Working Group, the Crown Prosecution Service's Violence Against Women and Girls External Consultation Group, and the National Police Chiefs Council's stalking working group. In 2014, Kristiana completed an MSc with the National Centre for Cyberstalking Research. Kristiana is currently Head of Research at the charity leaders' network ACEVO, where she works to champion the independence, expertise and value of civil society leaders.

Editors' note: We wish to acknowledge the writers of all the contributions written anonymously.

Foreword

Peter James

I'm blessed to have many readers who sign their communications to me as my 'Number One Fan'. Normally, that is just good humoured. They email, Facebook or Instagram me, or we talk on Twitter. I love having an open relationship with my readers and get a huge amount of feedback from it. Over the years, through interacting with them, I've built up a great research resource in a wide range of fields, from details of operating room procedures to, somewhat pedantically, 3,000 words explaining to me the difference between cement and concrete. And I once learned all about picking locks from a retired burglar fan – well, he said he was retired...

But there is a difference between those who write to me maybe once or twice a year and someone who writes many, many times a day, every day. When does a fan cross the line and turn into a stalker?

When it happened to me it started fairly low key. As a passionate supporter of libraries and bookstores of all kinds, both chain and, in particular, independents, I do events all over the UK, pretty much all year around, and regularly meet fans at book signings and at talks.

I was speaking at an event in Ipswich about 12 years ago, and noticed a woman in her mid-30s smiling at me very intently from the audience, as if she knew me, although I did not recognise her. I expected her to come up to me at the end and say hello, and probably get a book signed, but instead she vanished, like a ghost.

A week later I did a talk in Glasgow and saw a woman smiling and staring at me intently again. I thought she looked a bit familiar, but did not make the connection, and then I did a talk in Cardiff and she was there again. This went on for about a year. She turned up to every talk or event I did, anywhere in the UK, but always just sitting in the audience. Then she started coming up to me to get a book signed.

It began to get more serious when emails started coming. First, she wrote messages about how smart I looked in my black t-shirt, or that she liked the way I smiled at her. Then, if she was not going to be able to get to one of my events, for instance at a library in Winchester, she would apologise in advance, saying she hoped I would be OK if she was not there to support me.

Of course, I thought, I will be fine! I initially replied out of courtesy, but she would respond to any of my emails within minutes. Then, if I did not write back, another email would soon come, in which she said how worried she was that she hadn't heard from me and was I OK? She would write, 'It's been five hours. I am so worried you are lying unconscious somewhere.' You can put this down to someone simply being a bit obsessive, but it made me very uncomfortable.

I got very spooked one day when she sent me a photograph of her Peter James collection. It was like looking at a serial killer's dungeon. An entire wall, with candles burning in sconces at either end. On this wall were covers of every book I had ever written, including ones where I had only contributed a chapter as part of an anthology, and, even more scary, photographs taken with a long lens of me and my then partner coming out of bars and restaurants all around the UK, and, worse still, photographs taken from within the grounds of our very isolated and secluded Sussex home. It was like a shrine. Very creepy.

That was the point when I talked to the police and they did background checks on her. She didn't have any criminal history, and they thought she was probably just a harmless obsessive, but they warned me to take security precautions, saying there was nothing they could do unless she attacked me. Fortunately, for others in this position, the law has since changed.

We installed a £20,000 electric security system in and around our house and grounds. I was reminded of *Misery*, by Stephen King, and his obsessive fan who rescues him from a car crash before breaking his legs so he can't escape.

It got to the stage where, if I left a public event in the dark, I would check the streets for her. Our home was in a very remote area and our nearest neighbour was half a mile away. Despite the security system, we did not feel particularly safe after the situation began to become more serious. One night, when I was away in New York, someone tried to break in. As luck would have it, the camera pointing at the patio doors, where the intruder had smashed a pane, was not working, so we never knew if it was her. But whoever it was, the dogs – one of them a German Shepherd – scared them away.

After that, we made the decision to move. The attempted break-in was a major factor, but we might have felt differently had this not been going on. It was a definite trigger.

I do a huge amount of research into criminals and criminal minds. I am not saying she is a criminal, though. But, almost invariably, with a criminal there is an escalation. For example, during my research for my novel *Dead Like You*, which deals with the subject of rape, I read cases of many people who start out as minor offenders, such as flashers. That can escalate to rape, and even to murder. So, you have to look at it and ask, '*What is the tipping point?*'

As part of the research for my novel *Not Dead Yet*, featuring a female rock superstar turned actress who has a stalker threatening to kill her, I met and interviewed a number of obsessive Madonna fans. One was in the north of England. She was in her 30s and had a job in a law firm, but her entire life was Madonna. The upstairs of her home was dedicated to Madonna. She had spent £300,000 on seeing her concerts and on Madonna paraphernalia – even £150 on a balloon that was used in one of her shows.

In my past career in the film industry, I worked with many stars, including Al Pacino, Sharon Stone and Robert De Niro. But these people were shielded. If Madonna goes for a jog, she is surrounded by bodyguards. But at the same time, they need the oxygen of publicity. And they need their fans.

For years this woman would buy a book at almost every signing, so at one level she was definitely a good customer!

I get face blindness at times, if I am doing a big event, and I will not recognise someone out of context – for instance, a police officer who I know very well and who turns up out of uniform.

At an event in Leicester, my book was placed on the table and I looked up, but my mind had gone blank suddenly, and I could not remember her name. I asked her what name she would like it written to. She just shouted 'Mine!' and stormed off. Later on, she emailed me 10,000 angry words, saying, 'I have been your number one fan for the last 10 years and I can't believe you can't remember my name.'

I didn't hear from her again for two years, and that was a big relief. But, just as I was starting to think that was the end of it, in 2013, I was doing a book signing in Bristol and a hardback of my then most recent novel, *Perfect People*, was suddenly slammed down on my table.

xvi   OUR ENCOUNTERS WITH STALKING

I looked up and it was her. 'I have decided to forgive you,' she said. Great!

Every book I have ever written has some of my life experiences in it. But the Roy Grace thriller, *Not Dead Yet*, is the first one that was directly influenced by something truly scary that happened in my life. It tells the story of an obsessed fan who finally gets to meet the celebrity she loves but who goes murderously to pieces when she's rebuffed.

Around the time this book was published, in 2013, I did an interview with the *Daily Telegraph* and opened up to them about my stalker, essentially outing her. They ran with it as a full-page story, and it was picked up by a number of other papers and radio stations around the country.

It was the first positive action I had taken towards confronting my stalker. I had never confronted her directly and still have not. In a way, I didn't want to upset her, and I tried to play it down and hoped maybe her focus would shift elsewhere. Also, I was always worried direct confrontation might inflame the situation. Yet this 'outing' seems – so far at least – to have worked, and I've not heard from her in over three years. Perhaps it made her pause and reflect.

But I will never be totally sure I am free of her attention, although I know now that at least I can turn to the police if the situation ever escalates again. I'm hoping it does not.

As I said at the start, most of my fans are lovely and fun to engage with, and I've not let one bad experience cause me to retreat into a shell. But it has taught me just how terrifying it is when a stranger out there not only knows your every move, but also feels they have some kind of a claim on your soul.

Some people have not been so lucky. For another novel I wrote on the subject of stalking, I talked at length with a lovely lady, Trish Bernal. In 2005, her daughter Claire, 22, was working in the Beauty Department of Harvey Nichols in Knightsbridge and briefly dated a security guard there, 30-year-old Michael Pech. When she ended the relationship, he began to stalk her obsessively. Then, one day, he came into the store at closing time and shot her dead.

That is the ultimate nightmare for all victims of stalking – the obsessive who makes their victim live a life of fear, never knowing when he or she might strike – or what with. Sadly, the law today can only protect a potential victim so far. No law can ever protect a victim totally. And even when the offender is jailed, the victim lives with the fear that the stalker might one day be released and continue their deadly agenda, even more angry.

Preface

Sam Taylor

Helen, Alec and I began working together in 2011, following the publication of *Our Encounters with Madness*, a collection of mental health service user, carer and survivor narratives. Many of the contributors to that book told us how therapeutic it was to write about their experiences, and this inspired Alec and Helen to set up the Writing for Recovery community group. They successfully applied for Awards for All Lottery funding to run a series of service user-led creative writing groups, and later that year invited me to facilitate the groups.

The writing groups proved to be a positive and healing process for participants. They described feeling empowered through writing and sharing their stories, and at the end of courses we published an anthology of the work produced during the year. The experiences struck a chord with me in relation to the campaign work I was involved in, raising awareness about stalking, my own experience of being stalked, and its significant psychological impact.

The writing group participants felt stigmatised, betrayed and let down by 'the system' and were passionate about wanting to dispel myths of mental health illness, in just the same way that victims of stalking say they feel. These similarities inspired us to run the same project the following year, but this time for people who had experience of stalking, either personally or through their work.

Again, the participants fed back about the cathartic benefits from the writing process, and we produced an anthology of writings by the group, called *Talking Stalking*. We ran an event in 2015 where contributors presented their writing, which was both empowering for the authors and had a significant impact on people who attended the event, raising their awareness of what is it like to be stalked.

The natural progression from there was to produce a book on *Our Encounters with Stalking*. It was our belief that a collection of authentic voices of people with first-hand experience would speak directly and meaningfully to the reader, make a significant difference to current perceptions of stalking, and reach a wider audience.

It has taken considerable courage for the contributors to come forward to contribute to this book. For us, gathering national and international contributions was more challenging, for a variety of reasons. People were understandably reluctant to revisit their trauma; others were worried that it could put them at a greater risk (despite the option to remain anonymous), and some people's cases were ongoing so they couldn't write about them for legal reasons.

As you will hear from the first-hand experiences in this book, stalking is an incredibly complex crime, and learning and research in this field is developing all the time. We appeal to all those working in the sector to seek out and be always open to new learning, and, most emphatically, always to believe the victim. Our aim with this book is to challenge assumptions about vulnerability and about who the victims of stalking are and how they become victims, because stalking is a crime that can happen to anyone, and everyone has the right to live a life free from fear.

September 2017

Introduction

Alec Grant

Dictionary definitions of stalking include 'a person who harasses another person... in an aggressive, often threating and illegal manner', or 'a person who harasses another person, as a former lover, a famous person etc, in an aggressive, often threatening and illegal manner'. Although it is true that stalking is an illegal act, these definitions seem grossly inadequate in conveying its seriousness, extremely frightening nature, and the threat to the lives, relationships, jobs, financial security, integrity and mental health, and sometimes continued existence, of people who are unfortunate enough to experience it. Stalking at best can terrify, and at worst can kill.

The Crown Prosecution Service (undated) does not define stalking, but describes the offence as 'acts or omissions which, in particular circumstances, are ones associated with stalking. For example, following a person, watching or spying on them or forcing contact with the victim through any means, including social media'. However, Paladin (undated), the national stalking advocacy service, defines stalking as 'a pattern of repeated and persistent unwanted behaviour that is intrusive and engenders fear. It is when one person becomes fixated or obsessed with another and the attention is unwanted. Threats may not be made but victims may still feel scared. Importantly, threats are not required for the criminal offence of stalking to be prosecuted'.

Stalking is similarly defined in this book as 'conduct that constitutes a pattern of intrusions and harassment upon a person in a manner which would cause any reasonable person high levels of anxiety or fear' (Short and Barnes, in chapter 1). Taylor and Miles (chapter 4) describe it as 'a pattern of repeated and persistent behaviour that is intrusive and creates fear'. As will be seen throughout this book, stalking is also frequently associated with domestic violence, with partner and ex-partner abuse.

It is important at this point to unpack the definition provided by Short and Barnes. 'Conduct that constitutes a pattern of intrusions' translates as behaviour by stalkers that follows predictable and often escalating patterns, which, when put together, *are peculiar to the crime that is stalking*. These patterns will also become apparent to readers throughout this book, and are summarised in its concluding chapter.

Stalking is much worse and is much more than just harassment – an unfortunate fact that is often not recognised by people whose job it is to recognise the distinction. In related terms, the phrase '… which would cause any reasonable person high levels of anxiety or fear' signals a further distinction that needs to be made at this point – between reasonable and unreasonable people.

Stalkers are *absolutely not* reasonable people, so appeals to them to change their behaviour on the basis of morality, rationality and decency, made by public, professionals and our state protectors – the police and judiciary – are usually dangerously wasted effort. Unfortunately, just as they trivialise stalking as a bit of harassment, the public, professionals and state protectors often confuse stalkers with reasonable people, or behave towards them as if they are.

The assertion that those who are stalked experience 'high levels of anxiety or fear' is simultaneously true and a huge understatement. Those who are stalked often experience unbearable levels of terror, for very long periods of time. That this can have a damaging effect on physical and mental health is stating the obvious.

Victims

The characteristics and categories of stalkers and stalking, the effects on those who are stalked, and associated problems such as domestic violence in partner and ex-partner stalking, are discussed more fully in the rest of the book. Before you proceed beyond this introduction, however, it will help if you take some time to think critically about the key term that is often used to categorise the people on the wrong end of stalking. This term is 'victim'. Those who are stalked – mostly women, mostly by men – are often referred to as the 'victims of stalking'.

'How should they be described?' you may, reasonably, ask. A victim is a victim is a victim, surely? But it's not that simple. Language is never innocent; it is never simply a vehicle for describing events and people in straightforward, unproblematic ways that everyone can and will agree with in all circumstances and times.

Stalking is a vile act perpetrated mostly by men on those who are stalked, who are mostly women. That said, you may also reasonably think at this point that not all those who are stalked are women. This is of course true, as Peter James's foreword pays testimony to. However, most are, and this fact is significant in the broader context of human oppression in its current political, cultural and relational forms, and in terms of societal and gendered inequality.

Stalking is behaviour perpetrated by someone intent on damaging, hurting, sometimes killing, and certainly controlling another person. What does the word 'victim' actually mean in this context? And what does it mean to talk and write first-hand, lived-experience stories about stalking victimhood – the state of being a stalking victim, which is often gendered abuse of women?

To best answer this question, we need to understand how the language of victimhood in the broader context of human oppression has changed in recent years. The work of Rebecca Stringer (2014) is useful in thinking about this. Stringer argues that, as a style of political, economic and policy population management, the rise in neoliberalism from the 1980s has resulted in the development of specific forms of subjectivity, or self-knowledge, of women and men in modern societies. Key among those forms is the expectation that individuals assume responsibility for managing their lives and selves.

Victimhood

But our neoliberal times are contradictory. We need to look at who has the most power in society, to see the winners and losers in the 'personal responsibility' stakes. It's already apparent that gender power has a part to play in stalking, given the fact that women seem frequently on the receiving end of it.

But what about financial power? Global inequality is directly reflected in the upward distribution of wealth (Wilkinson & Pickett, 2009). The richest one per cent of people currently own more than the rest of the world; fewer than 100 people own as much wealth as half the world's population. And yet we are constantly given the message that we – ordinary, relatively non-privileged people – have *total* agency and responsibility for our lives, that we have *choice*. But choice is a luxury the relatively financially poor can often ill afford and rarely exercise.

The neoliberal message about the victimhood issue emphasises the subjective and psychological over the social and political. In neoliberal terms, victimhood doesn't 'happen to' someone. It somehow arises from inside of them, as a result of their having, for example, a 'victim personality'; or from making bad choices; or from poor risk management in their relationships; or from lack of personal discipline and positive thinking.

Stringer (2014) argues that this neoliberal world view has saturated contemporary consciousness to the extent that it often results in negative media, professional and lay attitudes towards 'victimhood' generally. Complaints about being a victim often evoke relatively unsympathetic responses from the public, and from professionals and the judiciary. These responses seem driven by the assumption that people are not living up to the self-management ideals expected of them in neoliberally governed societies.

As you will see throughout this book, authorities such as the police, the judiciary and other legal and professional services often act dismissively towards people – mostly women – who have been stalked. Their concerns are frequently trivialised; they are regularly treated as if they are 'putting it on'; as if their problems exist in their own minds, rather than in the real world; as though their complaints and behaviour signal 'an unhealthy attitude of resentment brought on by an individual's lack of personal responsibility, rather than a circumstance occasioned by wider social forces and the workings of power' (Stringer, 2014: 2–3).

Victim-blaming

Such 'victim-blaming' clearly deflects attention from the fact that suffering as a result of stalking violence deserves to be regarded as a social, political and collective problem, rather than a psychological, subjective and individual one. If stalking complaints were accepted in this way, they would be taken much more seriously. The consequence of viewing them instead as solely psychological, subjective and individual is that reports of stalking abuse are often trivialised and not taken sufficiently seriously, and those doing the reporting are treated very badly. This fact, backed up by stories of victims' lived experiences, will be repeated throughout this book.

Agency

For as long as our social, legal, judicial, professional, lay and social attitudes are shot through with gendered inequality, stalking is likely to continue to be regarded as simply part of life; as just 'the way things are'. But, contrarily, the neoliberal message is that we don't have to simply accept things 'just as they are'.

Stringer repeatedly points out that, in large part as a consequence of neoliberal population management and self-management, all of us today are expected to act responsibly, on the basis of personal agency. It is almost as if the antidote to being seen and treated negatively as a victim is to take responsibility to alter one's life and personal circumstances for the better.

On one level, with the right support, help and determination, assuming and striving for such agency is of course a reasonable thing to do in response to stalking. But this is only part of a much bigger picture. Gender, financial and material and social environmental constraints limit the power and effectiveness of personal agency. This is in spite of the encouragement and development of related personal qualities and behaviours such as 'resilience' and 'assertiveness' in self-help and facilitated workshops for the disempowered.

Good victims, bad victims and secondary abuse

Another problem with the idea of the power of personal agency is in the ways in which the category 'victim' is sub-divided in the public, professional and statutory consciousness. *Legitimate victims* are perceived to have problems that aren't easily solved, through no fault of their own. This group can be contrasted with resilient, self-determining agents, whose power, resources and support to alter their lives for the better make the 'victim' tag arguably inappropriate.

A further sub-division seems to be between legitimate victims and victims who are not accorded legitimacy. Legitimate victims are frequently romanticised as helpless and innocent, betraying a gendered view of (some) women as the powerless receivers of unreasonable dominance and violence. Legitimate victims are 'good' victims. They are good because they are seen to be forgiving, compliant, and no threat to the political, economic, legal, social and gendered status quo. These good victims are often regarded as genuine – as deserving of help.

In contrast, 'bad' victims are angry, vengeful and threatening to the status quo. They are frequently perceived to be manipulative, undeserving, motivated by resentment, and somehow 'fixated' on suffering. Bad victims are seen to lack credibility and authority, and are more likely to experience a second layer of (state-sanctioned) abuse. According to Stringer, this occurs when criminal justice responses attack and rubbish the complainant's (stalking victim's) credibility.

As a result of this, stalking victims are often positioned and treated as the guilty party, which effectively neutralises and invalidates their complaint. Ironically, the stories in this book testify to the many ways in which society should be deeply grateful to its bad victims.

Taking control

In keeping with the ethos of the *Our Encounters with...* series more generally, we aim in this book to celebrate the value and importance of knowledge grounded in lived experience. Stories of stalking, written by people who have experienced it first hand, will be complemented by professional, academic and third-sector accounts.

Our Encounters with Stalking challenges current unhelpful assumptions and incorrect knowledge about stalking, and attitudes towards the victims of stalking by providing more accurate and helpful ways of thinking and talking about the problem.

We want to help professions, institutions, the lay public and, most importantly, people involved at the victim end of stalking, to engage in a more helpful dialogue. As will become apparent, we hope to contribute to making stalking a *socially validated reality*, where the burden of its reduction and prevention is shifted from the individual to the state, and where stalking is seen as a political, social and economic reality, not solely an individual problem. Most importantly, we want to stop people (mostly women) being constantly regarded as blameworthy agents of their own victimisation, by helping them take back control.

Enabling stalking victims to take more control is reflected in how this book is structured and what it contains. It means helping people generally, and those affected by stalking specifically, find out more about stalking, through:

- de-mystifying and clarifying it
- finding out about the social psychology of stalking: the different forms of stalking; what motivates stalkers; what their characteristics are; the different types of stalker–victim relationships; who is likely to be stalked, and in what ways

- how people in non-statutory (third sector) organisations are combating stalking and influencing policy changes
- what the lived experience of stalking is like for those who have lived through and beyond stalking, either directly or by witnessing it
- making it real
- telling it how it is
- contributing towards the development of a valid and legitimate narrative and language of stalking, by writing it as a socially validated reality.

Socially validated realities

On the basis of the study of trauma in social history, Judith Herman (1997) argues that psychological trauma of any sort always involves an uneasy and unequal relationship between perpetrators, victims and bystanders. Each plays a different role in relation to traumatic events. Bystanders, who in this context can be members of the public, statutory professionals, or members of the police, legal services and judiciary, either witness the trauma event directly, hear and read about it, or discuss it. Perpetrators appeal to bystanders to do nothing. Victims, demanding action, ask bystanders to share the burden and pain of the trauma.

Herman (1997) argues that, in relation to the stalking events, the actions of the perpetrator constitute an 'appeal to the universal desire to see, hear, and speak no evil' (p7). In order to escape accountability for his crimes, the perpetrator's role, in concert with social structures and systems which are supportive of this role, is to promote forgetting. He does this through the deployment of secrecy and silence. If the strategy of secrecy fails, he has a pivotal role in the collective attacking and undermining of the victim and her credibility. If the victim cannot be silenced, he then plays a key part in the process of ensuring that no one listens, through the use of denial and rationalisation (excuses to justify his behaviour).

Bystanders are forced to take sides in a situation where the arguments marshalled in the perpetrator's defence are: the event/s didn't happen; the victim is lying or exaggerating; she brought it on herself; it is time to forget the past and move on. Herman (1997: 8) contends that: 'The more powerful the perpetrator, the greater is his prerogative to name and define reality, and the more completely his arguments prevail.' In this state of affairs, the socially and culturally weakest person – usually the victim – is the one who loses.

What is the broader social and cultural significance of this state of affairs? In terms of their gender, female victims of stalking are always already devalued, simply because they are women. It is in this social and cultural context that habitual ways of trivialising and dismissing the lived experiences of stalked and traumatised women maintains, in Herman's terms, *'socially validated reality'* – or what is regarded as 'right and proper' and 'just the way things are and should be' in our society. This keeps the cultural status quo and power relations untroubled, since the lived experiences of stalking victims always fall outside the realm of this reality.

For this reason, dominant ways of storying and responding to stalking events and victims need to change in a direction that favours and takes seriously the lived experiences of victims and the language they use to describe those experiences. Keeping hold of such 'traumatic reality… requires a social context that affirms and protects the victim and that joins victim and witness in a common alliance' (Herman, 1997: 9). This translates as victims who have the social support of friends, family, groups and informal and formal networks and societal structures. In turn, this requires the development of social and political movements that give a voice to the disempowered. Our book is a contribution towards this.

Chapters in the book

The chapters that follow are grouped according to content and category, although some degree of overlap is inevitable. In 'Setting the Scene' section, chapter 1 deals with the social psychology of stalking, looking at the varieties of stalking, the characteristics of perpetrators, victims and relational and environmental contexts. Chapters 2 and 3 in the next section are written by third-sector experts-by-experience at the UK's National Stalking Helpline and Suzy Lamplugh Trust. They address, respectively, the launch of the helpline, what has been learnt from it, and its future, the experience of working in the stalking sector, and the need to promote awareness of stalking.

The next section is 'The Police and the Courts', which the third-sector advocacy service Veritas-Justice opens with an exploration of the ways in which the Family Court is complicit in acting as the agent of stalkers. Chapter 5 comprises the transcript of the Sentencing Remarks made by the Hon Mr Justice Green at the trial of Michael Lane for the murder of Shana Grice in Sussex, and his statement in relation to the

Independent Police Complaints Commission. Chapter 6 ends this section with the three-way recorded and transcribed conversation between Veritas-Justice and Sussex Police.

Chapters 7 to 22 are the lived-experience stories of stalking victims. Some have decided to be named and others, for safety reasons, have made anonymous contributions.

Chapters 23 and 24, respectively, address the main themes and conclusions that emerge from the book as a whole and reflect on some of the editorial conversations between the editors of the book.

And, finally, there's section with useful contacts and information.

References

Crown Prosecution Service (undated). *Stalking and Harrassment.* [Online.] www.cps.gov.uk/legal/s_to_u/stalking_and_harassment/ (accessed 19 March 2017).

Herman J (1997). *Trauma and recovery: the aftermath of violence – from domestic abuse to political terror.* New York, NY: Basic Books.

Paladin (undated). [Online.] http://paladinservice.co.uk/ (accessed 19 March 2017).

Stringer R (2014). *Knowing Victims: feminism, agency and victim politics in neoliberal times.* London/New York, NY: Routledge.

Wilkinson R, Pickett K (2009). *The Spirit Level: why more equal countries almost always do better.* London: Penguin.

SETTING THE SCENE

1

Psychological effects of stalking

Emma Short and Jim Barnes

Stalking is defined as conduct that constitutes a pattern of intrusions and harassment on a person in a manner that would cause any reasonable person serious alarm, distress or fear of violence (Crown Prosecution Service, undated). Cyberstalking is the ongoing and persistent use of online and digital technology to pursue or intimidate people or groups. In the UK, between 12% and 32% of women report that they have been stalked; for men, the figure is between four per cent and 17% (Weller, Hope & Sheridan, 2013). Figures for cyberstalking are harder to establish, but it is estimated that 39.9% of people who experience stalking are also victims of cyberstalking (Suzy Lamplugh Trust, 2016a). Arguably, the anonymity, ease of access and the disinhibition generally encouraged by online communication are likely to increase the pool of potential victims.

Stalking is perpetrated by men and women. However, the overwhelming majority of stalkers are male. The most common scenario is a male perpetrator and female victim, and an estimated 70% of stalkers are male and 80% of victims are female (Suzy Lamplugh Trust, 2016b; Ostermeyer et al, 2016). Half of perpetrators, possibly more, are current or former partners, and only around 10–13% are unknown to the victim (Sheridan & Boon, 2002). It is not known if this also applies to cyberstalking, as this activity is different and much less well researched.

Characteristics and categories of stalkers and stalking

Most stalkers are motivated by a desire to force another into some form of unwanted relationship using insistent demands and attempts to create a level of intimacy that cause fear and distress in the victim (Spitzberg & Cupach, 2014). Perpetrators can be friends or loved ones. Former lovers are more likely to physically stalk their victim (Mullen, Pathé & Purcell, 2009). That said, use of electronic surveillance techniques by former partners to monitor, bully or victimise their victim is becoming increasingly common (All-Party Parliamentary Group on Domestic Violence/Women's Aid, 2017). Perpetrators who have no previous history of any relationship with their victim are common users of electronic surveillance.

Forensic behavioural scientists have established several categories of stalking behaviour. These are:

- ex-partner harassment/stalking
- infatuation harassment
- delusional fixation stalking
- sadistic stalking (Sheridan & Boon, 2002).

As many as 50% of stalkers have a mental health condition, such as personality disorder, schizophrenia or other psychotic disorder, depression or substance use disorders (McEwan, Mullen & MacKenzie, 2009; Mohandie et al, 2006; Rosenfeld, 2004). People who stalk strangers (including others they know only casually and celebrities) are more likely to have a mood, delusional or other psychiatric disorder, but less likely to pose a physical threat (Mullen et al, 2006). Those who stalk former partners are less likely to have a psychiatric disorder, but are more likely to be narcissistic or to have a personality disorder or drug or alcohol problems (Meloy, Davis & Lovette, 2001). This group is also more prone to envy and anger, and to have weak personal boundaries. This, in combination with the associated increased sensitivity to rejection, may trigger psychotic behaviour such as the obsessive pursuit of the target (from this point on the terms 'target' and 'victim' will be used interchangeably and should be regarded as synonymous), and the unshakeable belief that the relationship is continuing or will resume.

Less than 10% of stalkers are classified as having an antisocial personality disorder, which is surprising, given its over-representation in other criminal behaviour (Meloy, Davis & Lovette, 2001). However, given their profile, people with an antisocial personality disorder are more likely to be enraged when either a relationship is ended with them or their advances are rejected. However, they are also less likely to pursue a victim over an extended length of time. They are much more likely to follow a pattern of immediate angry response directly following the break-up, with a rapid de-escalation as time passes.

Stalkers who know their victim pose a much greater danger (Palarea et al, 1999). It is common for the stalker to have been in an intimate relationship with their victim, although it is not unknown for colleagues, neighbours and others who may have some form of professional relationship with the stalker (for example, health practitioners or public servants) to become targets. In the rarer scenario where the stalker stalks someone not known to them, the targets are often famous people. In these instances, the stalker may believe the target has romantic feelings for them, despite their never having met (erotomania).

Mullen, Pathé and Purcell (2009) have formulated a classification system that is commonly used to define all forms of stalking. Their categorisation considers the stalkers' motivations, personality, typical behaviours and the duration and type of behaviour, as well as victim characteristics, and separates them into:

- predatory stalker
- intimacy seeker
- incompetent suitor
- rejected stalker
- resentful stalker, and
- stalkers with erotomania and morbid infatuation.

The *'predatory stalker'* is motivated by the enjoyment, often sexual, of having power over the victim. These people often have low self-esteem, are typically of lower-than-average IQ and often unsuccessful in social or romantic attempts. The victims of such stalkers may be known or unknown to the perpetrator, and it is common for this kind of stalker to communicate with the target through unsolicited calls, spying, fetishism, exhibitionism or scopophilia (when someone derives sexual pleasure from looking at erotic objects, erotic photographs, pornography or naked bodies). This type of stalking is likely to last only a short time, although the stalker is more likely to resort to physical violence than other stalker groups.

The *'intimacy seeker'* typically tries to forge some romantic links with their victim. This often results in obsessive behaviours through which the stalker idolises the victim and thinks of them as the only person who can really understand them or satisfy their needs. They may often even believe the target reciprocates their feelings. They may ignore the victim's rejection of their advances, even when it is made clear that their feelings are not reciprocated. The intimacy seeker may believe that the target ought to feel the same for them because of the commitment they are showing by stalking them. These intractable beliefs may mean the stalking continues for longer than other types because the stalker is more obsessive. They are likely to regard anything the victim does to deter them as 'tests' whereby they can prove their strength of emotion, so attempts to stop them are unlikely to be effective. Typically, these stalkers are introverted and are not in any intimate relationship. As with predatory stalkers, their victims may be known or unknown to them. Methods include posting items or presents to the victim, writing them letters and making phone calls. If the victim tries to persuade the stalker that their feelings are not reciprocated, they may become angry or violent, and they are likely to be extremely jealous of any close relationships the victim may have.

The '*incompetent suitor*' often desires a romantic relationship with someone but is unable to achieve this because of their poor social skills. The incompetent suitor is likely to think they are inherently attractive and be unable to comprehend that the target does not think so. Typically, they stalk people known to them, but occasionally the target may be a stranger. The incompetent suitor may constantly invite their victim to go out with them, in spite of their negative responses, telephone repeatedly, or show inappropriate intimacy towards them, such as touching or hugging. This means the incompetent suitor does not stalk for as long as others, and may be convinced to stop their behaviour if encouraged to have counselling or threatened with legal action.

The '*rejected stalker*' is generally triggered by the breakdown of an intimate relationship. These stalkers are characterised by their attempts to either regain the lost partner or take revenge on the person that rejected them. As a result, they typically stalk former partners, although this may extend to other family members, friends or others who have had a relationship with the stalker. Almost all domestic violence cases involving stalking come under this category, so a history of violence in the relationship with the partner is not uncommon. In terms of personality, these stalkers have high levels of narcissism and jealousy. Rejected stalkers present as ambivalent about the victim and sometimes appear to want the relationship to start again. Equally, they can be angry and want revenge on the victim. They may also sometimes feel ashamed of their behaviour and show over-dependence. They may also have poor social skills, and therefore a limited social network. Their stalking is commonly a means of retaining contact or control over the victim, to increase their feelings of self-worth. Typically, rejected stalkers will strongly resist attempts to stop their stalking.

The '*resentful stalker*' aims to unsettle their victim, and may choose someone who has been involved with them in some previous, negative interaction, or a stranger who is related in some way to someone they think has upset them. They typically manifest irrational paranoia, and their behaviour is characterised by repeated obsessive behaviours, more often verbal than physical. If the behaviour is identified at an early stage, and legal action is taken, it may prevent further stalking, although if it continues for some time, this may have less effect.

The final category is stalkers with *erotomania and morbid infatuation*. They tend to fixate on celebrities and public figures, and are irrationally convinced that the target is in love with them, despite no evidence for this, and even when it is explicitly denied by their target. All actions or communication from the target are regarded as a demonstration of that love, which is hugely important to the stalker. Stalkers of this type are typically paranoid or delusional, and tend to choose as their victims people who are out of their reach in social terms. They will repeatedly try to see, speak or contact the target, and legal deterrents, such as imprisonment or restraining orders, rarely change their behaviours. However, psychological treatment is sometimes effective in stopping them.

Risk management and prevention

Given the diverse range of motivations and behaviour displayed by different stalker types, it is hard to devise an effective response to protect victims and manage the stalkers. A commonly used risk management tool is the DASH (Richards, 2009) – the domestic abuse, stalking and honour-based violence risk identification, assessment and management model, with further development with respect specifically to questions about stalking (Sheridan & Roberts, 2011). However, tools such as this are not consistently used across all police forces, and do not always include an assessment of online risk. There is a need to develop consistent, evidence-based risk assessment.

A better system of classification is needed to differentiate between types of stalking so the stalker can then be referred to the most appropriate form of treatment, whether educational or therapeutic (see MacKenzie & James, 2011). In addition, the escalation of cyberstalking is likely to require other ways of classifying motivations and characteristics of stalking behaviour (McFarlane & Bocij, 2003).

Strategies to reduce stalking, whether therapeutic, legal or physical, do exist, but more research is needed into further approaches and methods (see Mullen, Pathé & Purcell, 2009; Pinals, 2007). Some stalkers may require medical input and others may need detention. Stalking behaviours vary so much that curtailing it requires a range of approaches (MacKenzie & James, 2011). Co-ordination between medical and law-enforcement agencies and education is likely to achieve the best possible results and prevent the stalker from re-offending or lapsing. However, there are no clear referral pathways, due to a lack of research, and further work is needed on the management and treatment of stalkers, which should ultimately result in better frameworks of understanding.

The lived experience of cyberstalking victims

Research (Short et al, 2014) has identified five overarching themes in victims' accounts of their cyberstalking experiences:

* control and intimidation
* the determined offender
* escalation of the harassment
* negative consequences, and
* lack of support.

These themes are explored below using the words of victims themselves about their own encounters with cyberstalkers.

The theme of *'control and intimidation'* emerges in accounts where the stalking took place solely online or in combined methods that intruded into the victim's life and privacy.

The most obvious form of direct harassment includes making threats: 'Eventually the chat threads started becoming threatening, to me personally and to my family. In one instance, someone anonymously wrote they wanted to kill me.' People also report that cyberstalkers make false accusations against them: 'The person would make up channels saying I was a paedophile, woman abuser, dog molester, drug addict.' Other intrusions include hacking email accounts, sending viruses and posting intimate photographs: 'Setting up a Facebook account of me with intimate photos he'd refused to delete.' There are accounts of passwords being changed remotely by cyberstalkers, who then operate their victims' accounts. Methods of control and intimidation include complex behaviours and social manipulation such as tricking the victim into talking to the offender by creating alternative aliases and identities online: 'He created a fake journal and tried to become my friend'; or threatening suicide: 'Sent text messages indicating that he would commit suicide if I did not respond to him', and accusing the victim of being the perpetrator: 'She set me up to look like I'd stalked her by posting her email to the bulletin board.'

Indirect tactics can also be used, such as conversing online with the family or friends of the victim: 'Through her Facebook site... she contacted my daughter three times. Some of the things said to my daughter were both vile and completely untrue'; imitating the target: 'Impersonated me online sending out emails'; harassing their contacts via email or via online forums, and persuading others to pursue the victim: 'My address being posted in chat rooms', and watching the victim's online activity and gathering information to use against the victim: 'My stalker and her friends compiled information on where I worked, who my friends were, any new relationships.'

Many people also experience physical harassment, such as being followed in person, confrontation, letters, damage to property, and assault. Offline behaviours are often used either as a precursor to cyberstalking or in combination with cyberstalking: 'He started calling at all hours on the landline... the mobile... pay phones... He [then] overpowered and raped me, and continued calling and [instant messaging] me after that'; or, following cyberstalking: 'He posted aggressive and insulting messages on my Myspace profile. It escalated pretty quickly until one night he followed me home and tried to get into my house.'

The '*determined offender*' accounts highlight a number of common features. Most of these victims describe harassment as constant, relentless cyberstalking on a daily and ongoing basis: 'The texts and calls were relentless. At every work breaktime she'd phone over and over again and send text after text of nonsense. These could amount to over 30 a day'; 'Went on for three to five years from the same person.' The offender is often relentless, creating new ways to maliciously attack the victim if a method is blocked: 'Each time I shut down a means of communication from her she would find another way to harass me'.

As previously discussed, the motivations of '*determined offenders*' are very diverse. In this study, they ranged from intimacy seeking to anger and resentment to revenge: 'He kept calling and calling... trying to get me to go out with him'; 'He declared his love for me'; 'She was very angry and the harassment has continued ever since'; 'A friend's ex-wife blamed me for their divorce so started stalking my husband and myself'; 'I... stood up to them, they then embarked on a long campaign of harassment.' However, motivation can also be unclear: 'I started by getting a friend request on Facebook from someone I didn't know. Then they started sending me Facebook messages and it spiralled from there.'

The negative consequences of being cyberstalked are psychological, physical and social. Psychological responses include fear: 'My whole life stopped because I was in so much fear'; paranoia: 'I get paranoid very easily and reluctant to trust indirect communications', and anger: 'I am not so much scared by this, just really angry. Fear plays little part in it for me.' Almost 50% of women in the research felt they had to turn off their phone if they were not using it. Psychological symptoms can include panic attacks, flashbacks and post-traumatic stress disorder (PTSD). Victims report: 'I still have flashbacks and experience anxiety when going to my inbox. My health has not been the same since'; 'I became very ill… and now suffer complex PTSD/depression as a result of the harassment and abuse'; 'All the trauma and stress suffered from the stalking resulted in me miscarrying our child.' Social effects can include damaged reputation, damaged family relations and loss of work, either directly or indirectly as a result of the harassment and a damaged reputation; '[The cyberstalker] impersonated me online, sending out emails and status updates that ruined my reputation'; 'I have been unable to work properly, as I have felt sullied, damaged, and abused'; 'The stalking behaviour caused irrevocable damage to family relations.'

Victims of stalking express helplessness and a feeling that there is nothing they can do: 'He will follow me for the rest of my life and I can do nothing'; '... impotence at how little I can do is the main emotion I feel.' It seems that, as the offender increases control, the victim's perceived ability to do anything about it decreases: 'You are made to feel with less control of your life.' The sense of powerlessness may be exacerbated when the victim does not know the identity of the perpetrator. Unknown stalkers account for nearly half of all cyberstalkers and not knowing the identity of their stalker is reported by victims as particularly troubling (Maple, Short & Brown, 2011).

Some feel the level of harassment is influenced by how they respond: 'Ignoring him was probably the best response as any response from me appeared to either inflame him or make him happy'; 'It took a period of about two years for this to work, but it did work in the end.' The opposite effect occurred after responding to the offender: 'It is worse because I responded'; 'Contacting these attackers directly made the attacks worse – they seemed to enjoy knowing that they were getting to me'; 'Responding did not help. He just learned that the price for talking to me was calling 30+ times in a row.'

Many victims in this research highlighted the absence of support. Many reported that they got little help and that few people took them seriously: 'I completely despair at times of finding someone who will take this seriously'; 'My mother did not take this seriously at first, suggested I go out with him, and gave him my e-mail address.' There was even less support if the victim was blamed for the harassment: 'The police said it was my fault for putting the information online in the first place'; 'The police made us feel like we were almost to blame or that it was trivial.'

Effects of stalking and cyberstalking

Being the target of a prolonged campaign of stalking has long-lasting effects, whether it has taken place solely online or in a combination of physical and cyberstalking. People can be changed by their experience, and develop thoughts and beliefs about the world, themselves and their own responsibility for bad things happening around them. People who have been stalked and appear to have symptomatic PTSD (Weathers et al, 1994) feel more negatively about themselves, often describing themselves as useless and deserving the abuse. In line with PTSD symptomatology, they are less likely to trust others and are likely to blame themselves for negative experiences they have had (APA, 2013). Traumatic experiences in general cause most people to feel very anxious and distressed around the time of the event or events and for a short time afterwards.

In conjunction with the emotional and mental impact, stalking can influence the victim's life in numerous other ways. Indeed, 90% of people who discussed their experiences in a National Centre for Cyberstalking survey reported life-changing effects (Short et al, 2015). Nearly a third of victims report that stalking has negatively affected their ability to do their job (Maple, Short & Brown, 2011; Short et al, 2015).

As the ECHO survey indicates (Maple, Short & Brown, 2011), this largely affects males, who are more likely to report changes in their employment circumstances due to being stalked and, more significantly, more likely to be demoted or lose their jobs completely

Stalking and cyberstalking can impact on relationships, particularly if the victim gives up social activities, or cause the breakdown of an existing or new intimate relationship. Women are particularly likely to report negative impacts on their families, children and friends – often saying they have become more socially isolated as a result. The majority of the people surveyed by the National Centre for Cyberstalking said they had little support: 'I completely despair at times of finding someone who will take this seriously' (Short et al, 2014).

All types of stalking can result in social isolation, which can negatively affect the likelihood of the victims getting help. It can also intrude on a victim's work life. Often, this occurs when the offender includes people the victim knows in their harassment and attempts to isolate the victim from them. The victim can isolate themselves from others out of humiliation and embarrassment. Victims may become lonely, and may use drink and drugs to cope with the stress and trauma, which in turn can lead to long-term ill health.

Stress and trauma can also lead to long-term physical ill health, through the body being in a constant state of 'fight or flight'. In situations of danger and threat, neuro-hormonal changes, in the form of the release of cortisol and insulin, increase the heart rate, blood pressure and blood glucose levels. Where the threat is immediate, this mechanism is useful as it powers the body to respond quickly to danger. However, where it persists in the long term, without resolution, it can lead to major health problems (Selye, 1956), ranging from tension and migraine headaches to severe cerebrovascular incidents, such as heart attack and stroke. Gastro-intestinal problems, disruption in menstruation, erectile dysfunction and reduced immunity and increased vulnerability to infection are also common among people exposed to severe and unremitting stress (Cohen, Janicki-Deverts & Miller, 2007).

Conclusion

Stalking has major effects on victims' mental and physical health, on their social lives, work and other relationships, and on their wider family and friends. Cyberstalking is no less harmful in its effects. If you are being stalked, it is essential to report it to the police, as soon as possible. Every victim of a crime should expect to receive an appropriate response. There is guidance on what to expect when reporting a case of cyberstalking (Gilbert & Cobley, 2015) and the national Victim's Code (Ministry of Justice, 2015) sets out the minimum response people should expect from all criminal justice agencies and the minimum timeframes in which that should be done. If someone tells you they are being stalked, take their concerns seriously and encourage them to report it to the police, as it is essential that a risk assessment is done as soon as someone becomes aware that they are the object of someone else's fixation and this person has begun to intrude threateningly in their lives. Educate yourself about the psychological consequences of stalking and what you can do to support someone who is being targeted with stalking behaviours. Finally, check that the person you are supporting knows where they can get professional and practical assistance in order to stay as safe as possible.

References

All-Party Parliamentary Group on Domestic Violence/Women's Aid (2017). *Tackling Domestic Abuse in a Digital Age.* London: Bristol: Women's Aid. https://1q7dqy2unor827bqjls0c4rn-wpengine.netdna-ssl.com/wp-content/uploads/2015/04/APPGReport2017-270217.pdf (accessed July 2017).

American Psychiatric Association (APA) (2013). *Diagnostic and Statistical Manual of Mental Disorders* (5th ed). Washington, DC: American Psychiatric Association.

Crown Prosecution Service (undated). *Stalking and Harassment.* [Online.] London: CPS. www.cps.gov.uk/legal/s_to_u/stalking_and_harassment/ (accessed July 2017).

Cohen S, Janicki-Deverts D, Miller GE (2007). Psychological stress and disease. *Journal of the American Medical Association 298*(14): 1685–1687.

Gilbert J, Cobley P (2015). How to report cases of cyberstalking to the police and what to expect. In: National Centre for Cyberstalking Research (ed). *A Practical Guide to Coping with Cyberstalking.* Luton: Andrews Limited (pp136–144).

MacKenzie RD, James DV (2011). Management and treatment of stalkers: problems, options, and solutions. *Behavioral Sciences and the Law 29*(2): 220–239.

Maple C, Short E, Brown A (2011). *Cyberstalking in the United Kingdom: an analysis of the ECHO pilot survey.* Luton: University of Bedfordshire. http://hdl.handle.net/10547/270578 (accessed June 21017).

McEwan TE, Mullen PE, MacKenzie R (2009). A study of the predictors of persistence in stalking situations. *Law and Human Behavior 33*: 149–158.

McFarlane L, Bocij P (2003). An exploration of predatory behaviour in cyberspace: towards a typology of cyberstalkers. *First Monday 8*(9). http://ojphi.org/ojs/index.php/fm/article/view/1076/996 (accessed June 2017).

Meloy JR, Davis B, Lovette J (2001). Risk factors for violence among stalkers. *Journal of Threat Assessment 1*(1): 3–16.

Mohandie K, Meloy JR, Green McGowan M, Williams J (2006). The RECON typology of stalking: reliability and validity based upon a large sample of North American stalkers. *Journal of Forensic Sciences 51*: 147–155.

Ministry of Justice (2015). *Code of Practice for Victims of Crime.* London: HMSO.

Mullen PE, Pathé M, Purcell R (2009). *Stalkers and their Victims* (2nd ed). New York, NY: Cambridge University Press.

Ostermeyer B, Friedman SH, Sorrentino R, Booth BD (2016). Stalking and violence. *The Psychiatric Clinics of North America 39*(4): 663–673.

Palarea RE, Zona MA, Lane JC, Langhinrichsen-Rohling J (1999). The dangerous nature of intimate relationship stalking: threats, violence and associated risk factors. *Behavioral Sciences and the Law 17*(3): 269–283

Pinals DA (ed) (2007). *Stalking: psychiatric perspectives and practical applications.* New York, NY: Oxford University Press.

Richards L (2009). *Domestic Abuse, Stalking and Honour-Based Violence (DASH, 2009) Risk Identification and Assessment and Management Model*. London: Association of Chief Police Officers. www.dashriskchecklist.co.uk/wp-content/uploads/2016/09/DASH-2009.pdf (accessed July 2017).

Rosenfeld R (2004). Violence risk factors in stalking and obsessional harassment. *Criminal Justice and Behavior 31*(1): 9–36.

Sheridan L, Boon J (2002). Stalker typologies: implications for law enforcement. In: Boon J, Sheridan L (eds). *Stalking and Psychosexual Obsession: psychological perspectives for prevention, policing and treatment*. Southampton: John Wiley & Sons (pp63–82).

Sheridan L, Roberts K (2011). Key questions to consider in stalking cases. *Beha ioural Science and the Law 29*(2): 255–270.

Selye H (1956). *The Stress of Life*. New York, NY: McGraw-Hill.

Short E, Linford S, Wheatcroft JM, Maple C (2014). The impact of cyberstalking: the lived experience – a thematic analysis. In: Wiederhold BK, Riva G (eds). *Annual Review of Cybertherapy and Telemedicine 2014: studies in health technology and informatics, Vol 199*. Amsterdam: IOS Press (pp133–137) http://ebooks.iospress.nl/volumearticle/36403 (accessed June 2017).

Short E, Guppy A, Hart JA, Barnes J (2015). The impact of cyberstalking. *Studies in Media and Communication 3*(2) (accessed June 2017).

Spitzberg BH, Cupach WR (2014). *The Dark Side of Relational Pursuit* (2nd ed). New York, NY: Routledge.

Suzy Lamplugh Trust (2016b). *National Stalking Awareness Week 2016*. [Online.] London: Suzy Lamplugh Trust. www.suzylamplugh.org/past-national-stalking-awareness-weeks (accessed June 2017).

Suzy Lamplugh Trust (2016a). *Out of Sight, Out of Mind: an investigation into the response to stalking*. London: Suzy Lamplugh Trust. www.scaredofsomeone.org/wp-content/uploads/Report_consortium.docx (accessed July 2017).

Weathers FW, Litz BT, Huska JA, Keane TM (1994). *PTSD Checklist: civilian version*. Boston, MA: National Center for PTSD – Behavioral Science Division.

Weller M, Hope L, Sheridan L (2013). Police and public perceptions of stalking: the role of prior victim–offender relationship. *Journal of Interpersonal Violence 28*(2): 320–339.

THIRD-SECTOR EXPERIENCES

2

Experience of working in the stalking sector

Rachel Griffin

I joined Suzy Lamplugh Trust in 2012 from Victim Support, where I had worked on a range of projects and policy areas, mostly related to violence against women and girls. One of my responsibilities in my previous job had been updating policy on supporting victims of domestic violence, including requiring services to use the DASH risk assessment checklist (Richards, 2009). At the time, I didn't question why stalking (the 's' in DASH) was included as an indicator of risk to victims of domestic abuse: those who knew about these things had researched it and it was my job to make sure this was reflected in my organisation's policy.

I therefore arrived at Suzy Lamplugh Trust, which had managed the National Stalking Helpline since its launch in 2010, fairly confident that I knew something about stalking. I had read a fair bit about gendered violence, and understood that violence against women and girls existed on a spectrum, not in the traditional silos of domestic violence, sexual violence etc. I also knew that stalking was an indicator of risk of domestic homicide, and that this was one reason why the recent change in the law to place domestic homicide reviews on a statutory footing was so important, because there are so many lessons that can be learned from examining the events leading up to a domestic homicide.

However, this was when my real learning about stalking began, mostly thanks to Kristiana Wrixon, then manager of the National Stalking Helpline. From talking to Kristiana and others with experience of stalking, whether personal or professional, I began to appreciate the life-changing impact that stalking can have on its victims. In particular, I was struck by the diversity of people affected by stalking and the myriad ways that the impact of the stalking behaviour and its victims' support needs can be influenced by factors such as gender, the relationship between stalker and victim, the typology or motivation of a stalker and the length of time over which the stalking has been perpetrated. Four years on, I still feel that my learning about this complex subject has just begun, and I am very grateful both to fellow professionals in the stalking sector and to the survivors who, no less professional in their dignity and commitment to improving policy and practice, have generously shared their experiences with me.

Ours is a small but determined sector, driven more than most by the efforts of exceptionally committed volunteers and made up of a handful of national organisations working alongside a similar number of local partners. A reality facing our sector is that, in many parts of the country, the only way in which victims of stalking can access the support they deserve is for specialist stalking organisations to work in partnership with other organisations, whether in the wider voluntary sector or the public sector.

Therefore, with a view to informing the development of stalking awareness among a small but growing stalking sector, including those non-specialist organisations that are the first port of call for many victims of stalking, I have tried to summarise below some of the key lessons I have learned about stalking in the last four years. I hope they will be useful to those working with and for people affected by stalking.

Lesson one: stalking is a high-incidence, high-impact crime

Leading up to and during National Stalking Awareness Week 2016, Suzy Lamplugh Trust released research into the incidence of stalking, including cyberstalking (James et al, 2016).

This revealed that one in five women and one in 12 men have, at some point in their lives, experienced stalking. It reflects numerous other surveys in the UK and internationally, which find that stalking is far more common than many of us may assume (Tjaden & Thoenness, 1998; Office for National Statistics, 2016).

However, if you were to gauge the incidence and the impact of stalking on the basis of the priority it receives in public policy, especially criminal justice policy, you could be forgiven for assuming that it doesn't happen very much, or that it is merely a nuisance when it does happen.

One of the things I often find myself explaining in media interviews is that the individual actions that make up a pattern of stalking are, in and of themselves, often completely legal. Sending a text message, clicking 'like' against an image on Facebook, or even walking down someone's street, is not criminal on its own. It can be extremely difficult for someone who has not been on the receiving end of stalking behaviour (and I am one of these lucky ones) to understand just how frightening and life-limiting it can be to know that someone is obsessively and relentlessly fixated on you and that their behaviour not only will not stop but may escalate in frequency, seriousness, or both.

The flippant way in which the word 'stalking' is used in popular culture seems to me to fuel the perception of stalking as irritating but not very serious. A quick internet search will throw up countless T-shirts for sale bearing such slogans as 'I'm not stalking, I'm investigating' or 'Some call it stalking, I call it love!'. We have spoken to many victims, male and female alike, whose colleagues have trivialised their experience with comments such as 'Lucky you, I wish I had a stalker'.

Part of the problem is, no doubt, that stalking is often only taken seriously when it is understood to have led to physical violence. Waiting for non-violent behaviour to escalate to violence, rather than attempting to address it before it does, is generally a high-risk strategy. Research from the US found that 76% of victims of domestic homicide were stalked in the lead-up to the murder (McFarlane et al, 1999), and yet Suzy Lamplugh Trust recently asked local authorities how many domestic homicide reviews had identified stalking as a behaviour present before the homicide, and the response was only 27% of cases (Suzy Lamplugh Trust, 2016). Rather than indicating that stalking is less of a problem in England and Wales, this suggests to us a need to ensure that those carrying out domestic homicide reviews are trained to spot and name stalking behaviour.

A 2017 study, published by Suzy Lamplugh Trust, draws attention to the direct links between stalking and homicide (Monckton-Smith et al, 2017). The study explored this relationship in a sample of 358 cases of criminal homicide in the UK in the years 2012, 2013 and 2014. Stalking behaviours were present in 94% of the cases; recognised high-risk action markers were found across the sample: strangulation assault in 24%, threats to kill in 55%, and suicidal threats in 23%. The report highlights the key stalking behaviours leading up to the homicide: surveillance, including covert watching, was recorded in 63% of the cases, escalation in 79%, control in 92%, and isolation of the victim in 78%. Based on its findings, the study authors urged that the seriousness of stalking and risk to the victim should be measured not just by the severity of the stalking actions but by escalation in frequency or severity of stalking behaviours, which is frequently triggered by separation or threat of separation, loss of control over the victim, or revenge and resentment.

Besides the obvious risk of allowing stalking to tip over into physical violence, minimising stalking also ignores the psychological harm experienced by many victims. I suspect this is one reason why so many victims in general feel short-changed by the service they receive from the criminal justice system. 'Come back when he does something' is a phrase that victims hear all too often when they have reported stalking to the police.

What those victims tell us, and what research carried out on cyberstalking demonstrates, is that the stalker has already done considerable damage (James et al, 2016; Maple, Short & Brown, 2011). The *Stalker in Your Pocket* research report identified that, of those stalked online, one-third felt fearful about their personal safety and one in 10 moved home as a result of the stalking (James et al, 2016).

Lorraine Sheridan's 2005 research found that the effects of stalking could be physical as well as emotional. Her study identified that 58% of victims were very frightened, 92% reported emotional effects and 98% reported physical effects (Sheridan, 2005).

The startling gap between the seriousness of stalking, as measured in its prevalence and its impact, and the prevailing public perception places an additional burden on organisations in the stalking sector. It can be difficult to get decision makers, including politicians and public services commissioners, to commit to providing support for the victims of a crime that they don't understand. A good part of our work as a sector, therefore, is educating those in and around the criminal justice system to recognise just how serious the crime of stalking is. Only when we have their attention can we begin to work with the system to bring about changes to policy and practice.

Lesson two: stalking isn't just perpetrated by former intimate partners

On joining Suzy Lamplugh Trust, I was unsurprised to learn that 90% of those who contact the National Stalking Helpline are stalked by someone they know. Having understood the prevalence of stalking following the ending of a relationship – indeed, this was the only context in which I had really read much at all about stalking – I had assumed that the calls the service was answering were predominantly related to stalking by ex-partners. I was shocked to discover that 50% of those contacting the helpline are being stalked by someone other than a former intimate partner.

The other 50% of victims who contact us are stalked by acquaintances (15%), neighbours (9%), colleagues and ex-colleagues (6%), family members (5%) and various others (4%), leaving 11% of victims who are stalked by either a stranger or someone whose identity is still unknown.

Over the last few years, we have seen a gradual increase in acknowledgment by public and voluntary sector partners alike of stalking as a crime of violence against women, including the government's inclusion of stalking in its Violence Against Women and Girls strategy (Home Office, 2016). This is extremely welcome to us at Suzy Lamplugh Trust. Stalking, like violence or financial abuse, can intersect with so many other forms of gender-based violence, especially domestic abuse, but, like violence or financial abuse, it has its own characteristics and complexities. It is critical that the risk factors specific to stalking, particularly the dangers associated with obsession and fixation that underpin stalking behaviour, and the likelihood of stalking escalating to serious physical violence, are understood by services supporting victims of domestic abuse where the perpetrator is also stalking them.

While I am encouraged by the increasing awareness and understanding of stalking and its impact in the context of violence against women and girls and domestic abuse in particular, it is frustrating that progress is relatively slow in the development of provision for victims stalked by someone other than a former partner.

Suzy Lamplugh Trust first took up the cause of stalking in response to campaigners like Tracey Morgan, herself a victim of a sustained campaign of stalking from a former colleague, which culminated in her attempted murder, because people like Tracey simply had nowhere to go to get the support they needed. Tracey's stalking experience began in 1992, and she, with the support of the Trust, successfully campaigned for the introduction of the Protection Against Harassment Act 1997. Some 20 years later, it is depressing to see that, if Tracey were seeking support now, she would not find many more specialist stalking services available to her than in the 1990s.

Suzy Lamplugh Trust recently asked all the police and crime commissioners in England and Wales how many specialist services they had commissioned for victims of stalking in their areas. We learned that, in 42 police areas, including London, where the powers of police and crime commissioner sit with the mayor, only nine police and crime commissioners (PCCs) had commissioned any stalking-specific services between April 2013 and February 2016 (Suzy Lamplugh Trust, 2016).

Looking at this problem from the perspective of individual victims, rather than as a set of statistics, this means victims of stalking have no access to refuge or other safe housing provision, are invisible to risk-management structures such as multi-agency risk assessment conferences (MARACs), fall outside the remit of most independent domestic violence advocate (IDVA) services, have limited access to advocacy support from someone who understands stalking, and face significant challenges in accessing legal aid. This dearth of support at a local level means that national services like the National Stalking Helpline are both heavily over-subscribed and seriously limited in the range of services to which they can refer clients for ongoing support.

The prism of domestic abuse through which many organisations, particularly in the criminal justice system, tend to view stalking – if they recognise it at all – is characterised by the common response we at the Trust hear from representatives of police forces when we ask what they are doing on stalking. This response will often begin, 'Our violence against women team is doing…'

While I wholeheartedly commend the work of specialist violence-against-women-and-girls (VAWG) teams, public protection units and others for increasingly recognising stalking as one of a number of VAWG strands, I would challenge police forces and those responsible for commissioning victims' services to look at their provision for victims of stalking who have never had an intimate relationship of any kind with their stalkers. This diverse group, frequently invisible to service providers, also often passes under the radar of existing services that might be well placed to help them.

We regularly give talks on stalking to groups of police officers, and it is not unusual, when we report some of the frustrations with the police response that victims tell us about, for officers present to insist that their colleagues would never treat a victim so dismissively. On further probing, it often emerges that the officers we are speaking to work in a specialist unit to which victims are referred, and are not representative of those frontline officers whose role it is to recognise stalking when it is reported to them.

Victims of stalking by former partners also report a police response that is far from satisfactory. But I am particularly worried that victims who have a different, or, indeed, no relationship with the stalker not only find that their experience is not recognised but also have precious few support options available to them if it is.

Lesson three: stalking is seriously misunderstood – sometimes by those who need to understand it the most

I have alluded earlier to the difficulties victims tell us that they encounter when reporting stalking to the police and in finding support to deal with their experiences. Around half the victims who call the National Stalking Helpline have already reported it to the police, and of those who have, fewer than one in five report feeling satisfied with the response they have received. In 2017, HM Inspectorate of Constabulary, with the HM Crown Prosecution Service Inspectorate, published a highly critical report on the police and CPS response to harassment and stalking. Its findings make for grim reading to those working in the sector, and living with stalking:

> We found that stalking in particular was misunderstood by the police and the CPS. As a result, it often went unrecognised. The police sometimes mis-recorded stalking offences, or worse, did not record them at all. Prosecutors on occasions missed opportunities to charge stalking offences, instead preferring other offences, particularly harassment.
>
> We also found that the absence of a single accepted, consistent definition of stalking is a very significant contributory factor to the unacceptably low number of recorded crimes and prosecutions. It is also one of the main reasons that police officers, staff and prosecutors gave us varying interpretations of stalking.
>
> The result for victims was that offences were not dealt with appropriately by using stalking-specific powers (for example, the power to search premises and seize evidence). Incidents of victimisation were dealt with as isolated cases and were not treated seriously or quickly enough, and victims were left at risk. In some cases, the charges did not reflect the seriousness of the offending. (HMIC, 2017: 7)

The report also found a failure in crime recording: incidents were not recorded, were mis-recorded, or were wrongly recorded as harassment: 'The evidence suggests we cannot be confident about the accuracy of the recorded crime figures for stalking in any of the forces we visited' (HMIC, 2017: 7).

The cyberstalking research that we published with Drs David James and Raj Persaud and YouGov (James et al, 2016) revealed that less than half of those who reported the stalking to the police found their response in any way helpful at all. Considering that the law on stalking was introduced in November 2012, it's frustrating that it seems to be taking so long for policy to be turned into practice.

I regard the lack of mandatory stalking training for police officers as a key to this problem. The brief, e-learning module that officers can undertake at their desks, at the discretion of their chief constable, cannot be enough to enable someone to understand even the law as written, let alone the complex factors of risk, relationship, stalker typology and length and nature of stalking that combine to make each case unique. These must be understood thoroughly in order both to carry out an effective investigation and to protect the victim.

A particular concern is the response to cyberstalking that many victims tell us they encounter when they report it to the police. We are still hearing of victims being advised by police officers not to look at their emails/text messages/social media feed. As well as being completely impractical, when so much of our work and social lives are lived online, this advice assumes that victims will not be concerned if they cannot read what is being said about them online. Moreover, if what is said is, in fact, a threat to harm or kill, ignoring it could be very dangerous.

There also seems to be a persistent attitude that there is some distinction to be drawn between stalking that happens online and stalking that happens in 'real life'. Modern life involves the complete integration of online and offline communication, work and socialising, and this needs to be understood by those taking reports of stalking. Indeed, most of the victims we talk to have been stalked by a combination of online and offline means.

I can think of no better solution to this problem than to invest in stalking training for police officers and frontline civilian staff. This should explore myths and stereotypes around stalking– debunking, for example, the myth that the typical stalker is a stranger hiding in the bushes – and focusing on the fact that most stalkers are known to their victim.

Training should look at the lessons learned from cases where indicators of risk were missed or ignored and how to prevent tragedies like these recurring. Perhaps most importantly, it should examine how stalking differs from other sorts of harassment. The law does not help to explain this difference. It simply cites a number of examples of 'acts or omissions which, in particular circumstances, are ones associated with stalking', including following, attempting to contact someone and loitering. It does not actually state in which 'particular circumstances' these behaviours would be 'associated with stalking' (Protection of Freedoms Act, 2012).

Suzy Lamplugh Trust describes stalking as characterised by the stalker's obsession and fixation with their victim, and we encourage those we have the opportunity to train to understand that it is this particular characteristic of stalking, a crime of *persistence*, that means it can escalate to serious violence.

Suzy Lamplugh Trust and partners such as Veritas-Justice have begun to see some progress, in that more decision makers are embracing the need to provide training in stalking to police officers and staff. A partnership project in Sussex, for example, funded by the police and crime commissioner, has allowed us to deliver face-to-face training to 70 people working in and around the criminal justice system, all of whom play a critical role in determining what kind of experience victims of stalking receive when they make their first report.

Even the best classroom training, on its own, will not always get across to the learner the aspects of the stalking experience that can only be understood by hearing from the victims themselves. My ideal stalking training syllabus for professionals within and around the criminal justice system would therefore combine face-to-face training, as Suzy Lamplugh Trust and Veritas-Justice have delivered in Sussex, with the first-hand accounts of those who have experienced stalking. I recommend *Our Encounters with Stalking* as background reading for anyone wanting to understand the impact that stalking can have on its victims and some of the very individual ways in which, through telling one's own story, the individual process of recovery can begin.

References

HM Inspectorate of Constabulary (2017) *Living in Fear: the police and CPS response to harassment and stalking.* London: HMIC,.

Home Office (2016). *Ending Violence against Women and Girls: strategy 2016 to 2020.* London: HM Government. www.gov.uk/government/publications/strategy-to-end-violence-against-women-and-girls-2016-to-2020   (accessed June 2016).

James D, Persaud R, Suzy Lamplugh Trust, YouGov (2016). *The Stalker in Your Pocket.* London: Suzy Lamplugh Trust. www.suzylamplugh.org/2016/04/stalker-pocket/ (accessed June 2016).

Maple C, Short E, Brown A (2011). *Cyberstalking in the United Kingdom: an analysis of the ECHO pilot survey.* National Centre for Cyberstalking Research. Luton: University of Bedfordshire. www.beds.ac.uk/__data/assets/pdf_file/0003/83109/ECHO_Pilot_Final.pdf (accessed November 2012).

McFarlane J M, Campbell J C, Wilt S, Sach CJ, Ulrich Y, Xu X (1999). Stalking and intimate partner femicide. *Homicide Studies 3*(4): 300–316.

Monckton-Smith J, Szymanska K, Haile S, with the Homicide Research Group, University of Gloucestershire Centre for Learning and Innovation in Public Protection (2017). *Exploring the Relationship between Stalking and Homicide.* London: Suzy Lamplugh Trust. http://eprints.glos.ac.uk/id/eprint/4553 (accessed August 2017).

Office for National Statistics (2016). *Intimate Personal Violence and Partner Abuse.* [Online.] www.ons.gov.uk/peoplepopulationandcommunity/crimeandjustice/

compendium/focusonviolentcrimeandsexualoffences/yearendingmarch2015/
chapter4intimatepersonalviolenceandpartnerabuse (accessed June 2016).

Richards L (2009). *Domestic Abuse, Stalking and Honour-Based Violence (DASH, 2009) Risk Identification and Assessment and Management Model*. London: Association of Chief Police Officers. www.dashriskchecklist.co.uk/wp-content/uploads/2016/09/DASH-2009.pdf (accessed July 2017).

Sheridan L (2005). *Key Findings from www.stalkingsurvey.com*. Leicester: University of Leicester supported by Network for Surviving Stalking. www.le.ac.uk/press/stalkingsurvey.htm (accessed June 2016)

Suzy Lamplugh Trust (2016). *Out of Sight, Out of Mind: an investigation into the response to stalking*. London: Suzy Lamplugh Trust. www.suzylamplugh.org/Handlers/Download.ashx?IDMF=0d387e89-1fb4-48cd-818e-138dc84563eb (accessed June 2016).

Tjaden P, Thoennes N (1998). *Stalking in America: findings from the National Violence against Women Survey*. Washington, DC: National Institute of Justice/Centers for Disease Control and Prevention. www.ncjrs.gov/pdffiles/169592.pdf (accessed June 2016).

3

About the National Stalking Helpline

Kristiana Wrixon

'Mine first – mine last – mine even in the grave!' (Alcott, 1997). This quote is from a novel called *A Long Fatal Love Chase*, written in 1866 by Louisa May Alcott, an author best known for writing the children's classic *Little Women*. *A Long Fatal Love Chase* tells the story of a woman who is chased around the world for years by her cruel, estranged husband. At the end of the novel, he accidentally kills her while trying to murder her new partner and proclaims, 'Mine first – mine last – mine even in the grave!' This quote is so chilling because, during my time managing and operating the National Stalking Helpline, many victims of stalking have told me that similar things have been said to them by their stalker. *A Long Fatal Love Chase* shows us that stalking is not a new crime or a crime of celebrity; it is a centuries-old crime of fixation and obsession that causes harm and can lead to murder. Despite this, there is a still a startling lack of knowledge about stalking and a dearth of support services.

Before I started working for Suzy Lamplugh Trust, I was a civilian officer with Devon and Cornwall Police. My job involved me recording details of crimes attended by police officers, including entering data relating to domestic abuse risk assessments that had been carried out by response officers. During my time there, the constabulary changed from the SPECSS+ risk assessment model to DASH (Domestic Abuse, Stalking and Honour-Based Violence) (Richards, 2009). So, I was aware of stalking and I knew it was a risk indicator in cases of domestic abuse, but I knew very little about the complexity and impact of the crime until I began working directly with its victims.

The launch of the National Stalking Helpline

I was hired by Suzy Lamplugh Trust in March 2010 to set up and launch the National Stalking Helpline. The helpline started taking calls on 26 April 2010. It was the first service in the country specifically dedicated to victims of stalking, and, as far as I am aware, remains the only national helpline in the world providing expert stalking advice.

From the helpline's very first day, it was apparent that the service was desperately needed. During the first three months of operation, the National Stalking Helpline dealt with 454 emails and phone calls. However, a further 658 calls did not reach an advisor because the line was engaged. Within six months, Suzy Lamplugh Trust had recruited an additional staff member to help to respond to the demand and the helpline has continued to steadily grow. We now (2016 figures) respond to just under 3,000 calls and emails a year, and there continues to be a higher demand for the service than we have resources to meet.

During my first month working for Suzy Lamplugh Trust, I met and learned from campaigners who had personal experience of stalking and who had campaigned tirelessly to improve the experiences and services available to victims of stalking. I met Tricia Bernal and Carol Faruqui, whose daughters had been murdered by their stalker ex-boyfriends. I listened to Tracey Morgan, Alexis Bowater and Ann Moulds speak at awareness-raising conferences about their experiences of stalking. I learned that, in some cases, stalking ends in murder, and in all cases it destroys a person's sense of peace, wellbeing and safety, causing significant emotional harm.

As well as talking directly to victims of stalking, I read research papers by stalking experts, which gave further insight into the complexities of stalking. One paper, by Dr Lorraine Sheridan (2009), included a case study that demonstrated the extremes of fixation that victims of stalking can experience:

Maureen was 20 when she turned down Richard's advances in 1962. Their families were part of a very close-knit and isolated religious community in Wales and they tried to pressure Maureen into marrying Richard. She refused and married someone else. Her family rejected her because of her choice and Richard stormed the wedding ceremony and made a scene. He had to be physically removed. Throughout her four-year marriage, Maureen was often confronted by Richard. He followed the couple, insulted her husband, and continually stated his commitment to Maureen. After four years, her husband could take no more and left. He moved away, leaving Maureen and her infant daughter.

Richard stalked Maureen for 43 years in total. His belief that they belonged together and that they would one day be married never wavered. Maureen was diagnosed with a nervous disorder and was never able to form another romantic relationship. Richard made it his business to put off any potential suitors. Maureen encouraged her daughter to move away at an early age so that her life would not be blighted by Richard's activities. When Maureen died in 2005, her daughter attended her funeral, and this represented the point that Richard transferred his attentions to the daughter. Maureen's daughter says: 'He killed my poor mum. He hounded her to death but he won't do the same to me. He is old now and has nothing. I have a degree and a work permit for the USA... I have to go if only to stop myself murdering him for what he did to my mum... He destroyed her. He killed her... I can't believe that no one ever did anything.'

This case study demonstrated to me a level of fixation and obsession that I had simply not previously thought possible. No one should have to live their life trapped by the suffocating, unwanted attention of another person.

Before the helpline launch, many survivors of stalking and bereaved relatives had bravely spoken out about their experiences with stalking. However, many people still assumed that stalking was not a particularly widespread crime and that relatively few cases were as 'serious' as those experienced by campaigners. When the National Stalking Helpline began, some questioned whether there would be sufficient demand for such a service. Six years on, with the helpline responding to just under 3,000 contacts a year and an increasing demand for the service, it is unarguable that more services for victims of stalking are needed.

Learning from the National Stalking Helpline

As well as providing information and support, the National Stalking Helpline has enabled us to capture more data on stalking than has previously been possible. Helpline advisors record anonymous information from people who make contact with us, recording information such as the behaviours experienced and the relationship between the perpetrator and victim. This information has enabled us to have a better understanding of stalking than ever before. Our statistics show that 78% of victims of stalking who contact the helpline are women and 74% of perpetrators are men. Only seven per cent of people who contact the helpline are being stalked by a stranger, and the largest category of victim/offender relationship is former partner (53%).

Our data also give us information about stalking victims' experiences of seeking help from the criminal justice system. Half of those who contacted the helpline in its first year had previously spoken to the police about what was happening to them, and of these, only 13% were satisfied with the response. This figure has not changed significantly since 2010. Furthermore, three-quarters of those who contact the helpline have not sought civil legal assistance. In many cases, they are unaware that this route is available to them, but in other cases they report a lack of available legal services with expertise in stalking and harassment. Protective orders such as non-molestation orders or injunctions under the Protection from Harassment Act 1997 are also often prohibitively expensive.

Creating change

Six months after the National Stalking Helpline started, I was asked to speak at my first conference about the lessons that could be learned by police and prosecutors from those contacting the helpline. The subjects I chose to speak on were the three most common problems raised by callers to the helpline:

1. inappropriate use of police information notices (PINS)
2. limited awareness and understanding of stalking and the Protection from Harassment Act
3. a dearth of specialist support services, especially at a local level.

It is fair to say that all three of these points are still cause for concern. However, there has been significant progress in all three areas, and this should not be overlooked.

1. Police information notices

There is no legal basis for PINS; they are not referred to in the Protection from Harassment Act 1997 or in any other statute or regulation. It is said that PINs make prosecutions easier because they make it more difficult for an alleged perpetrator to deny that he knew that his behaviour was regarded by the victim as harassing. In my experience, in the majority of cases dealt with by the National Stalking Helpline, the offending behaviour is intended to harass. The inept suitor who accidentally goes too far is more unusual than the stalker who makes silent phone calls, sends abusive emails or puts up defamatory websites. This stalker does not need a PIN to tell him that what he is doing amounts to harassment.

Victims who contact the National Stalking Helpline also often report feeling reassured by officers issuing a PIN because they think it is a restraining order. For instance, many victims report being told by police that a PIN can stop a perpetrator coming within a certain distance or entering a certain area, and that breaching it will result in arrest. Victims also tell us that police have told them that the PINs are valid for a specified amount of time, usually a year. There is no legal basis for either of these statements. The result is that when, as often happens, the perpetrator makes contact again and the victim reports this 'breach' to the police, the victim then becomes very frustrated when she is told that the stalker cannot be arrested for 'breaching' the PIN.

Police officers appear to hold a common misconception that a PIN has to be issued first, before any other action can be taken. We have also heard from victims that police officers have told them that, if a perpetrator refuses to sign a PIN, there is nothing further the police can do. Neither of these is true, but they often lead to victims being misinformed and to unnecessary delays in steps being taken to arrest and prosecute stalkers.

Overall, we believe that PINs are more dangerous than helpful. They appear often to be used as a quick and easy method of appearing to deal with stalking without actually tackling the crime. They are creating confusion among victims and perpetrators, without, very often, having any effect on the stalking behaviour at all.

In response to these concerns raised by charities and campaigners, it has been acknowledged that the use of PINs needs to be reviewed. Assistant Chief Constable Garry Shewan, the National Police Chief Council stalking lead, has said that 'some cases that had resulted in a victim being killed had followed inappropriate use of PINS at an earlier stage in the process' (Home Affairs Select Committee, 2015). To date, we are still waiting for the release of the updated stalking Authorised Police Practice (APP), which is expected to contain updated guidance for police officers on when to issue a PIN, which will be rebadged as an Early Harassment Notice. This is a positive step forward, but I remain unconvinced that an updated policy will effect real change, and I hope that, alongside this, the police monitor when the notices are used and how effective they are.

2. Awareness and understanding

There has been a significant improvement in awareness and understanding among police, the Crown Prosecution Service (CPS) and the general public over the last six years. This is in large part due to a number of successful campaigns that have resulted in new stalking legislation in Scotland, England and Wales. Awareness of stalking has also been raised because a number of high profile individuals, such as Emily Maitlis (Hughes, 2016) and Lily Allen (McVeigh, 2016), have spoken out in the national press about their personal experiences of being stalked.

However, the National Stalking Helpline still frequently gets calls from victims who have been given misinformation about the law by the police. Comments such as 'We can't do anything about it until s/he does something physical', 'It is not stalking if they are using the internet', and 'S/he is allowed to stand outside your house if they want, it's a public footway' are still too common. It is not just the police who could do a great deal better; we also receive calls from people who are frustrated with the CPS for not knowing the full history of the case when communicating with the victim and/or not asking for restraining orders as part of court proceedings.

There is also evidence from people contacting the helpline that local agencies such as housing associations, non-specialist victim services and social services are missing key warning signs that have been identified in the Stalking Risk Checklist (https://www.stalkingriskprofile.com). The checklist should help professionals to identify behaviour of significant concern, such as escalation in the number of incidents, visiting the home and criminal damage. Phrases like 'If I can't have you, no one else will' don't seem to raise the appropriate level of concern among agencies dealing with stalking victims.

Training needs to start at the point of report. Call handlers should be trained to recognise risk factors that warrant a swift response from the police so that they do not dismiss callers, who may then be reluctant to try to report the stalking again. Response officers and detectives should be able to conduct meaningful stalking risk assessments, and victims should be signposted or referred to appropriate support agencies.

There are pockets of good practice and some excellent practitioners. However, this is not widespread. We believe this is due to lack of training and awareness. While training often features in the national debate about how to improve the police and CPS response to stalking, it is important that it is detailed and includes direct reference to the 'victim's experience'. We remain concerned that training is not of sufficient depth to bring about the cultural and attitudinal change that needs to occur if stalking is to be dealt with as seriously as it should be.

3. A lack of local support services

The National Stalking Helpline was the first specialist stalking support service in the UK, but thankfully is no longer alone. In 2013, Paladin, a national stalking advocacy service, was launched to provide casework to high-risk victims. Veritas-Justice was also established in Sussex in 2014, and provides valuable support and advocacy to stalking victims, as well as signposting to local support services. A number of other charities, such as Aurora New Dawn in Portsmouth, have also started to provide specialist stalking support services.

While these services are a vital resource, support for victims of stalking is still inconsistent and varies significantly nationally. A report released by Suzy Lamplugh Trust (2016) to mark National Stalking Awareness Week in 2016 found that only nine out of 43 police and crime commissioners had funded any specialist stalking services since they were elected in 2012. Only two police and crime commissioners had funded services that lasted for longer than one year.

Stalking is a complex crime and victims are entitled to support from services that fully understand it. All National Stalking Helpline workers receive training in stalking and intersecting criminal behaviour, such as revenge porn, honour-based violence and domestic abuse. They also receive ongoing training on related issues, such as the family courts and immigration. This level of expertise should be available to all victims of stalking and for this to happen funding needs to improve. Where you live should not determine the services available to you. All victims of stalking deserve safe, specialist services, no matter where they are in the country.

The future

We will continue to monitor and campaign for improvements in all of these areas, and others where callers to the National Stalking Helpline tell us they want improvements. Among the most pressing issues are abuse of process and the need for an expert stalker perpetrator intervention programme.

Abuse of process occurs when stalkers make vexatious complaints to the court in order to further their campaign of harassment. Examples of vexatious complaints told to the National Stalking Helpline include reports to police and social services of child abuse and allegations that the victim is her/himself stalking the stalker. Action is needed to close the legal loopholes that result in victims of stalking experiencing trauma in the family and civil courts due to vexatious complaints by stalkers.

Ultimately, we cannot address the issue of stalking – which is the result of obsessive behaviour – without looking at ways to intervene in the perpetrator's behaviour. Stalkers are known to be recidivists (Mullen, Pathé & Purcell, 2009), and many of the people who contact the helpline have achieved a successful prosecution of their stalker in the past only to continue to be stalked after their conviction. The only existing perpetrator intervention or treatment for stalkers in the UK is at the Fixated Threat Assessment Centre, and this is reserved for high-profile cases, such as stalkers who threaten senior politicians or members of the royal family. While models have been developed for work with stalkers (by, for example, the UK's National Stalking Clinic,[1] the US Stalking Resource Center,[2] and the Victorian Institute of Forensic Mental Health;[3] see also Warren et al, 2005; MacKenzie & James, 2011) there is currently no intervention or treatment available for the vast majority of stalking perpetrators in the UK.

Learning by listening

The most important thing that a professional working with a victim of stalking can do is to believe them and to listen to them. The direct experiences of those who are stalked should inform the development of support services and policies. That's why this book is a valuable resource to anyone wishing to learn about stalking, because it focuses on the experiences of those affected by stalking.

References

Alcott LM (1997). *A Long Fatal Love Chase*. New York, NY: Dell Publishing Company.

Home Affairs Select Committee (2015). *Police Information Notices: fifteenth report of session 2014–15*. London: the Stationery Office. www.publications.parliament. uk/pa/cm201415/cmselect/cmhaff/901/901.pdf (accessed June 2017).

Hughes T (2016). Newsnight's Emily Maitlis reveals she has been stalked for 25 years by schizophrenic man who was at university with her. *Daily Mail*; 14 May (updated 16 May).www.dailymail.co.uk/news/article-3590003/ Newsnight-s-Emily-Maitlis-reveals-stalked-25-years-schizophrenic-man-university-her.html (accessed June 2016).

MacKenzie RD, James DV (2011). Management and treatment of stalkers: problems, options, and solutions. *Behavioral Sciences and the Law* 29(2): 220–239.

---

1. See www.beh-mht.nhs.uk/mental-health-service/mh-services/national-stalking-clinic.htm
2. See http://victimsofcrime.org/our-programs/stalking-resource-center
3. See www.forensicare.vic.gov.au/

McVeigh T (2016). Lily Allen on being stalked: 'I was asleep. He steamed into the bedroom and started screaming. *The Observer*; 16 April. www.theguardian.com/music/2016/apr/16/lily-allen-stalked-singer-police (accessed June 2016).

Mullen PE, Pathé M, Purcell R (2009). *Stalkers and their Victims* (2nd ed). New York, NY: Cambridge University Press.

Richards L (2009). *Domestic Abuse, Stalking and Honour-Based Violence (DASH, 2009) Risk Identification and Assessment and Management Model*. London: Association of Chief Police Officers. www.dashriskchecklist.co.uk/wp-content/uploads/2016/09/DASH-2009.pdf (accessed July 2017).

Sheridan L (2009). *Stalking: cause and effect*. Unpublished research. Leicester: University of Leicester. www.le.ac.uk/ebulletin-archive/ebulletin/features/2000-2009/2007/07/nparticle.2007-07-17.html (accessed August 2017).

Suzy Lamplugh Trust (2016). *Out of Sight, Out of Mind*. London: Suzy Lamplugh Trust. www.suzylamplugh.org/Handlers/Download.ashx?IDMF=0d387e89-1fb4-48cd-818e-138dc84563eb (accessed June 2017).

Warren LJ, MacKenzie R, Mullen PE, Ogloff JRP (2005). The problem behavior model: the development of a stalkers clinic and a threateners clinic. *Behavioral Sciences and the Law* 23: 387–397.

POLICE AND THE COURTS

4

Stalking by proxy – the Family Court as the stalker's agent

Sam Taylor and Claudia Miles

Veritas Justice is a community-based, professional service-user-led organisation. Our unique approach combines legal, therapeutic, creative and academic skills, which we have used since our participation in the parliamentary inquiry into stalking in 2012 (Justice Unions' Parliamentary Group, 2012). We have been privileged to collaborate with passionate professionals, students and survivors in all our work.

Stalking became a criminal offence in England and Wales on 25 November 2012, as a result of an amendment to the Protection from Harassment Act 1997, which introduced two new specific offences of stalking. For the purposes of this chapter, we will define stalking as a pattern of repeated and persistent behaviour that is intrusive and creates fear. It occurs when one person becomes fixated with another and attempts to call, text, follow or contact them, and this behaviour is unwanted and carried out in a manner that could be expected to cause alarm, distress or fear.

Stalking is one of the most debilitating crimes that can be experienced. Its relentless nature gives victims no respite and few opportunities to recover. Stalkers can involve other people, services or professionals in their harassment and stalking campaigns to contact or track their victims. Often, they unwittingly help the stalker perpetuate the stalking, even without the perpetrator's involvement. This is particularly true when stalkers use legitimate processes to access and control their victims and their families. This involvement of third parties is known as stalking by proxy.

In addition to the overwhelming number of calls, text messages, emails and threats (to name but a few of the forms of contact) a victim receives, we argue that the Family Court assists perpetrators to indirectly use the children to gather information about the victim's movements, habits and networks of support. These terrorising behaviours become invasive and all-consuming, posing significant risks to the safety of women and children.

Stalking by proxy

'Patterns of stalking can be particularly difficult to resolve when the stalker and victim share children. Stalkers, who may have previously shown little or no interest in their children, view child custody hearings as another chance to maintain contact with the victim and to punish them' (Mullen, Pathé & Purcell, 2009).

Stalking by proxy does not exist in isolation; it is part of a wider pattern of coercive control. It is important that these behaviours are recognised and dealt with in context and that comprehensive responses are devised to reduce the long-term impact on the whole family.

It is important first to outline the current legal position in relation to childcare arrangements in England and Wales.

Section 11 of the Children and Family's Act 2014 (England and Wales) amended Section 1 of the Children Act 1989 to include a provision relating to parental involvement in the assessment of a child's welfare. This new section (2a) provides that 'a court is to presume, *unless the contrary is shown,* that involvement of both parents in the life of the child concerned will further the child's welfare' (our italics).

The wording of the legislation seems to provide an opportunity for parents and courts to address the risk of harm to the children if contact is to be established with both parents. However, from our work with women who have experienced stalking and harassment after separation, we know that the risks are not always identified, understood or taken into account, and that contact with abusive fathers is almost always viewed in the 'child's best interest'.

We know, from our research, experiences and supporting women through the Family Court process, that stalking is the most prevalent form of post-separation abuse, and it is now widely acknowledged that perpetrators abuse the Family Court system (England and Wales) to continue to torment their victims. This has recently triggered a significant, widely publicised and much overdue review of the family justice system and its treatment of victims of domestic abuse, stalking and harassment.

It must be acknowledged that not all victims of ex-intimate partner stalking have experienced physical violence before separation, but they will, more commonly, have experienced various forms of coercive control. However, the impact of stalking on the whole family due to the persistent, coercive and controlling behaviour that continues post-separation is routinely misunderstood in the Family Court process, if stalking is not identified and dealt with.

Furthermore, the reduction of Legal Aid has meant that the situation for women in the Family Court system is getting worse. Many stalking victims are not able to provide the strict forms of evidence required to be eligible for legal aid and are therefore forced to represent themselves in court, cross-examine their stalkers and be cross-examined by them. Courts are thus faced with an influx of women who are representing themselves and, through the complexities of our legal system and fear of their stalkers, get locked into arrangements that are inappropriate, unsafe and unworkable.

Vexatious applications

'We know that less than one per cent of child contact applications are refused and stalking features in around 70%– 90% of cases going through the courts. This includes public as well as private law proceedings' (Women's Aid, 2016).

This suggests that stalking is commonly perpetrated through multiple and often malicious applications in the Family Court. This is also echoed by our own data, collected in our stalking advocacy pilot project in 2016 (see below), which show that 70% of our clients and their children have experienced stalking by abusive partners through the Family Court, through vexatious applications for childcare arrangements (Veritas Justice, 2016).

In another study, published by Suzy Lamplugh Trust in 2017 (Monckton Smith et al, 2017), the researchers singled out the presence of vexatious or baseless allegations and court actions as key markers of risk in cases where stalking led to the death of the victim, and highlighted that they were frequently not recognised as stalking, and should be.

Concerns about the merits of those applications are often minimised and dismissed, thereby validating the stalker's activities and rewarding them with more control of their ex-partners and their children. 'Research shows that custody arrangements provide stalkers with further opportunities for intruding on the victim, either during visitations and exchanges or less directly, through the children (Mullen, Pathé & Purcell, 2009).

Our clients have routinely described how former partners can make repeated court applications for child contact, the aim of which is to continue their stalking and harassment campaigns rather than establish a long-term, meaningful relationship that is in the best interest of the children.

In fact, most mothers and their children see some value in father and child relationships, provided that they are well informed and safe for both mother and child(ren), and not abused as a source of information and continued contact between women and their stalkers.

We argue that the current and popular co-parenting post-separation narrative ignores the lived experiences of women and children who are being hunted down by their stalkers through the Family Court, which forces them to agree to unsafe childcare arrangements that may ultimately not be in the best interest of the child. This provides the stalker with opportunities to instigate repetitive and sometimes malicious court applications, gratifying them with the attention they so desperately seek.

What stalking through the Family Court looks like

Stalkers who abuse the legitimate opportunities provided by family law for parents to maintain long-term meaningful contact with their children rely heavily on a culture where a father's good faith is presumed, all but irrefutably, by those making the decisions about the child's welfare.

The picture is one of judges striving to establish meaningful and enduring parent–child relationships, social workers directed to make recommendations aimed at establishing co-parenting, articulate and credible stalkers playing the master puppeteer, and emotionally distressed and traumatised mothers forced to balance the conflicting demands of keeping their children safe while working in 'partnership' with their stalker.

Each part of the process plays a role in further enmeshing the victim in their stalker's long-term obsession through child contact disputes. Stalkers will capitalise every possible avenue to continue their campaigns.

Mothers' voices

As reported above, Veritas Justice ran a pilot Stalking Advocacy Service from November 2015 to November 2016, during which time we supported 22 women (we did not collect data on the number of children the women had, but whether children were subject to Family Court proceedings). We found:

- 100% of service users were women
- 70% cases were stalked by an ex-intimate partner
- 100% of ex-intimate partner stalking cases involved children
- 70% involved Family Court proceedings
- 95% of victims said their experiences affected them and their children psychologically, socially and emotionally, regardless of whether they were physically assaulted or not
- 80% were dissatisfied with the Family Court's understanding of stalking risks
- 60% represented themselves in the Family Court but did not feel confident about their ability and knowledge to navigate the system
- perpetrators used the Family Court process to maintain contact with the victim (Veritas Justice, 2016).

Patterns of stalking can be particularly difficult to resolve when the stalker and victim share children. Stalkers who may have formerly shown little interest in their children view child custody hearings as another chance to maintain contact with the victim and to punish them for trying to end the relationship (Mullen, Pathé & Purcell, 2009: 169).

The case studies below are a sample from our client group. These are three families that have been affected by stalking through the Family Court process. We have chosen them as representative of the majority of the stories we hear.

In Mary's case, the father had an extensive criminal history and stalked her and her family after attempting to kill her. He'd exhausted all other avenues for contact with Mary when, two years after the couple separated, he issued an application to the Family Court for contact with the children, even though social services had deemed him unsafe. Despite all the professionals involved being greatly concerned about the risk he posed to Mary and her children, proceedings continued for over a year.

During this time, the father committed a string of offences against Mary and others, breached court orders and terrorised the family. He spent several months in and out of prison. Significantly, he underwent a psychiatric assessment that concluded that, despite his being a significant danger to women, children and the public in general, he was not a danger to his own children, and some form of contact was recommended for consideration.

Laura, a professional woman, was pursued for seven years through the Family Court by her wealthy ex-husband, during which time 11 orders were issued in relation to arrangements for the child. The husband used a contact book diary to abuse Laura after every contact visit. He sent messages via their four-year-old child threatening to cut Laura's throat, and even refused to sign the authority letter for the child to join school.

He attempted to financially control Laura by refusing to support the child financially, and even made false allegations to her employers and her professional regulatory body. Throughout the seven years, the courts and the professionals described the case as 'warring parents', and suggested that, given their financial and educational backgrounds, 'they just needed their heads banging together'.

Jo also spent several years in the Family Court process. The children returned from contact with their father significantly distressed on each occasion. Every time Jo bought new outfits for the children, the father would deliberately cut them up during contact visits, and went on to report Jo to the children's teachers and social services, accusing her of not buying the children any clothes and neglecting them.

When Jo reported him to her social worker for destroying the clothes, she was told they couldn't prove it was him. There was a restraining order in place, due to previous harassment convictions, for which he had served a custodial sentence. However, the Family Court suspended the effects of the order for the purpose of contact handovers, so Jo was forced to have direct contact with him at these times.

During the five-year Family Court process, the father stalked, abused and terrorised the family, until he was eventually deemed by the courts to be unsafe to have contact with the children. However, his behaviour towards the family during the years of unsupervised contact has had significant long-term psychological and emotional impact and the children now require specialist educational support.

'In addition to orchestrating protracted disputes over child custody, stalkers continue to dominate their victims' lives through the disputes over property and child support payments, exerting considerable influence over the victim's welfare through these measures' (Mullen, Pathé & Purcell, 2009: 169).

Courts, professionals and agencies

'It is, in my view, high time that the Family Justice System abandoned any reliance on the proposition that a man can have a history of violence and abuse to the mother of his children but, nonetheless, be a good father' (Lord Justice Wall, 2006).

Family law has traditionally adopted a stance of downplaying family violence and abuse, in an attempt to concentrate minds on the discourse that parents' involvement is in the best interests of the children, thereby suggesting that children's wellbeing is intrinsically linked to continued contact with their father, on occasion regardless of the safety and value of such contact.

Use of stalking behaviour to subjugate women is not new. In fact, mothers who oppose contact with abusive fathers are often put under considerable pressure from judges, solicitors, court welfare officers, mediators and even the media to withdraw their objections. The courts have taken an increasingly critical and punitive view of mothers who resist contact, regardless of the circumstances.

Unfortunately, the gaps in legal processes and training for professionals allow stalkers to use the justice system as an agent for their stalking campaign. Poor understanding of context (which is essential in identifying stalking) has meant that professionals consistently believe the vexatious accusations and reinforce the father's claims that the mother is being obstructive about contact with children.

While the comments of Lord Justice Wall above highlight the very important cultural changes identified and called for by the judiciary itself, it is also evident from the words he uses that risk of physical violence continues to dominate thinking in this sphere. There is an underestimation of significance of coercive control and abuse in the context of wider patterns of stalking behaviour, yet these are frequently a factor in post-separation abuse and very often missed in risk assessments and case management in child contact disputes.

The practical consequences of this narrative are that mothers are frequently expected to separate the children's needs and experiences from their own. This ignores the fact that the children have in most cases witnessed and/or experienced the same abuse, and the mothers have usually been the children's primary caregivers, so post-separation violence, abuse and stalking will victimise them all.

There seems to be a contradiction between the legal provisions attempting to criminalise stalking as a form of violence against women and the developments in the law relating to family justice. While the first encourages women to report violence, abuse and stalking and to leave abusive relationships in order to protect their children, the latter places woman at risk by forcing them to comply with arrangements for the stalker to have contact with the children.

'Perps are adept at exploiting weaknesses in any system and the legal system in particular offers stalkers ancillary methods of harassment and a ready vehicle for stalking by proxy' (Mullen, Pathé & Purcell, 2009).

Victim- and mother-blaming

Women and their children also experience violence and abuse not only through the legal processes that affect their lives but also through the narratives of victim- and mother-blaming.

> *Women who assert the need for protection from further domestic abuse (and stalking) when arranging child contact are in danger of being viewed as selfish, obstructive or hostile to the father as a parent and hence to the welfare of the children. Responsibility for any harm that is caused to the children when contact is set up with an abusive man is shifted back onto the mother. Her fears of the father, rather than the persistent abuse that gave rise to them, are invariably deemed to be the chief source of damage to a child and the main obstructive forces to continue contact. Responsibility also shifts back onto her to continue to manage the man's abuse after separation.* (Radford et al, 1997)

Our advocacy work for stalking victims has provided us with a valuable opportunity to share learning, working with survivors and professionals alike. Some of the reflections of this work would suggest:

- there is a socially accepted narrative among professionals that mothers are the main problem and barrier to establishing contact between abusive fathers and their children
- the continued involvement principle places a hidden burden on professionals to encourage women to ignore their concerns about safe contact in favour of contact at all costs, which is often perceived to be in the children's best interests
- mothers who dare to challenge this presumption and highlight the risks and inconsistencies during the process are routinely viewed and treated as hostile and obstructive by the courts
- having escaped their abusive relationships, women find that, despite the perpetrator's continued violence, abuse and stalking, they are now viewed as good-enough fathers
- stalkers often present as credible and calm, in contrast with their terrorised, traumatised and apparently 'over-reacting' mothers, making it difficult for professionals to identify the fathers' manipulative nature
- popular discourses suggest that women frequently make false allegations to gain an advantage in child contact disputes, contrary to statistical findings.

'In a study of over 9,000 divorce cases, it was found that less than two per cent included false allegations of domestic abuse' (Theonnes & Tjaden, 1990).

The children's rights

The right to know and have a relationship with one's parents has been recognised by the UN as a basic human right (United Nations, 1989), so, undoubtedly in principle, contact between children and their parents is a positive thing. However, entitlement to this right is less clear when that contact is not safe or it is used to inform and facilitate a stalking campaign.

The impact of stalking on the whole family due to the stalker's persistent, coercive and controlling behaviour, which carries on after separation, is routinely misunderstood in the Family Court, and there is a lack of training, understanding and support around stalking when it is perpetrated by fathers through child contact.

In the *Nineteen Child Homicides* report, Women's Aid (2016) drew attention to the deaths of 19 children who were deliberately killed by a parent who was also a known perpetrator of abuse. Stalking behaviours were described throughout this report, yet stalking was not identified or named.

According to the report:

- 19 children were killed
- two children were seriously harmed through attempted murder
- in seven out of the 12 families, contact had been ordered through the Family Court.

'The *Nineteen Child Homicides* describes one devastating consequence of the Family Court's failure to make safety a priority in contact orders and the huge gap that separates justice for abused women' (Women's Aid, 2016).

These killings were made possible through unsafe child contact arrangements with abusive fathers (stalkers) in their efforts to maintain contact with their victims. In over half of these deaths, contact with the children was ordered by the Family Courts.

It is not in dispute that children can benefit from the positive influence of both parents, and, in turn, children usually wish to remain in contact with both parents after separation. However, we must not ignore that some of these parents will not be able to put their children's needs before their own obsessions.

Significant misconceptions of mothers being obstructive and a barrier to meaningful father/child relationships are based on scanty evidence and a thriving culture of victim-blaming, where it is widely accepted that, unless there is physical evidence of abuse, then accusations must be untrue.

Lessons to be learned

Co-parenting with a stalker as ordered by the courts seriously disrupts victims' lives and creates understandable distress. It also reinforces their feelings of powerlessness and undermines all hope of escaping their situation.

Undoubtedly, professionals, agencies and the judiciary work tirelessly to provide best practice and advice. However, to truly 'learn lessons' from the horrific cases such as those reported above, they must resist the desire to view parents as 'equals'. To do so is to grossly (and potentially fatally) underestimate the complex experiences of women and children terrorised (stalked) by abusive fathers through the family justice system.

Despite changes in legislation, lack of training and support for the courts, and, for some, inadequate information from professionals, means that our justice system will continue to fail victims of stalking and their children. This is not just because of the glitches and inadequacies inherent in any social system; insensitive practices and legal loopholes, at their worst, allow the stalker to use the legal system as an agent of their campaign of abuse, harassment and stalking.

What has become apparent through our analysis of academic research and serious case and domestic homicide reviews is that, while stalking behaviours are described throughout the literature, stalking is rarely mentioned or identified. We would hope that our work contributes to raising awareness of this longstanding problem and helps communities, survivors and professionals better protect those victimised by this devastating crime and hold the perpetrators to account.

The social, political and legal battles in which children are used as emotional capital has had a profound effect on the way stalkers misuse the family justice system to impose continued contact on women and children. Allowing stalkers to manipulate professionals and agencies in this way at worst puts women and their children at risk of being killed, and at best condemns them to a life of constant fear.

In the words of Nev Kemp, writing when he was still Chief Superintendent with Sussex Police:

I am regularly upset, angered and also inspired by the stories of domestic abuse and stalking that I hear day to day from officers and staff describing the cases they are involved in. I am upset by the effect on the survivors and sometimes those close to them, including children, angered by the destructive acts perpetrated by controlling, selfish individuals. (Kemp, 2015)

References

Justice Unions' Parliamentary Group (2012). *Independent Parliamentary Inquiry into Stalking Law Reform: main findings and recommendations.* London: Justice Unions' Parliamentary Group. http://paladinservice.co.uk/wp-content/uploads/2013/10/Stalking-Law-Reform-Findings-Report-2012.pdf (accessed June 2017).

Kemp N (2015). Foreword. In: Biswas Sasidharan A, Podd N, Miles C, Taylor S (eds). *Talking Stalking: writing for recovery.* Brighton: Writing for Recovery Group, University of Brighton.

Monckton-Smith J, Szymanska K, Haile S, with the Homicide Research Group, University of Gloucestershire Centre for Learning and Innovation in Public Protection (2017). *Exploring the Relationship between Stalking and Homicide.* London: Suzy Lamplugh Trust. http://eprints.glos.ac.uk/id/eprint/4553 (accessed August 2017).

Mullen PE, Pathé M, Purcell R (2009). *Stalkers and their Victims* (2nd ed). New York, NY: Cambridge University Press.

Radford L, Hester M, Humphries J, Woodfield K (1997). For the sake of the children: the law, domestic violence and child contact in England. *Women's Studies International Forum 20*(4): 471–482.

Theonnes N, Tjaden PJ (1990). The extent, nature and validity of sexual abuse allegations in custody and visitation disputes. *Child Abuse & Neglect 14*(2):151–163.

United Nations (1989). *United Nations Convention on the Rights of the Child.* New York/Geneva: United Nations.

Veritas Justice (2016). *Stalking Advocacy Pilot Report.* Unpublished report, produced for Sussex Police Crime Commissioner. Brighton: Veritas Justice.

Wall N, Lord Justice (2006). *Report to the President of the Family Division on the Publication by the Women's Aid Federation of England entitled* Twenty-Nine Child Homicides: lessons still to be learnt on domestic violence and child protection with particular reference to the five cases in which there was judicial involvement. London: Courts and Tribunals Judiciary. www.judiciary.gov.uk/wp-content/uploads/JCO/Documents/Reports/report_childhomicides.pdf (accessed March 2017)

Women's Aid (2016). *Nineteen Child Homicides.* Bristol: Women's Aid. www.womensaid.org.uk/child-first-research/ (accessed March 2017).

5

Sentencing remarks and IPCC statement in the murder case of Shana Grice

The Hon Mr Justice Green

This chapter reports verbatim the public records of the sentencing remarks and the Independent Police Complaints Commission (IPCC) statement by the judge, the Hon Mr Justice Green, in the case of Michael Lane, who pleaded not guilty to the murder of Shana Grice at his trial on 23 March, 2017. The documents highlight the mindset of Michael Lane during his stalking activity and after the murder of the woman he professed to adore.

After sentencing, the judge explicitly highlighted his concerns about the way in which the police handled the complaints made to them about Lane's stalking activities by Shana and others. Their response was typical of those highlighted by service users and professionals throughout this book.

R v Michael Lane, Lewes Crown Court, 23 March 2017

1. Michael Lane, the jury has found you guilty of the murder of Shana Grice. You killed Shana by slitting her throat. You set fire to her room, intending her body and the scene of the crime to be burnt beyond recognition. You stole her money. Shana was 19 years old when she died, still a teenager.

2. Everyone in this Court heard Shana speak when the recording of her conversation with you about the theft of the key was played. We heard the clear tones of a confident and vibrant young woman. You robbed Shana of her life and you have caused grief untold to her family and friends. They have attended this trial together and provide support to each other and they have had to sit

through harrowing and demeaning evidence about Shana's love life and her death.

3. The Court has heard from Sharon Grice, Shana's mother. She spoke of the enormous gulf that Shana's death has left in the lives of family and friends. She described her only daughter in these terms: 'Shana was a beautiful, bright and bubbly, kind-natured 19-year-old who brought joy to all those who knew and loved her. She was popular throughout childhood; she made friends easily and was never grumpy. She loved life and was enthusiastic. She particularly enjoyed spending time with her grandparents, with whom she had a very strong relationship.'

4. She also said: 'We have lost our beautiful, kind and thoughtful daughter; we miss her giggles and laughter, the jokes we shared and having her to hold and share our future lives together as a family.'

5. No sentence that I impose can ever begin to compensate them for their loss.

6. I am quite sure that you have caused despair to your own family and friends, who will be bewildered and at a loss to understand your actions.

Conclusions on the facts

7. It is now my duty to sentence you. I do this only upon the basis of facts that I am sure of. The evidence against you was overwhelming.

8. In the months before the murder, you had a relationship with Shana. Throughout that period, you exhibited obsessive behaviour which can only be described as that of a stalker. You were jealous of the fact that she was at the time in a long-term relationship with another man. You would hang about where Shana lived. You sent messages to her boyfriend telling him that Shana would always cheat on him. You were jealous of any relationship she had with other men. On one occasion, this led you to follow Shana down the road and then you grabbed her phone from her hand, hitting her in the process. You secretly placed a tracker on her car so that you could follow her movements, and you would follow her car in yours. Every few days you would sneak back to her home and covertly recharge the battery in the tracker without her knowing. You stored embarrassing text messages between you and her and were prepared to use them as pressure against her, as a form of moral blackmail. You also used

such messages to persuade the police that, when she complained to them about you, it was she that was the wrongdoer and not you. You deflated and slashed her car tyres so that you could then help repair them and appear in a good light to her. You stole her rear door key and used it to enter her bedroom at 6.00 in the morning so that you could peer at her whilst she slept. You engaged in silent, heavy breathing telephone calls to her. You even sent her threatening legal letters about a debt you believed that she owed you.

9. It is undoubtedly the case that this was a complex relationship. On the one hand, Shana was sufficiently concerned about your conduct to make repeated complaints to the police about you. But on the other hand, she was also attracted to you. Because of her age and inexperience of life, Shana did not know how to deal with you. And, tragically, when she sought help from the police, she received none.

10. On 23rd August 2016, Shana decided that her relationship with you was at an end. This split occurred in a hotel in Hove that same evening. You then plotted revenge.

11. I am sure that your revenge was premeditated. This is clear from the evidence given during the trial. You told a young woman in the pub that, when you split from Shana on an earlier occasion, you were upset and depressed and you told her that Shana would 'pay for what she had done'. That was an indication of your general state of mind. On 24th August, the day after the final split, you purchased petrol in a can. You told the Court that you were intending to commit suicide by setting fire to yourself. That was untrue. You purchased the petrol because you intended imminently to cause terrible and fatal harm to Shana and then to destroy evidence with a raging fire. You also set out on the morning of the 25th August with your disguise in your hands. This was the high visibility jacket and a peaked cap to pull over your face. All of this shows a high degree of calculated planning and premeditation. I am in no doubt, therefore, that, when you set out from your home in your car at just before 7.25am on 25th August 2016, you had already formed an intent to kill.

12. At shortly after 7.30am, you went into Shana's bedroom, knowing that her house mates had left for work. We will never know for certain what then passed between you and Shana. At about that time a neighbour heard a raised female voice coming from Shana's house. But there was no screaming or shouting. Shana knew her assailant, and it was you. You took a knife, almost certainly from the kitchen,

which has not been found, and you slit her throat. In all likelihood, you did this from behind her. She would have been conscious for some time before she died slumped by the side of the bed.

13. You killed Shana in the few minutes either side of 7.40am. Having killed her, you searched for her bank cards. Then, in your disguise, you walked out on to the street. You were at this stage wearing a hoodie, which you had obtained I suspect from Shana's house, and the high visibility jacket and the blue cap on your head. The hood of the hoodie was pulled up over the cap and you were looking downwards to avoid being recognised.

14. And then, to add insult to injury, you headed for the nearest ATM, which was close by on Graham Avenue. You can be seen on the CCTV within 20 metres of the cash machine at 8.06am. This was the time when Shana's bank card was used to steal her money. You knew the pin. You accepted in evidence that you had used that pin in conjunction with her card some months earlier. You clearly stored the pin number and now you used it again. You attempted to steal a sum from her account, which was roughly the same as that you believed she owed you as a debt. But Shana did not have that amount of money in her account. So, instead, you checked her balance and then you took out £60, which was just below the balance. There was a small service charge to pay but the machine only issued the amount you keyed in, namely £60. It is no coincidence that two £20 and two £10 notes, totalling £60, were later found by the police in your car.

15. Having stolen Shana's money, you went to your car and, having driven around and purchased some water, you returned to Shana's house, because you needed to destroy the evidence of the murder. It is probable that at some point you transferred petrol into that water bottle. You can be seen on the CCTV at about 8.22am going back into Chrisdory Road, to Shana's house, carrying a bag. And, even though you denied this was in fact a picture of you, nonetheless you also accepted in evidence that you were indeed at the house at that very time. You re-entered her house with the petrol and you moved Shana's body onto the bed. You doused the floor and bed with petrol and you ignited the fire. You left, closing the door behind you. The fire quickly took hold and, because it was a confined space, the heat built up rapidly to a high temperature. Shana's body was burned but the oxygen in the room soon became depleted, and the

fire extinguished before the body and room burned down and all of the evidence was destroyed.

16. Having left Shana's house, you went home and showered to remove incriminating bloody stains, and you set about hiding all of the clothes and shoes that might be contaminated with Shana's blood. You disposed of the murder weapon.

17. This was a cold-hearted murder. I have not detected in you any appreciation of the devastation you have caused to Shana's family and friends. Nor have I detected remorse. In so far as I have detected emotion in you, it has been a determination to do all you can to protect yourself, and you have been the one person you have felt sorry for.

Sentence of life imprisonment

18. There is only one sentence that in law I am allowed to impose upon you and that is imprisonment for life.

Minimum term

19. I am also required to set the minimum term, which is the number of actual years that you must serve before you are able to apply to the Parole Board to be released on licence. Lest there be any misunderstanding, the minimum term is not the point in time when you will be released. Whether you are released then, or indeed ever, is a matter for the Parole Board, not for me.

20. The starting point for determining the minimum term is the guidance set out in the Criminal Justice Act 2003. Under that Act, I must determine the seriousness of the offence and any related offences. The facts of the present case do not fit exactly or neatly into any of the categories in the Act, as is accepted by the Prosecution and by your own counsel.

21. In my judgment, this was a murder following significant premeditation. When you set out on 25th August, you intended to kill Shana in her own home. You knew where you would find an appropriate killing weapon in Shana's kitchen, and it was a part of your plan to use this knife. This was a long way from a spur-of-the-moment killing.

22. You also combined murder with arson. If you had not closed the door behind you when you left Shana's bedroom, then the fire would have been fed by oxygen from outside the room and there is a real likelihood that the house would have burned down and Shana would have been incinerated. There is also a risk that the fire could have spread to neighbouring homes, causing a danger to the lives of others.

23. I also cannot ignore the theft. This was a cold-hearted and callous action. It reveals a lack of remorse on your part; having, just minutes before, murdered the young woman you professed to adore, you set about stealing her savings. I do not believe, however, that theft was the main motivation for the murder. That was a combination of anger at Shana for having split with you and jealousy of any other man, such as her longstanding boyfriend, Ashley, that she might replace you with.

24. I must also take into accounts the efforts you made to conceal your own clothes from being found with incriminating evidence upon them.

25. I do take account of your age. You do not have previous convictions. I take account of the grief and pain that you will have imposed upon your own family and friends. This was in my view a crime committed from the profoundly misguided and irrational emotion. You have suffered from depression and suicidal tendencies in the past, which may well be connected in some way to these events.

26. I do not apply a mechanistic approach to sentence. I have taken full account of the guidance and starting points set out in the Criminal Justice Act 2003. Ultimately, I have to stand back and look at all of the evidence in the round to assess the overall seriousness of the crime and to consider what is just in all the circumstances.

Sentence

27. Michael Lane please stand.

28. The sentence of this Court is one of life imprisonment

29. You will spend a minimum of 25 years in custody before you can apply for parole. Whether or not you are released is for the Parole Board. You have been on remand since 3rd September 2016. The time you have spent in custody on remand will count towards this minimum term.

Please take him down.

Statement: IPCC investigation

1. Having listened with great care to the evidence in the course of this trial, there is one matter that I wish to make some observations about.

2. Shana Grice was murdered by Michael Lane in August 2016. Between February and July 2016, Shana or persons on her behalf made five complaints to the police about the behaviour of Michael Lane. On the second occasion in March, a complaint was made about an alleged assault by Lane upon Shana. When questioned by police, Michael Lane showed them text messages passing between himself and Shana which indicated that he and she were in a sexual relationship. The police then treated the complaint as being based upon the deliberate supply of false information. Shana was issued with a fixed penalty notice and a fine for wasting police time; in other words, she was treated as the wrongdoer and having committed a criminal offence, and Michael Lane was treated as the victim.

3. There was seemingly no appreciation on the part of those investigating that a young woman in a sexual relationship with a man could at one and the same time be vulnerable and at risk of serious harm. The police jumped to conclusions and Shana was stereotyped.

4. The position adopted by the police had three potentially serious consequences.

5. First, following this incident, the police treated all further complaints by Shana with scepticism. In particular, three further complaints were made over the course of the short period between 9th and 12th July 2016. The first related to theft of a door key by Lane, which he then used to enter Shana's bedroom to peer at her in her bed at 6.00am in the morning. The second concerned the sending of silent, heavy breathing calls to Shana, believed to have been from Lane. The third concerned an incident when Lane was seen following Shana. In relation to the use of the stolen key to enter Shana's bedroom, Lane received a caution for theft and a low-level warning to terminate contact with Shana. In relation to the subsequent complaints, Shana was told, in effect, that no further action would be taken. The incidents were classified as low risk. Shana was murdered six weeks later.

6. The second consequence was that, when further incidents of stalking occurred, Shana did not complain to the police because she felt that her complaints would not be taken seriously. Evidence was given to this effect during this trial by those close to Shana.

7. The third consequence was that Michael Lane felt that, if he continued with his obsessive stalking behaviour, it was most unlikely that the police would do anything to stop him. And he did continue, even though he had been warned by the police to keep away from Shana.

8. I would emphasise that my concern lies with the way in which the complaints were handled. Following the murder, the investigation and prosecution of this case has, in my view, been conducted by the police professionally and efficiently.

9. I am aware that the Independent Police Complaints Commission (the IPCC) is investigating, and, indeed, officials from the IPCC have been observing this trial. I am therefore directing that my concerns be brought to the attention of the IPCC so that they can be taken into consideration in the course of that investigation.

6

The really critical thing is the impact on the victim

Sam Taylor, Claudia Miles and Richard Bates (transcribed by Helen Leigh-Phippard)

This chapter is the transcript of a three-way recorded conversation between Sam Taylor (ST) and Claudia Miles (CM) from Veritas Justice and Detective Chief Inspector Richard Bates (RB) from Sussex Police Safeguarding Investigation Unit, on 11 April 2016. It is the result of an ongoing dialogue and work that Veritas Justice undertakes alongside Sussex police, trying to raise awareness of the issues around stalking.

The conversation took place just four months before Shana Grice was murdered on 25 August 2016 by her stalker, Michael Lane. Shana had made five separate reports of stalking to Sussex Police; not only was she disbelieved and her complaints dismissed as not serious, she also received a Fixed Penalty Notice for wasting police time.

Her tragic death is a stark reminder of the deep misunderstanding of the dynamics of stalking that is endemic within the criminal justice system and the urgent need for victims' complaints to be taken seriously and concrete plans put into place to support them when they seek help.

ST: Shall we start by discussing issues around identifying stalking?

CM: I wanted to pick up on something that you said a bit earlier about how the stalking offence is described in law and the difficulties trying to prove it for prosecution purposes. Mostly, what people understand is that you only need to receive contact or communications that you don't want and that are causing you distress, anxiety or fear, and that the person sending them knows or ought to know that the attention is unwanted. What we hear from victims at Veritas is that, when they receive unwanted communications and they report them to the police, sometimes they're not taken seriously, or the incidents they describe are viewed in isolation, rather than part of a wider pattern of behaviour.

ST: … or not addressed or understood within the context of stalking

CM: So, in your view, how many contacts are sufficient to demonstrate stalking? How many times do you have to tell someone 'Don't contact me anymore', and how realistic is it to not have contact with them if you have children with the perpetrator, or friends and colleagues keep in touch with the perpetrator and don't always appreciate the risk?

RB: The Protection from Harassment Act, which has been on statute for many years now, sets out the offence of harassment, a core requirement of that being that the perpetrator pursues 'a course of conduct'. That is more than one incident; it can be as few as two incidents. It will always be something of a moot point as to how wide apart those two incidents are before they become separate incidents, as opposed to a course of conduct, but in the strictest sense, two incidents is a course of conduct.

The stalking legislation was brought in by a new Act of Parliament, The Protection of Freedoms Act 2012. That new Act updated and amended the original harassment offence (Harassment Act, 1997). It's added new sections of the law that say that, if you commit the offence of harassment and your behaviour amounts to stalking, then you commit this new offence of stalking. So, in order to commit the offence of stalking, you must, by definition, have committed the offence of harassment first.

I think the difficulty with the new law, and what we need to learn to work with, is that people recognise stalking when they see it, but it can be really difficult to articulate and define it in legislation.

The legislation gives examples of the types of behaviour that could be construed as stalking and that most people would be able to understand as stalking, but it's not a definitive list, so it's actually created an offence that's really, really broad. It's very much down to what an objective person might consider stalking, or not. For me, the really critical thing is the impact on the victim.

So, there's two elements to the offence. One is causing the victim to fear violence, which I think is probably going to be easier to identify and recognise. The second is causing significant alarm and distress. I think we've got to be really cautious that we don't make a judgment as to whether the behaviour would cause us personally that level of alarm and distress, because it's the perception of the victim that matters. That's what the law talks about: that it's caused the victim significant alarm and distress. For me, it's really important that we listen to the victim, and that we look at the wider context and understand why that particular behaviour could, in those circumstances, cause that level of alarm and distress to the victim. Because it's the history that gives it the context for the victim, and it's the history that is going to cause the victim to interpret that behaviour in their own very personal way, which is going to manifest as the alarm, the distress, and the personal impact on them.

CM: So you think it's central that stalking has a subjective test to it – that what defines a behaviour of stalking is the perception of the victim of the consequences of that behaviour, which seem innocent or normal to the normal or reasonable person?

RB: Yes.

CM: But what seems to be the problem is that people choose not to report because some of the ways in which they present themselves don't seem to be normal or typical, and that often makes it harder for them to access the services. I'm thinking of people with acute trauma or mental health difficulties. In fact, this is one of the classic stalker allegations – that their victim is mentally ill, that they imagined the behaviours. So how do you think police work and deal with this difficult dynamic? Because you may have someone reacting to a very extreme set of circumstances in a very extreme manner and you may have your perpetrator or your suspect behave in a really plausible manner. If the test is subjective, how can you subjectively find the difference between the two, because I think it is really difficult for the police officer?

You may have an interview with someone who has been arrested by appointment, and they are credible and plausible and rational, and you can have a conversation with them, whereas the victim may be crying and shouting, and she may have a history of previous domestic abuse in the relationship, or substance misuse, or a whole range of issues, and who's telling the truth?

RB: It is really difficult, and we know that a lot of the behaviours of stalkers, when looked at in isolation, might seem innocuous. They can be explained away, and that is part of the coercion and control, and that's very similar to the questions we have about the new coercive control legislation: that someone who is stalking a victim may well have an understanding of the law; they might well understand where that line is that they're going to tread, and they're really conscious that they need to be able to explain away whatever they do, and one of the easiest ways is to blame the victim and that, in a way, exacerbates that victimisation, that victim-blaming. Part of the impact of stalking is that the victim starts to doubt themselves and starts to doubt whether they're seeing it for what it really is.

So I think we police officers need to make sure that we really know the legislation, and understand how stalking can manifest itself, and how the cumulative effects of seemingly innocuous incidents build and build and build, and really understand it from the victim's perspective. When they're looking at, say, the most recent incident, their perception of that and their interpretation of events is going to be influenced by everything that's gone on before, whether that's previous stalking, the previous relationship or the perpetrator's behaviour within that relationship. It all gives a context, and a very real context for them as victims, that is going to influence how they are perceiving it and influence the fear and anxiety that they might feel as a result.

So, for police officers, I think the challenge for us is to first make sure we're looking at that broader picture: we've really got to get an understanding of the wider circumstances, rather than looking at incidents in isolation. But also, we have to be sure we are really listening to the victim, because, if something seems innocuous but the victim is clearly distressed and anxious about it, we've got to be asking ourselves why that is. What is it about these circumstances that has caused the victim to perceive them in that way? And, until we're doing that consistently, that for me is where we risk missing opportunities to identify stalking.

Of course, the next challenge, once we've got that awareness, is to present the evidence in a way that is objective and that can stand up to scrutiny in a court. Courts work on evidence; it's about proof rather than truth, so that's the next challenge for us, as police officers. But, of course, the victim is central to that, and again, it's making sure that they are at the heart of it and have the opportunity to articulate why it's having that impact on them.

CM: Do you think that your partners, and I'm referring specifically to the Crown Prosecution Service (CPS) and the judiciary, are working as hard as the police to take into account these issues and to support your work? Or is there a recurrent theme of 'Let's go for the easier charge', 'This is easier to prove', masking the reality of something that is quite serious? If you think about sentencing, let's take the example of harassment, you can have an argument with your neighbour about a hedge, that is harassment. It's quite different from stalking and the consequences and impact are quite different.

In relation to the CPS, do you feel supported in the pursuit of stalking charges? Do you feel that they're working as hard as you say the police are to identify and properly charge perpetrators under the new stalking legislation, rather than just harassment?

RB: Sure. I absolutely don't feel unsupported. I think everyone in the criminal justice system has got that shared sense of trying to achieve justice for the victim, trying to safeguard the victim. It's all part of a wider public service, so to doubt anyone's commitment to that would be wrong. I think the different organisations involved in the criminal process have very clearly defined roles and come into the process at different stages, which can present its own challenges. The CPS, when they're considering charges, can only consider the evidence that we're presenting to them, and they consider the case as it's presented to them. They will advise from an expert point of view, but it is incumbent on us to be aware of all the offences that could be committed and to gather all the evidence that's relevant and to present a good, well-articulated case to the CPS, in order for them to consider the charges.

With the courts, again we've got a well-established judiciary. To me, there's no reason to think that the judiciary is any less committed to enforcing stalking legislation than any other legislation. I don't think there's any evidence for that at all. I think it perhaps links back to what I touched on earlier – that, having recognised stalking is being committed, its very nature can make it difficult to build a really rational, objective, evidence-based case, because a court can only work on evidence. It has to work on evidence; it can't work on a gut feeling; it can't work on an overall perception; there's got to be evidence. So, these cases can present challenges at every stage of the justice process.

There is another interesting aspect of stalking legislation – a good number of the behaviours described in the legislation that could amount to stalking are actually offences in their own right, so I suppose that presents some interesting questions for the CPS.

Where the stalking does amount to other offences that are perhaps easier to evidence, then is it the right thing to do to charge the individual with those offences and to pursue a criminal justice outcome for those offences, rather than pursuing a conviction for stalking? This might, I suppose, give the perception that they're taking the easy option. I don't think it's necessarily taking the easy option, but they need to take a really objective view as to whether there's a reasonable likelihood of a case being successful at court.

CM: Maybe easy isn't the correct word. I think a better phrase would be 'the more dangerous option', because if you pursue someone, let's say, for criminal damage, they will (especially if it's their first offence), more likely than not, get a suspended sentence and a fine, but not a custodial sentence, or the option of work that they can undertake to correct their behaviour. They could probably explain it as a fit of anger or something like that, and most people that commit just criminal damage – break your car window – will probably just go away and you will never see them again.

With stalking, the likelihood of that happening is very, very small; they will come back for more. So, when you choose a charge like criminal damage, which, quite often, will represent a small part of a whole stalking scenario, you are ensuring that that person has walked away with it and your victim is still at risk. So, it seems like an incredible amount of resources, time and work are being invested here that, in the longer term, won't hold up to scrutiny, because the chances are that the perpetrator is going to come back for that victim. So, I hear what you say, and I agree with you: I think everyone is trying to do their best work.

But there certainly is an issue with the lack of training, and stalking is a crime that can't be understood without robust training in place. There needs to be more understanding of stalking as a 'course-of-conduct crime', otherwise it just won't be picked up, the links won't be made and stalkers won't be dealt with under the stalking legislation.

RB: Sure. And for me, there's no question that we should be taking the easy option. Where there's a clear case of stalking, we should pursue it, and we should be pushing for that to be reflected in the charges. I think it's important we don't lose sight of the bigger picture for the victims as well, because convictions at court are important for getting justice for victims. The sentencing for any offence will balance a number of issues, but mainly there'll be a punitive element, and then there'll be some sort of safeguarding element. So, if a person is in prison, then there'll be an element of their sentence that is a punishment, and then at some point they become eligible for parole, and that's where it becomes more about safeguarding. We can impose conditions and the like to ensure that further offending does not take place and risk is managed. And that would be the same, regardless of what offence is charged and what offence is convicted.

But it's almost inevitable that, even if there's a period of imprisonment, the perpetrator will come out at some point, and it's the nature of stalking that, whether they're in prison for a year or five years or longer, that risk is still going to be there when they come out. So, I think that, while convictions are a really important part of the whole approach, in themselves they only provide a short-term safeguarding for the victim, and that's where we need to be looking at work with partners, at other opportunities within the law – some of the civil orders, ancillary orders – to make sure we've got a really tight package to support the victim in the longer term. That, in a way, is the greater challenge, I think, than getting a case to court, when we've got identified offences.

CM: I was just saying that because, if you have a stalker, a convicted stalker, then I think there needs to be a wider policy question around what more needs to be done with the perpetrator. Because, as you mentioned, they will be let out; that's inevitable. So, if I know what this person's problem is – obsessive and fixated behaviour – is there any work I can do with this person to address it? How effective that intervention is will probably have an impact on the victim staying safe.

If someone has been convicted for criminal damage, we should be having a different approach and different rehabilitation programmes: for instance, a week attending anger management could work for that person, but it won't work for a stalker. And I know there is not enough funding at the moment to invest in national stalking clinics, or that sort of thing, but there should be, and the more convictions and prosecutions and charges we have for stalking, the more we increase the case for that funding being made available and for those people having those interventions.

Controversially, I think there is a case for doing some proactive and preventative work, rather than purely reactive work, because if we only concentrate our efforts on protecting victims at highest risk, and they are quite rightly going to be prioritised, there is a whole load of other people constantly suffering because they don't reach those thresholds that we talked about.

I would argue that, if more work is done to identify and name stalking, we would get a better chance to work with the person who has an obsessive disorder or a fixated disorder before the next victim comes along, or, when the same victim comes with a new report, we will know what the problem is.

ST: But then you need people like psychologists and psychiatrists to appropriately assess what they're dealing with, and I've sat in on assessments of perpetrators where the psychiatrist or psychologist has an understanding of some of the behaviour, but not an understanding of the context.

RB: For me, it's almost a more basic question. In terms of the context we're in as a society at the moment, I think it absolutely makes sense that we should be working with perpetrators and we should be breaking that cycle of offending, because we know that perpetrators go on to form new relationships. We see it with domestic abuse and if we can break that cycle of offending, we clearly ought to be doing this. I think in Brighton one of our real strengths is the partnerships we've got. We work really well with people like Veritas Justice, with Survivors Network, with Rise, with the commissioners at the City Council. I think the Office of the Sussex Police Crime Commissioner is really well engaged with the partnerships and is investing and contributing towards commissioned services. But the wider context is that we're still in the depths of austerity, which presents some really difficult decisions as to how you prioritise spending, and I think it's reasonable that, when you've got someone who is being victimised right here, right now, today, the funding is prioritised to make sure that they've got appropriate support and they're safe and that their needs are met. So, I think, in the longer term, absolutely we need to do more around perpetrators, and I think that will be an area that I hope will grow and develop over the coming years, but it's really difficult to find a balance when there's finite funds available. I think the challenge for all of us is to work together to make sure we get the biggest impact from those funds that are available, recognising that the criminal justice approach is only a part of that wider process. It's a really important part of that process, but a prosecution in itself can't keep a victim safe forever; there needs to be something wider and something more structured; we need to get that real, long-term safeguarding in place.

CM: I think that, if the ultimate goal of the criminal justice system, or the basis of it, is rehabilitation and reintegration, if you don't charge people with the correct charge, that ultimate end is not being fulfilled. The focus of the criminal justice system is obviously the perpetrator, and he or she ought to be found guilty and punished and offered an option of rehabilitation, and that doesn't happen with stalkers, and I don't think it facilitates anyone's work when we don't know exactly what people's needs and difficulties are.

RB: In a way it links back to that challenge around the legislation identifying behaviours that might amount to stalking but actually are criminal offences in their own right, and some of those are really serious criminal offences. The law talks about sexual abuse and sexual assault, violent assault, so I think, when we're looking at an individual case, it may well be that there's more serious offences, as the court would see it, and it's right that they would be charged, because we are choosing the most serious offence that it's appropriate to charge and to pursue.

I get a real sense, speaking to people like you and stalking victims, that the introduction of the offence of stalking is really important because it identifies it and acknowledges it and recognises it, and names what people have been subjected to, and we don't want to lose sight of the importance of that, because justice, as delivered by the criminal justice system, can mean lots of different things to different people. And I suppose that's where, throughout our investigation, our conversations with the victim need to be really open, really transparent. We need to really understand what the victim needs from that investigation and what a positive outcome looks like and might feel like for that victim. It is difficult, picking that right charge: justice is quite objective, whereas everything about stalking is much more complex, isn't it? It goes to the heart of who we are as people and our emotions, and the anxiety and the stress that's caused, and measuring that is really, really difficult.

CM: I don't want to take anything away from the good work that's happened here in Sussex, and I think we do have pretty good work going on here, but we have supported people who have had less happy experiences, let's just say, even in their involvement with the police. One particular case comes to mind, and we have supported this person, and from that point of view I think, yes, it is a challenge sometimes, even for those of us who support victims. But it seems, or what has been fed back to us, is that victims who experience mental health difficulties, or may have been the perpetrator at some point in the context of domestic violence, or whose stories don't quite add up, are treated less favourably, and their very credibility has been questioned because of the issues they have experienced, and their experience of services is that they are not believed, thereby giving the perpetrator a platform to continue the abuse. And this evidence that these people have been talking about is the kind of evidence that doesn't have any objective element to it. It's the belittling; this person has been told things like, 'Well, it's not a criminal offence to drive down somebody's road', and of course it's not. 'It's not a criminal offence to stand by the traffic lights next to your ex-partner.' No, of course it's not…

RB: But it's the context.

CM: It's the context. And yes, victims lie – they lie, like perpetrators do, like professionals do, like everybody else does. You don't tell your friend, 'Oh my god, that lipstick looks awful on you!' when they come in in the morning, even if you think that, because you don't want to hurt their feelings.

RB: When you look at some of the types of offending that we didn't recognise, we didn't identify, they were always there. When we look at how alive we are now to child sexual exploitation, how much better our response is now to domestic abuse, I think our awareness and understanding of stalking is probably one of the more recent developments, and that's why the stalking legislation has only been in place for a short period of time. It reflects that developing understanding. And I think, not just the police, particularly, but other organisations, partnerships, their understanding, their response to these sorts of issues will also develop over time as recognition improves.

Then our response can be tailored and can improve. I've seen quite a lot of changes within the organisation in recent years. So, my team, for example, has gone through a significant restructure: we've merged adult protection with child protection; we've brought on board the investigation of all rapes and serious sexual assaults;

we've got our domestic abuse case workers; we've got officers at the MASH (Multi-Agency Safeguarding Hub). So, we've brought together a whole range of people, both police staff and police officers, with some really specialist skills, who are really tuned into the safeguarding element of these investigations, as well as the criminal investigations.

So, I think that's indicative of the police as an organisation recognising that we need the specialist skills, we need officers with that knowledge, who've got that understanding of these more subtle types of offending, or offending that can be presented as more subtle – obviously, it's not subtle for those who experience it themselves. They understand that they need to look at it differently, that they need to look at that broader picture, that they need to see it from the victim's perspective and try to understand what's causing those levels of anxiety and distress.

And so, I think we're in a better position now as a police service to respond to victims and to give that service and I think, within the city, we've got a good network of partners. Because we see, with a lot of offending that's perpetrated against the more vulnerable people in our society, that the vulnerability presents challenges in itself. They might not recognise what's being done to them: if they've experienced a kind of long-term abusive relationship, at what point does that become the norm for them?

And I think we need to recognise that, while we do everything we can to build trust in the police among the community and among victims and to encourage confidence to report and to speak to us, there are still people who are more confident and more comfortable speaking to partner organisations, and we have lots of skills within the city. And so I look at the network, and I look at the structure that we've got within the city, and my hope is we have more opportunities now for people to have contact with people whom they trust and can talk to about what they're going through, and that we're sufficiently joined up so that, when someone makes that disclosure, there is support to help them navigate the criminal justice system as well as access the help they need.

I think our services will continue to evolve. I think they need to, because I think our understanding as a criminal justice organisation will continue to develop and improve. And it will continue to improve working with organisations such as yourselves and listening to and hearing those first-hand experiences of stalking.

CM: Do you think that there is any reluctance from the police to intervene in cases where there are children involved and where there are Family Court residence and contact orders?

RB: Not per se. Are you thinking of particular circumstances?

CM: Well I'm thinking that some of the women we support have children with the perpetrators and, if there is a court case, often perpetrators who were not previously interested in the children become so when separation takes place, and children are frequently used as a means of maintaining contact with the victim. So, contact handover, for example, becomes the perfect opportunity to shout abuse at the victim or follow her back if she's living in a different place, and the very existence of refuges and that sort of thing gives you an idea that someone is being tracked down, and now there is an offence that is called stalking but we hardly ever use the word stalking for that sort of situation.

A Women's Aid survey (Women's Aid, 2013) found that 50% of women who separated did so because they feared something would happen to them or their children of they continued the relationship, and it goes on to show that 76% of applications to the Family Court were made by perpetrators to track down the families. It gives you an indication that there is an element of stalking embedded in some of these: we are talking about at least 76% of the cases in which there is a Family Court order in place, and, given that only one per cent of applicant fathers are refused contact, we are talking big numbers.

But when these women we support call the police, whatever their concern is, as soon as they mention that there is a court order in place and the father has contact with the children, the police say, 'Oh well, you know, he is the father, what can we do?' and, while he may not be an immediate threat to the victim or the woman who appears to be the victim, she is vicariously at risk when the children are at risk, if we're talking about the mother. Do you think there is a general reluctance from the police to intervene in those cases because there is a sense that the judiciary has already made a decision on how those family dynamics need to play out or how those timetables should play out?

RB: I think, where there's court orders in place, then we have to respect those court orders, and that doesn't mean I'm not alive to the ways in which a perpetrator might seek to use the Family Court in order to continue the abuse and the control. I can recognise that, but we have to recognise the Family Court as a legal entity in this country, the same as the Magistrate's Court and the Crown Court, so, if orders are made, we need to recognise that.

ST: If an unsupervised contact order has been made, then the civil justice system is saying that there are no child protection issues present. A lot of the women that we support come to frontline services with their concerns around child contact issues, and I'm just wondering, at what stage would those cases come to the recognition of your particular department?

RB: Well, the police's role primarily is to enforce criminal law. Of course, over the years, the role of policing has become much, much broader than that. We do a lot of things across the community, much of which has got very little to do with criminal law, but principally our role is criminal law. And so, for me, this just highlights the importance of having a really joined-up approach. Stalking's not something the police can tackle in isolation: it needs to have a really structured approach with lots of partners, lots of organisations, recognising the whole breadth of ways in which the perpetrator can exert control and continue to exert control on their victim.

And that's where I think our response to stalking as a society is going to continue to develop, as the conversations keep taking place. As well, I've got some optimism within Brighton, because I know those conversations are taking place and I see the strength of the partnerships and the real desire to improve the services. But we need to recognise what each particular agency brings to the issue and what contribution they can make and what the limitations might be – whether they're limitations of resources for some organisations, or whether they are limitations in terms of powers and legislation. Stalking, as you know, is really, really complex, so our response to it needs to be agile and adaptive and co-ordinated.

CM: On that front, I'm thinking about the 36.8% of people who have been stalked who have also been stalked online (Suzy Lamplugh Trust, 2016). I think stalkers have this amazing ability to adapt to the times and online access is so readily available and is now used so often to track down victims. This is, like you say, something that we should all do in partnership, because all of these devices are constant transmitters of our activities, of our information, private or not, and as much as some of those can be used to help parents keep their children safe and all of that, they can also be used for much more sinister means. Very few of the people we support who have experienced online stalking actually reported it to the police. I do wonder if, when we see someone coming to the criminal justice system for support with online stalking or cyberstalking, we start looking immediately for other crimes that may have been committed under the Malicious Communications Act, as a way of supporting that other charge. Or is that something we still need to get to grips with, because it's moving so much faster than we can possibly update our systems?

RB: I think it's really interesting when you look at how far technology has developed in our generations. The world's just changing, it's changing constantly, and, I suppose, not just with stalking, with many types of offending.

Criminals out there are often the first to recognise new ways to exploit new technology in order to continue to perpetrate whatever offences they're perpetrating. We see it with online sexual exploitation, we see it with online fraud, we see it with stalking as well. The challenge for a police service and for society is to keep track with those changes, with the developing technology. I think we need to recognise, and we do recognise, as a police service, that so much more offending is taking place online, and actually the traditional structures that we've had, of bobbies on the beat, is not effective at tackling some of the new kinds of cybercrime. We need to adapt to that, we need to restructure, we need to start putting resources, or continue to put more resources into those high-tech investigation units so that we've got the capability and we've got the ability to respond.

In terms of our response in a broader sense, I think exactly the same challenges apply. We've got behaviours that could be construed as stalking and could amount to an offence of stalking, but in themselves could be other offences as well, whether it's malicious communication or other offences taking place in a cyber environment. The challenges are the same: we still need officers to be looking at the individual circumstances and recognising the wider context of what's taking place, recognising the impact it's had on the victim. It might be something that, in itself, might be relatively minor or innocuous – someone's changed their password to their email or has posted something on their Facebook page. We need to understand the context of that and understand why it's different to an isolated incident, why it's different in the circumstances. So, it's new challenges, but it's a challenge for us all as a society, as technology improves, to continue to adapt our response accordingly.

CM: On that note, we were concerned to hear a police officer say that, if you are being harassed and stalked online, you need to shut down your Facebook account.

ST: It's expecting victims to change *their* behaviour.

RB: It's absolutely not a solution and, again, my view is that, while the online world is really new and it's continuing to evolve and change, the principles are not so dissimilar to the real world. When I leave my house, I lock my front door. When I leave my car, I lock the car. I take reasonable precautions. What I absolutely shouldn't have to do is change my routine, lose my freedoms, and that equally applies to the online world. I've got a Facebook account and I've set the privacy to the level that I'm comfortable with, because I want to exert some control over who can see what I post. I think it's right that people have an awareness of what steps they can take to protect their security and their personal information online, but it is recognising the point at which they are being forced to go further, or if there's any pressure on them to go further than make those free choices.

So, I think the two worlds are not wholly different. I suppose the difficulty with new technology is that the vast majority of society sees new technology as an opportunity, as something new and exciting, and it presents really positive experiences. And then you get a very small number of people who'll seek to exploit it, and so I suppose it's about deciding what's reasonable for society as a whole to do to respond to that and protect themselves online.

ST: And also, I've heard police officers telling people to change their mobile phone number or change their phone, and I suppose there's a whole issue there around getting rid of evidence, essentially. So, if people change their number, they'll no longer have the evidence of the 50 texts that they've been sent overnight.

RB: I think it's important not to confuse personal safety advice with the evidential needs of an investigation.

ST: That's not what's being advised though, around securing evidence; that's the issue.

CM: How do we ensure that people get the right advice when they first access services or support or report a crime? Because I am sure, as you go up the ladder in different organisations, you get people with more and more and more expertise, but when your frontline response isn't up to scratch, people lose confidence. One of the big struggles we have is that, for any of the people we support, I don't think we are the first service that they have approached. They have been through other services, and we say, 'OK, you must report it to the police, you must report everything, because, if stalking is a course-of-conduct crime, you need to prove that there was a course of conduct, and the only way that you can get them on board is if they know that this happened and it happened again and again. So, you must give them the evidence that they need to help you.'

But, we do hear a lot from them, 'Oh, I've been so many times to the police and they just said that there is nothing they can do. I won't report it.' So then you think, well, I can't force people to report incidents, and if they don't give me permission to report it, I can't report it either. But there is an issue of confidence, of what that first advice is like. So when you say to someone, 'Oh well, just get rid of your phone', or 'Come off social media', you're asking them to shut down their lives and this will not only prevent them from engaging with services but also it's damaging in terms of gathering evidence.

RB: I think anyone who's advising a victim to change their number as a solution to being stalked is not recognising that person as a victim of stalking, because it can never be an answer to that. It just can't. You know, if someone's being stalked, it's going to manifest itself in so many different ways that, for me, it's suggestive of their missing the opportunity to identify a person as a victim of stalking. And that's where we've got to continue to work to build awareness, to build knowledge, so that officers are going out and consciously looking and holding those conversations and asking those broader questions of the victims to understand the context. It all goes back to the context. It is about the early identification, undoubtedly; we need to get better at that and we'll continue to get better at that.

I think that confidence is really important as well. As a service, we do lots of work to try to build confidence among our communities to report matters to us and we continue to see increased reporting in domestic abuse and significantly increased reporting for rapes and sexual offences. There are really positive trends around these vulnerability offences, so my hope is that, as awareness of stalking becomes more commonplace, more people will have the confidence to come forward, officers will get better at identifying it, that we'll provide a better response, and that in turn will perpetuate increased confidence.

Establishing confidence takes time, because when you're let down once, the impact can be massive, and it can take a long time, if you ever get that opportunity, to make amends. We have to keep improving. But I think, with the development of specialist teams such as my own, we do go out to events with partners, and we talk about the work that we do and we really try to get across the message that we're *more* than just police officers, *more* than just investigators. I think we can be an access point for the support services, to cover that whole safeguarding package. And, as awareness of our advocacy work at Veritas builds, then that perhaps will contribute to building confidence in reporting, alongside, of course, the work that you and other partners are doing across the city. Again, it needs that whole joined-up approach, because it is difficult to build confidence and it takes time and we've got to be relentless and committed and consistent, and, when people do report, we've got to do the best we can to provide the level of service that they deserve.

CM: I think, especially with stalking, because it's such a debilitating situation and people have so much to respond to in dealing with all the little things their stalkers do, that if keeping on an investigation means one more task, it might just be that one more task that you just don't have any more energy for and then you think, 'OK, well, they arrested him and let him go, he'll be here next.' I think that it's a very, very difficult line to tread, because you can have only so many expectations and so much trust in what police can do in an emergency.

I think those initial conversations are *so* important – the 'I'm going to keep you informed', 'This is what's going to happen' conversations. I think that's incredibly easy for the police to do, and for the person accessing the service, it's so reassuring because you know, 'OK, I'm going to be kept informed. No one's promising anything but I am going to be kept informed. I am a part of this.' So, in that sense, like you say, all that initial work, either with the police or with other agencies, is *so* important to keep someone engaged.

RB: I think it's about the whole process in that, quite often with an early report of stalking, the behaviours that are reported to us can appear quite minor and maybe don't amount to a criminal offence in themselves. It's when they're taken together that we start looking at the offence of stalking. To progress a case to court and for the CPS to authorise charges or proceed with a case to court, then it needs to pass the evidential test.

There needs to be sufficient objective evidence in order to achieve those charges, and it might be the case that, at that first opportunity, there just isn't sufficient evidence. But, because we know that stalking's different to other types of offending, that it doesn't end, it's going to carry on, for me the challenge is how do we make sure we work with the support organisations so, when the criminal investigation perhaps comes to an end for a period of time, there is a pathway for that victim to continue to receive support and easily access the police again, should it continue. That's about relationships, that's about my team working with your organisation and other partners around the city and it being an ongoing relationship with the victim, so that the support continues.

I suppose it's different to other types of offending where the offence might be committed as an isolated incident or over a very short time period; this is long-term stuff, so our response needs to reflect that, and our response needs to reflect the fact that it's broader than just a criminal justice response. The police can deliver the criminal justice response, and if that's not achievable at a particular time, we can look at what other options are available – the civil orders or ancillary orders and the wider safeguarding that is still going to be ongoing. So, it needs that longer-term approach, recognising the different roles of different organisations in providing that package for the victim.

CM: Do you think the new offence of coercive control is going to present very similar challenges as stalking because, from what I can see, it's exactly the same offence, it's just got a cut-off point in a timeline. Do you think the two offences are going to become ancillary to the other in relation to increasing prosecutions for both offences?

RB: I think there's an awful lot of similarity between the two offences, so I think they will continue to develop almost in parallel: the coercive control legislation will apply to people still within the intimate relationship, and the stalking to those not in an intimate relationship. The similarities are quite clear. There is something about the criminal justice system in this country that the offences as set out in law tend to focus very much on physical harm to an individual, so the seriousness of an assault charge is determined by the level of physical injury.

The courts work on evidence, on proof rather than truth. So, you can assault someone with psychological harm, it's there within statute, but actually the prosecutions that would take place for psychological harm are going to be a minority in comparison with physical assaults. So, I think the challenge is there in both the coercive control and the stalking legislation for investigators to recognise it from the victim's perspective, to understand why there is that level of anxiety and distress, and to work with the victim to articulate that and turn it into evidence and present it to the courts.

We will continue to get better at it. With the specialist officers in my team, we have got the skills we need. When we look at the approach we might take with victims of rape and serious sexual offences, with the video interviewing, we've got specially trained officers that work with the victim to capture their evidence, so there's lots of skills that we can transfer across. It's a different question as to how the courts will view the cases as more of them progress to court and how judges will interpret the sentencing. I think, in many ways, that will reflect society's recognition of the impact of both stalking and coercive control – society recognising the real impact on the victims, that it goes beyond physical injury. So, in many ways, I think our criminal justice system reflects society's wider thinking and we need that thinking to develop across the board, not just within certain organisations. We need to recognise that psychological harm is every bit as damaging and hurtful and painful as physical harm.

CM: So what needs to be done for that to become more of a norm, I wonder? Because the literature about the impact of psychological abuse on adults and on children who witness it suggests it is so much longer lasting and more damaging than the physical abuse.

ST: Victims themselves describe it as being much worse and that physical harm is easier to deal with than the long-term impact of psychological abuse.

RB: Of course, at times, it feels like society's moving far too slowly and things could happen a lot quicker. I often reflect back on the years

I've spent in the police and the really significant changes that have taken place. By way of example, in law a husband couldn't rape his wife, and you look at that now and it's absolutely staggering that society could think like that. Of course, it feels at times as if society is moving far too slowly but, actually, I think it can change quickly, but the challenge for us is how do we encourage that change, how do we encourage that momentum to continue? For me, it's about conversations and visibility and awareness, making people consciously confront their thinking on it and question what they think is acceptable.

ST: People think, 'What happened in her childhood to make her end up in an abusive relationship?' It's seen as a crime that the victim brings on themself – that's the issue with domestic abuse and stalking and rape – that there must be something about the victim that encouraged this to happen.

RB. Yes, undoubtedly there's people out there who think like that. As always, that's the challenge we've got with so many of these different types of offending – there's such a range of understanding and perceptions and opinions.

ST: I spoke at a coercive control conference in Ipswich and we had a magistrate, a female magistrate, probably in her 60s, and she sat through the entire conference, and then she rounded up what she had heard and it was just all about that we were all anti-men, and we shouldn't be blaming them. It was almost as if she hadn't heard anything that had been said, by men themselves as well. It was staggering.

RB: We need to recognise that we've got to keep on working to tackle homophobia, we've got to keep on working to tackle hate crime and racism and ignorance of all sorts and all kinds.

CM: When we were doing National Stalking Week last year at the university, we got young men saying, 'Oh no, stalking is for girls.' Stalking is for everyone. Anyone can be stalked.

RB: It's a really interesting point, actually, because we still see under-reporting of domestic abuse by men. We still see under-reporting of rape and sexual offences by men. There are a lot of people who will make judgments around men experiencing those sorts of crimes and we've got an enormous amount of work to do here in raising public awareness. We see the same with child sexual exploitation. We need to raise awareness and recognition that it can happen to anyone, and that it's never the victim's fault – man, woman, child, it doesn't discriminate.

CM: It's really difficult with some of the students that we work with, the students that we teach too – with men not reporting or not being victims, or women deserving it – equally, they just assume that these things only happen to certain groups in society.

ST: I have experienced domestic abuse and stalking and I didn't recognise domestic abuse in my own situation at all. I lived with him for five years and, because he wasn't physically violent – I always knew that if a man touched me, if he was physically violent towards me or sexually violent towards me, that would be the end of the relationship, and it would have been – but this was so unrecognisable, what was happening, that I didn't see it at all. Thinking back to my own perceptions of domestic abuse, it only happened to women on the Jeremy Kyle Show; it didn't affect people like me. So, although I recognised that he was very verbally abusive and that he made me extremely unhappy and that he was a heavy drinker and had inappropriate behaviour, I did not recognise myself as a victim of domestic abuse at all, and it took a friend of my mum's to name stalking. I didn't know I was being stalked. I knew I was terrified and I felt I was being hunted down, but it wasn't until she actually used that word that I really realised just the level of risk that I was at.

RB: It is that level of complexity. It's about the authorities and the police recognising it, and it's about the people experiencing it recognising it, and their friends and family.

ST: Yes, my friends and family didn't recognise the domestic abuse side of it at all, even in the context of his broader offending behaviour. My best friends, who are very articulate, middle-class, educated people, still supported him and visited him in prison, even though they knew his past behaviour. It wasn't until they were personally affected by it that they recognised it themselves, and that was two years down the line from the initial disclosure.

RB: And that's really interesting, when it's gone through court, and the court has said, on the evidence, you are guilty, and the gravity is such that we are sending you to prison, and still people are reticent to recognise that person as an offender.

ST: It was only when their own daughter was harassed by him online that they actually recognised that behaviour, and they now have a restraining order against him. I think that's part of the complexity and challenges that you're up against – if it's not affecting you personally, it's that much more difficult to understand.

RB: It's difficult because it's almost unimaginable that someone who says they love you can behave in that way towards you. But the work that you do with your organisation, sharing victims' experiences, is a window, a small window, into that world, which is so important and so powerful.

References

Suzy Lamplugh Trust (2016). *Out of Sight, Out of Mind.* London: Suzy Lamplugh Trust. www.suzylamplugh.org/Handlers/Download.ashx?IDMF=0d387e89-1fb4-48cd-818e-138dc84563eb (accessed June 2017).

Women's Aid (2013). *Women's Aid Annual Survey 2013: domestic violence services.* Bristol: Women's Aid. https://1q7dqy2unor827bqjls0c4rn-wpengine.netdna-ssl.com/wp-content/uploads/2015/10/Womens-Aid-annual-survey-report-2013.pdf (accessed August 2017).

FIRST-PERSON ACCOUNTS

7

Can't let go

Rachel Williams

My name is Rachel and I was a victim of stalking. I didn't know that I had actually been stalked until it was brought to my attention by a trustee of Network for Surviving Stalking.

I was in an abusive relationship for 18 years, which consisted of sly punches to the back of my head and spitting in my face. My hair was pulled and I was controlled about what I could wear and where I could work, along with other abuse too. I was constantly walking on eggshells.

The 9th July 2011 was the day that I finally told myself I was going to leave him. This was after he tried to strangle me and slit his wrist in front of our son, who was 16 years old. The fear of staying with him now became greater than the fear of leaving him. I thought, if he can do this in front of our son, then what else is he capable of doing? It was not long before I found out.

I called the police and gave a historical statement, filed for divorce and started with procedures to sell the home, because I knew that he would never agree to me staying in the house, and I didn't want this to be a reason for any contact. I needed to sever ties completely. This is something that I had never done before, and this really shook him up.

Over the next few weeks, my estranged husband was arrested for the assault and was bailed for a later court date. During this period, he had taken an overdose… this is part of an abuser's tactics in trying to woo the victim back, which didn't work! Now all his pleading and saying sorry fell on deaf ears because I had repeatedly heard it over 18 years.

On 19th August, my estranged husband came to my place of work, a hairdressers, armed with a sawn-off shot gun. There was a battle in the salon, he hit me on the head with the butt of the gun and I landed on the floor. I managed to pull the reception desk over me for cover. He then kicked this away from me, and I was exposed to him. He was siux foot, seven inches, and 22 stone – 22 stone of muscle, as he was a body builder. My abuser was now standing over me pointing a gun at me. At this point, I had pulled my knees up under my chin to shield myself for what was coming next. He aimed the gun at my chest and told me that he loved me and pulled the trigger. The first shot blasted my left knee and shin, the second shot skimmed past the right side of my head.

He then put the gun down to reload. I remember the gun very vividly – it was silver with ornate engraving on it. I grabbed the gun and the battle commenced. I fought tooth and nail to keep hold of the gun. I found a supernatural strength. I won this battle, and he then, in frustration, repeatedly stamped and kicked all over me. Thankfully, I never lost consciousness and was fully aware as to what was happening. After this beating, he then fled the shop and was later found hanged.

I was taken to hospital, where the surgeons were fantastic and managed to save my leg. This was after I was initially encouraged to have it amputated. I spent six weeks in hospital and I still had black eyes after my hospital discharge.

On 23rd of September 2011, I was discharged from hospital and went home to recover. I was still wearing a leg brace; this was going to be a slow process.

Three days after my discharge, our son, who had witnessed the domestic violence and the attack on 9th July, committed suicide. He was 16 years old. He was the innocent victim of domestic violence and he now is another statistic in a report. This is the reality of domestic abuse and violence.

I want to say that, during the six-week period between 9th July and the shooting, my estranged husband stalked me, but I never knew his behaviour was stalking. This was something that hadn't entered my head, but it was made clear to me once I spoke to Network for Surviving Stalking, and they actually told me his behaviour was stalking. During the six weeks, he sent me unwanted text after text and repeatedly phoned me. He also parked outside my place of work and chillingly stared at the hairdressers.

Unbeknown to me, this was the start of the tragedy that was shortly to unfold.

Stalking can kill.

The video telling Rachel's story, 'Trouble with an Ex', made by the Network for Surviving Stalking, is on YouTube at www.youtube.com/watch?v=vnntNrSFuEY

8

The unravelling

Amy Barlow

It began as most love stories begin. Nervous, excited encounters initially, heady passionate romance. It all felt a bit quick though. I was in a tough place. I'd been a single mother for two years, and was lonely, struggling, and looking for romance. With hindsight, I was a bit vulnerable. Prior to the birth of my daughter, I had my first experience of extreme psychological distress, and found myself detained under the Mental Health Act. For those two years, I had tried really hard to keep on a level, without much direction or support.

I longed for a father for my daughter – a reliable, non-alcoholic one. I wanted to share the intense relationship we had with another person, have some fun. Most of all, I needed support, which was severely lacking. No close relatives nearby, my friends had equally small children, or they were childless and still partying.

The headiness lasted three months, and I started to feel a bit trapped, a bit controlled, a bit manipulated. I also started to question this man's reliability around my daughter. Doubt set in, mistrust and dark thoughts. I no longer felt able to leave him alone with her. I kept thinking it was all in my mind – unreal, paranoid, haunting glimpses of my own abuses were rising from the depths. I didn't share these thoughts with my friends. I persisted with the relationship for another three months, the nagging feeling inside growing. We went to a local, small music festival. I was working there doing stilt walking, the most fun I'd had in a long while. However, there was a reason I had been avoiding festivals, as I soon became over-tired, increasingly unstable emotionally, and I unravelled.

I blurted out accusations and ended the relationship. Interestingly, the friend I turned to, who let us sleep in with them that final night at the festival, could see the truth in my utterances. I was a wreck. I continued to not sleep, unravelling more by the second.

I had planned to perform at another festival in Ireland, a paid stilt-walking gig, at a much bigger and well-known festival, while a friend looked after my daughter. I arrived there a mess, got lost, and became a missing person for 24 hours. Again, I was detained and given drugs that made me see double and slurred the edges of my world. I didn't know how I had got to this place. I gathered up my sanity and, with the help of an amazing friend, came back to the UK.

I wasn't going to mention my mental health but I think it's pertinent. The weeks that followed consisted of increasing instability. I partied, I enjoyed myself and I certainly did not recognise I was losing touch with myself again. The fear that something had happened to my daughter consumed me, and the regret that I'd allowed someone untrustworthy into our lives was intolerable.

Although my daughter was only two and a half, she revealed three months after I ended the relationship with my ex that some form of sexual abuse had occurred. Three months of doubt, worry and suspicion came to a horrendous head of realisation that this probably did happen. During those three months, I had had a barrage of text messages from him. Phone calls to my landline and mobile were around 20+ a day. For three months, I felt increasingly paranoid, untrusting of anyone, and feeling less and less safe in my own home.

One day, during those three months before my daughter disclosed my ex's treatment of her, I caught sight of him through the window, opposite my flat. I lived on the first floor on a busy main road. He was pacing and peering. I'd had enough. Toddler in the buggy, I approached him and warned him quite loudly in public that this was unacceptable, and I would call the police if it happened again.

After the disclosure of his abuse from my daughter, I experienced a period of not knowing what to do, a spell of tightly coiling terror mounting in my head. My daughter's father had told some of his traveller friends – new travellers who lived in vehicles around the Brighton area – who wanted to retaliate with violence. Her father also attacked me at my shop and the police were called. I also accidentally bumped into my ex and he threw his glass in my face. On Boxing Day, we told the police, as we thought this was the right thing to do. I unravelled again.

I felt physically very unwell. My stomach turned in knots constantly. I was doubled over in pain a lot of the time. I didn't sleep. I drank very heavily, when not with my daughter. I felt like I was losing control of my very core being. All that I held dear, trust in loved ones, reality, all started to feel like they were spinning out of control. I became very paranoid about everyone, I trusted no one. Reality began to blur and every day there was more drama. It really was too much for me to bear. I think, if I had enjoyed a stable upbringing myself and had solid early childhood relationships, then maybe I could have coped better, but I just did not have the emotional resources at this point in my life.

I was reported missing again. I was detained again.

The terror I felt about my ex seeking vengeance was totally overwhelming. The sighting of him opposite the flat, the dozens and dozens of calls, the shouting at me in the street. I was living among a very liberally-minded community, many of whom would describe themselves as anarchists. We were trying to live in an alternative way, one that thrives on co-operation and mutual aid. Many people lived in vehicles, as new travellers, around Brighton and the UK, in more sustainable ways, off grid, free from high rents and social norms.

This subculture, the travelling community and the anarchists, has a strong belief that the state, especially the police, should not be turned to for support or to punish members of the community. This was at odds with what I believed should happen in this situation. This tight-knit community I lived in didn't believe me, because of my mental health problems. I really believed he would try to hurt me in my sleep, break in, even perhaps kill me. I couldn't stay there any longer.

Social services wanted me to prove that I was taking every step available to 'protect my family'. That's my daughter and me, my family. After my ex threw a glass in my face, I reported it to the police and they put a marker (quick response alert) on my phone and my address. Under the guidance of social services, I asked for a restraining order, so that my ex could be charged if he approached me or tried to contact me. It was at this point that I told my neighbour what had been happening. She told me she had seen him near the entrance to our flats almost twice a day for the past few months. Even with the threat of a restraining order, he approached me, but I was feeling much stronger by then. I reported this again to the police and he was given a warning.

The cruellest aspect of the whole experience was not only the terror and the fear that his constant lurking and relentless, hateful texts and phone calls evoked. It was clear to me that, in his mind, he had a convenient excuse: I was mad; I was delusional; I had been detained three times; I needed medicating. By my behaviour, I had undermined the beliefs of my community in endeavouring to find a way, mutually and co-operatively, to smooth over problems in relationships. I was the one in the wrong. In my mind, however, I was a vulnerable single parent, living off small means, alone, without close family nearby. He and others of his ilk are the ones in the wrong. In relation to the stalking, the police helped me feel safe through the marker and having a female officer, whom I felt I could relate to, come into my home to talk to me.

They took me seriously, which I didn't feel was happening in my community, and it felt like things were more on my terms. The police were also very clear about what support there was, and what to do if something happened with my ex. I felt listened to, and this did help my feelings of insecurity and fear somewhat. However, the experience of reporting the alleged abuse to the police was not a positive one. I think that the timing of it, over the Christmas period, and a lack of police personnel, delayed the process significantly. It was obviously complicated by my detention, but I felt the police should have had clearer guidelines and protocols that could have been communicated to me.

I did not think I would ever get through this. However, I had an amazing student social worker who believed I could, and I believed in him. Immediately after having my detention revoked, I stopped drinking alcohol and have stayed off alcohol now for eight years. This has helped my recovery immensely and my ability to single-parent my child. Slowly, the wounds began to heal and, about a year later, I took myself away and lived on a boat for a while, the distance helping both socially and emotionally.

I returned six months later, a bit braver, less anxious and ready to begin life again. I decided to train to become a health professional, as I wanted to give back some of the compassion I had received, and to challenge what I saw as wrong with mental health services. My true friends stayed by my side and supported me, and continue to do so today. The perpetrator was never convicted, as my daughter was too young to question. He still lives in the same town, and is still connected to youth services, which is troubling. My daughter is no longer troubled by what happened, thankfully, and is a bright, shiny, brave girl.

9

You couldn't make it up

Sam Taylor

Oh, the noble traditions of British justice, but fuck me, it's 1830 – I must get my chimney swept.
(Abi Grant, 2009)

I've written about my experiences of being stalked to the point of boring myself (and others) unconscious on the subject, in a desperate attempt to make sense of what became my life, and almost my death, over a period of four years from 2008 to 2012. I wrote personal diaries and a screenplay. I wrote statements for the police, victim personal statements for the Criminal Court, response statements for the Family Court and letters to my MP. I wrote and gave evidence to a parliamentary campaign on stalking law reform, and made it the focus of every paper, dissertation and article I've written since.

This shit takes hold of your life and relentlessly batters you, waiting for a moment when you might not be focused; a moment when you might get distracted by normal life and it can take you down. Preparing for battle becomes your normality. Not just against the stalker but against an entire system that disadvantages people who have never been in trouble, at each turn giving the perpetrator every benefit of the doubt.

I had to speak out and write about what it was like to be stalked. That's what kept me sane (that and pogo dancing around my living room to 'Pretty Vacant' by the Sex Pistols full blast). A lot of people feel ashamed or embarrassed. But what have I got to be ashamed about? I'm bloody livid.

So, I wrote about it and talked about it, until I literally felt 'stalked out'. I found it almost impossible to focus on anything else, although for much of the time there's little choice to do otherwise if you want to survive. I needed to know what was happening. Most of the time I couldn't believe what was happening as things turned from bad to catastrophic, and I experienced every emotion available to human beings, not only due to the behaviour of my stalker but also because of the archaic way in which the 'system' deals with cases such as mine.

I never shied away from my experiences. On occasion, I would be advised to keep silent in order to protect others from the terrible details of my situation. 'They won't understand' and 'People will judge you,' I was told, which is incredible, considering how understanding people were on discovering he'd raped a 14-year-old girl eight years before I met him. 'Poor dad; he just wants to see his kids.'

I was informed he was on the sex-offender register while I was still living with him and when my children were both under the age of three. The police had known he was living with me but he'd lied to them about having kids and therefore they didn't view me as at risk and didn't think it necessary to tell me. I asked him to leave the family home and he wouldn't go, which ended in him trying to break my neck after I had put the children to bed one night. The children and I were escorted to my parents' house and were unable to return home for the next six months because of the threat he posed.

About a week after the attack, I met a woman who advised me, 'The safest thing you can do is tell everyone,' and, terrified of my stalker and utterly horrified at what was happening, I took her advice. He'd been arrested, charged with battery and released on bail, leaving him free to get back to his job, keep in contact with my friends, family and neighbours, and continue hunting me down. I had to start sharing my story until people listened.

My expectation of telling people what had happened was that naturally they would believe my side of the story – the truth. In stalking cases, however, particularly ex-intimate partner cases, things are not quite that clear-cut. People had known him as a local gardener, a neighbour and a father. I won't go as far as to say he had friends, but some people liked him and now supported him, and saw me as a hysterical, neurotic woman who was embellishing the truth. Perhaps it was just too terrible for people to accept.

I was living in a world of utter confusion, and at times I would question myself over what had actually happened. I remember thinking I must be dead, he must have succeeded in killing me. I was living in some strange, parallel universe, where what was happening wasn't really happening and I was watching everything from the other side of a cracked and frosted window. The wrong decisions were being made at every turn and, no matter how much I protested, they were going to happen anyway. And they did.

Every experience I went through was at odds with normal, logical thought or reason. On one occasion, while he was in prison on a 32-week sentence for breaches of the restraining order, I was told by the police that I had been assessed as at 'high risk of homicide'. A couple of weeks later, he was released from prison and permitted to live five minutes walking distance from my house. When I expressed my concern to the authorities, the response was, 'Oh I know, it's not right is it, but the police can't be your personal bodyguards can they'?

So, my children and I were sent to a refuge, out of the area and away from our entire support network, where I had to take unpaid leave from work, go on income support and get put on a housing list. I was sent away with a one-year-old and three-year-old in tow, to a place where I wasn't permitted to let anyone know where we were staying and where the local police were not familiar with my case, should I need to ring them in an emergency.

It was at this point that I started writing to my MP. I'd been a bit nervous to write before, but now I was furious with the position I'd been put in. Some serious action needed taking. It took several months for the MP's response to land on the desk of the police department dealing with my case, but once it did, they started taking more notice. I had the Chief Superintendent in my living room, apologising profusely for the catalogue of mistakes that had been made in my case and reassuring me these mistakes wouldn't happen again.

At the time, this felt like a minor victory, but soon the situation started deteriorating again. My stalker went on the run, having breached his restraining order again. The police could never find him, but he would turn up everywhere I went. At one point, I even suggested borrowing a police uniform so I could go and arrest him myself. This led to me having to write to my MP a further 11 times.

The problem is a systemic one. You meet individual police officers who say all the right things, which they genuinely mean at the time of saying them, but this good will isn't enough to make the changes required and they don't seem to have a lateral understanding of stalking. They seem only able to deal with one incident at a time, thereby missing the links, the patterns, and a course-of-conduct behaviour. And so it goes on: the situation isn't taken seriously enough, the perpetrator receives a clear message they can carry on as ever, and all this leads to two women a week being murdered by an ex-partner in the UK.

Since the attack, I'd been suffering from post-traumatic stress disorder, but there was barely a moment of respite. His behaviour was relentless and you couldn't second guess what the hell he might do next or how seriously the next police officer, solicitor, barrister or judge would take it. Access to justice from the victims' perspective all becomes a bit hit and miss.

When the reality of the situation became too overwhelming, I would sometimes escape into another world. I'd imagine I was actually working as an undercover researcher for a screenplay I hadn't written yet. I'd feel exhilarated at the idea of writing it up later and sharing what I'd written with others. I'd even imagine who I might get to play the various roles for each character. Often, I would think of cutting scenes out because they seemed too exaggerated, all while these real-life events were actually taking place.

I'd imagine being filmed in scenes as they were happening. I would visualise a TV camera on wheels following me down the wood-panelled police corridor, or the camera would zoom into a close-up as I was opening yet another poisonous letter from my stalker's solicitor. The credits would start to roll and I wouldn't have to deal with any more shit until the following week. I'd get time for a breather from the daily feeling that I might be murdered today while getting my make-up redone for the next shoot.

As I'm writing this, it occurs to me to describe 2010 as a real low point in my case, but actually, looking back and reading my diaries, at that time I was as high as a bloody kite on adrenaline. The year was topped and tailed by two Crown Court cases, and for nine months in between I had the fight of my life in the Family Court, and the previous year I had enrolled myself onto a full-time masters in creative writing and personal development – guess what I wrote about for the duration of the course?

I desperately needed an outlet for the growing trauma that had become my existence and which reached new and dizzy heights that year. Suffice to say, I didn't do much parenting of my by now three- and five-year-old children, leaving that responsibility to my parents.

The Crown Court episodes can only be described as a farce: 'a comic dramatic work using buffoonery and horseplay and typically including crude characterisation and ludicrously improbable situations' (Oxford Living Dictionaries, 2016). But it was happening for real.

He was brought into court from prison having pleaded not guilty to breaching the restraining order for the about the 70th time by trying to contact me indirectly via text messages to my parents and a letter to a close friend. He'd been recalled to prison from an offenders' hostel after being caught in possession of several mobile phones.

I was met by a CPS barrister who had approximately five minutes to skim-read my case file, which was now about three inches thick. The defendant, however, had a defence barrister who had spent three months working on the case. I was given special measures in court, meaning I could enter the court via a separate entrance, wait in a separate area and be cross-examined from behind a screen.

We all thought it was an open-and-shut case, including the police. We were confident that the evidence spoke for itself and he would inevitably be remanded in custody. But the jury weren't given the full context and background of his behaviour, he was able to speak for a day and a half in court without being cross-examined, and the shock outcome was that he was found not guilty and was released just in time to attend the Family Court a week or so after.

Later that year, we were back in the Crown Court, as the stalking continued after his release and, once the police could actually find him, he was arrested, charged with harassment and released once again into the community. Again, he pleaded not guilty and I was about to be called for evidence when the court process was paused while he had a chat with the judge to ask what would happen if he pleaded guilty at the last minute. He was advised that, if he admitted what he had done, he wouldn't be returned to prison, but would most likely be released on a suspended sentence. We were all sent home while he decided what to do, and the following day he pleaded guilty and was released again, almost without punishment – a ludicrously improbable farce.

But the Crown Court was an absolute pleasure in comparison with the Family Court process, for which I could never have prepared myself. You could liken it to the ducking stool, a medieval way to identify witches. If the witch floated and survived, it was deemed that she was in league with the devil, and hanged. If the witch sank and drowned, she was innocent (but conveniently dead anyway).

It's the same with this judicial process.

After receiving the application the father of my children had made in order to have contact with them (which arrived through my letterbox on Christmas Eve 2009), I started to feel as though I had found myself in a place that didn't exist – I was somewhere, but nowhere. He had been prevented from seeing the children since the attack on me, until a very helpful female solicitor touting for business in the local prison advised him that every sex offender has the right to see their children. All of this was done with absolutely no consideration for the devastating fear he'd caused the children through his unhealthy obsession with their mother.

The judges in the court had a similar attitude, camouflaged by a repetition of the phrase 'in the children's best interest', a term that slips easily off the tongue when making decisions about other people's families.

As a woman, if you live with an abusive partner, every expectation is on you to be the protective parent. Some women have had their children removed for not being protective enough, and yet, when you get into the Family Court, should you dare to make an allegation of domestic abuse and stalking, you will be viewed as obstructive to contact and the likelihood is that an abusive father will be rewarded with unsupervised contact.

In my case, a psychiatric assessment of the father was undertaken and he was found to be a 'psychopathic paranoid narcissist' – a triple whammy! That said, the psychiatrist went on to state that, while the father was a significant danger to women, children and the public in general, he did *not* consider him to be a physical danger to his own children.

I just wanted to scream at them all , 'Let him see your fucking kids then!'

At this point, I was ready to walk away from my children altogether and leave them with my parents because I had run out of ideas on how to protect them. I knew he would seriously harm them as revenge for me not giving into him, and the more I tried to protect my children, the more potential risk they seemed to be placed in.

Fortunately, a final report was made, challenging the psychiatrist's findings, and the father eventually withdrew his application.

By now, and very much addicted to the adrenaline that had come from living in constant fear for three years, I didn't quite know what to do with myself, with no court case looming on the horizon. I heard that my stalker was in a new relationship and things went quiet for several months. But I wasn't comforted by the feeling of relief I'd been so desperate for, and began itching around to find ways of busying myself to feed my now deeply rooted 'fight or flight' addiction.

During my masters course, which I'd somehow successfully completed and passed, I wrote a poem entitled 'This is Where I Shelter When I Shelter'. I'd shared the poem with various professionals who'd supported me through my case, and consequently I was invited to present at several public events, including police and domestic abuse training sessions. Having never been one for public speaking, this challenge gave me the buzz of anxiety I had been so frantic to replace.

There were a couple of additional benefits to sharing my story in this way. Seeing the look of horror on the faces of those hearing my story for the first time helped me to realise that:

1. I hadn't over-reacted and imagined what had happened to me after all, and

2. if I could educate or change the attitude of just one person in a room, it might start to improve the way in which stalking victims are dealt with.

That same year I was invited to give evidence as part of the Stalking Law Reform Campaign, which came about due to all-party parliamentary support for an independent inquiry. Being asked to speak in Parliament was an exciting opportunity. I'd written a nine-page statement on my case, specifically outlining the stalking issues involved, and I was eager for those in positions of power to hear the account of my experiences.

But what became most apparent on that day was that I was the only surviving domestic abuse stalking victim to give evidence. All other evidence was being given by parents of murdered daughters.

The impact of these first-hand accounts led to the aims of the campaign being achieved in a remarkably short time. Victims' voices were heard, taken seriously and on 25 November 2012 the Stalking Law was introduced. At the time, this was an incredible achievement, and all of those involved were very optimistic about the changes this would make to the way in which stalking cases would now be dealt with. We'd all given countless television interviews on BBC, ITV and Sky News and we felt the message would be having a wide-ranging impact and would influence all the right people.

But, frustratingly, since the law was amended, we have seen little change in attitudes towards stalking in the agencies who are supposed to protect victims, and this seems to be down to a significant lack of education and understanding across the board. All of the awareness-raising that has taken place seems to have only had small pockets of impact. Women continue to be murdered, patterns of behaviours are missed, and stalking is rarely identified in most cases (even in domestic homicide reviews).

In 2014, together with a couple of friends, I set up a local community interest company in Brighton, Veritas-Justice, which combines specialist expertise with personal experience. We advocate for victims of stalking while also addressing trauma and recovery through creative writing and peer support. We have joined forces with other stalking charities across England and Wales to create the National Stalking Consortium, where we continue to campaign for multi-agency stalking training to be rolled out across the UK.

In August 2016, a 19-year-old woman was murdered in my area by a man she knew. She had reported to the police on several occasions that she was being stalked and that she was significantly afraid of this man, and, although the risks to her were evident, she wasn't taken seriously, and the worst possible outcome occurred.

Sadly, victims continue reporting to us at Veritas that they feel let down and, in their own words, 'fobbed off' when trying to access help. And so I continue preparing for battle, although these days through speaking out and writing about it in publications such as this.

Unfortunately, while I was writing this piece for the book, my dad died. I wanted to mention him here because he unfailingly supported me through some of the most difficult and challenging times of my life, and was the most inspirational father to me and to my children, in the absence of their own.

References

Oxford Living Dictionaries (2016). [Online.] https://en.oxforddictionaries.com/ (accessed July 2017).

10

On the outside looking in

Liz Godfrey

I'm one of Sam's friends, and watching her story unfold over the years was like watching a bizarre slow-motion terrorist attack. A lone attacker, not a suicide bomber. An insurgent hiding in the hinterland and creeping around, spreading fear and dread... for years.

Before stalking and abuse happened to Sam, I didn't know the statistics, I had no idea the judicial system sucks and I thought the police were there to protect us. Ha! What a lot you can learn through someone else's experiences.

Sam's journey saw her transformed from light-hearted filmmaker to terrorised single mum and out the other side to campaigner and advocate. I walked beside her through much of her story and it became, in many ways, my story too. Like the outsider peering through someone else's net curtains at the fireside within, I learned what horror is, what friendship is, what society can and won't do. I learned about the power of women and their resilience. I learned that I am not a fighter and Sam is.

Sam and I share a sense of humour, which saved her and me from insanity. There have been so many hysterical events and we have shared such laughter. Like the wartime spirit of the blitz, we came through. I have memories of the most intense conversations about life and death (literally) in sunny playgrounds, with the children racing about – the juxtaposition of real life and judicial and forensic chaos.

I remember Sam's stories of survival in the women's shelter alongside a collection of women driven mad by trying to salvage a way forward with their children and no money. Escaping from the detritus of their shattered lives while cooking sausages and discussing injuries and assaults with equally traumatised women in plaster casts and with black eyes.

We met a woman who told us a story. She was in the car being driven by her violent, icy-faced husband, with her two children in the back. He had already threatened that he would kill her and she was terrified. He inexplicably threw her bag with money, keys, phone etc out of the car. He then drove a bit along the road and stopped and told her to pick it up. Should she? Was he going to drive away and kidnap her children? Was he going to reverse the car into her and kill her? What would happen if she got out of the car? He forced her out. She went back for the bag, came back to the car and got in.

He smiled.

When she got home, she rang the police and told them. They said they couldn't really do anything about it...

'But', asked the nice policeman, 'Was the bag damaged?'

'No', said the woman

'Oh pity – we could have charged him with criminal damage.'

The story of the handbag has stayed with me. The 'system' works if there is actual 'blood on the carpet' or actual damage to property. But in the absence of visible damage to handbags, or women or children, the 'system' is impotent and we are all on our own.

One day I went to Sam's house.

'Wow! Come in let me show you my new fence!' she shouted above the mayhem of kids, chaos, a Chinese exchange student, piles of books and of course a crazy dog...

'Come and see, isn't it wonderful?!'

'Err, no Sam *(I think inside my head),* it's hideous ... a mile-high fence around the back garden to stop your terrorist gaining access. It's ugly and unthinkable. But, of course, if it's that or being murdered, then a mile high fence is...'

'Wonderful' *(I say out loud).*

Well, it complemented the panic alarm, sealed windows, extreme locks, letterbox protector, restraining orders... But, funnily enough, no one had thought to seal the trap door to the attic... and that was another story!

Sam had to go and face her terrorist in the Family Court – again. Magistrates' Courts, Crown Courts, Family Courts ... she and I learned the nuances of each with an intensity that should have earned her a PhD. There was a restraining order from the Court to stop her personal terrorist going anywhere near her, but the Court said they both had to come to court to discuss access to the children. So, despite all the paperwork proving that he was a psychopathic, narcissistic paedophile, and all the paperwork proving he was violent and had tried to kill her, and all the paperwork to say he had no intention of complying with anything, and paperwork showing he had terrorised a previous barrister off the case, Sam had to face him again to try to stop him accessing the children. And, of course, with no funding, she had to represent herself: in court, face-to-face with her own personal nightmare-terrorist.

Her sitting room turned into Mission Impossible as she prepared for Court. We laughed and cried our way through the paperwork, the complications of 'Applications' and 'Submissions' and what to wear. Lipstick? Is crying a good thing or a bad thing in court? If you are too controlled, will the Court think you don't care, and if you cry will they think you are a numbskull or Section you? How do you convey years and years of abuse, fear, intimidation and torment without coming over as loopy?

The Judges are judging you!

The Judges can take away your family!

They can order you to hand over your little toddler to a terrorist for the weekend for years!

And when you arrive at the Court after all the planning and waiting, you find it is a grubby building, with grubby waiting areas and grubby-looking toilets. The down-at-heel women court clerks move about like mini-daleks on silent shoes, occasionally dropping a bit of paper or offering advice like 'wait there'. They slide along corridors of closed doors with huge handles. When the moment comes and your court time (allotted by a million bits of administration) finally arrives, you are ushered into a room that is embarrassing in its banality. So many lives – the futures of your children – will be decided in this public space, little better than a condemned library foyer. Chipped chairs, chipped walls, chipped everything. And barristers, who should look like TV barristers, are actually old and bored and dusty and rather pathetic, with shabby bat-like gowns and comb-over hair and tatty black shoes. A Dickensian vision of ineptitude.

Yep – hysterical covers it.

The wonderful workings of the judiciary mean you can literally be 'in the Family Court' system forever – or at least until the children grow up. Years go by. You can (as Sam did) redecorate your home twice, get a new job, study for an MA, enrol your children in nursery school, and then two years later in primary school, and change your hair colour three times... and still be 'in Family Court', waiting for the next trial date, the next submission, the next social services report...

I arrived one day for our now very regular hysterical laughing sessions in Sam's heavily protected home, where we would drink tea and eat carrot batons with tikka chicken bits, French bread and hummus. Like someone driving slowly past a car crash, I was eager to know what was happening. I cannot lie. Painful as the unfolding story was, and horrific as some of it sounded, I still wanted to know. I needed to know. I had absorbed it and it had become part of my history too.

'So, what's the latest?' I ask, slumping into a creaking, near-dead dining chair and grabbing another carrot baton and slathering it with couscous.

'Another new bloody social worker arrived to see if I was a fit mother and I had to go through and explain absolutely everything again. He was wearing shiny bright new WHITE shoes!'

(Much laughter)

(I think inside my head) 'So did it go well or did you get cross and shout and be indignant and belligerent and enraged and wind him up?'

(Out loud) 'Oh, how was it?'

'He thinks I shouldn't have anything to do with my terrorist and I told him I was trying not to have anything to do with my terrorist. I explained about the recent attempted murder.'

'Oh'

'He said terrorists were bad for the children and had I thought about that?'

(I think inside my head) 'But I thought we were going to talk about your terrorist trying to break into the house last night and you calling the police on the panic button and it turning out to be the recycling bin falling over and you overreacting!'

(Out loud) 'Oh,' I said. 'Was he a trainee?'

'I don't know... he had bloody dreadful shoes and he has to write a report on me as a parent and whether to take the kids into care. He has total control over my family and all I could think of was he had bloody dreadful shoes.'

(I think inside my head) 'The Child Protection hearing must be soon ... dear God, I hope she was nice to the man in white shoes.'

(Out loud) 'Went well then?'

'Cake?'

One day the police asked Sam and me to give evidence in the Crown Court about the terrorist breaking restraining orders. He was in prison for related offences (or was he out of prison again before going into prison again, I can't remember?) Anyway. we went to the Crown Court. So, the basis of the police case was that the terrorist was a proven terrorist and had been sent to prison for breaking his restraining orders (often) and for his attacks on Sam and was now contacting me (Sam's friend, whom he disliked) as a way to get to Sam and circumnavigate the restraining orders. He wrote me a letter from prison about Sam and obviously meant for Sam (so yes, he was in prison, I remember now). So, the police wanted this prosecuted in the Crown Court because he was such a git. When we got to court the judge ruled that the jury weren't to be told that he was a terrorist or that he had ever been in prison or that he had ever tried to kill Sam. So, the jury obviously thought I was mad, giving evidence that he had written to me from prison. He was allowed to charm the jury for two days, regaling them with jolly tales and japes. Of course, the jury had no idea what was going on and why the police minded him writing to me about Sam and why we were in Crown Court, and of course they found him not guilty.

Go figure! Early on in the story, when 'he' had tried to kill Sam, the police had an arrest warrant out for him again. A mutual friend phoned Sam to say 'he' was in the pub up the road. Anyway, she phoned the police, who took eight policemen and raided the pub. They raced slowly into the bar and more or less looked vaguely everywhere but couldn't find 'him'.

'Bloody hilarious,' said Sam to me later (hil-ar-i-ous being her favourite word that year...). 'He was standing at the bar drinking and watching the police looking for him and then, just for a laugh, walked out past all eight of them!'

(I think inside my head) 'If he is in the local pub and meeting with his old friends, will he come and attack Sam again? Last time he was seen locally, he broke in and turned off the power and melted all her frozen food and pissed on a bed. Shouldn't we do something? Phone someone?'

(Out loud) 'Crumbs.' I said. 'Shall I put the kettle on?'

'Yeah ... look, my Dad put up the trampoline in the garden and the kids love it.'

Yep. And that is the story of stalking and abuse. By the time you have navigated your way through violence, purgatory, extreme fear, extreme poverty and terrorist threats, you come to a place where it all feels normal.

Sam had her own private terrorist. The clear and present danger has passed away at last, but the memories, the hinterland of fear and dread, are still there – very distant echoes of another world and another life lived a long, long time ago in a landscape far, far away.

And in a way, that is the sad end to this tale. The terrorist-paedophile-crazy still lives on to fight another day somewhere else. But, thankfully, the children are growing up and thriving, and their mother has become a heroine disguised as a normal person. The judicial system has moved on to the next victim, the next injunction, the next family fleeing terror...

Two deaths a week.

11

Margaret's story

Dear Dan,

I don't expect you to understand what I am about to say, predominantly because I believe that you think the way you have treated me and, as I have recently learnt, previous partners, is totally normal and acceptable. It's not, and you have destroyed me.

I spent 10 years in a relationship with you, five of those married to you. I loved you, I truly did, and I believed that I couldn't live without you. But not only did I love you, I was also terrified of your temper, terrified I was never good enough, terrified I would lose you. I spent most of the time believing that I was disappointing you.

I spent our relationship believing that I caused all of the problems that we had and blaming myself for everything. In fact, you spent our relationship blaming me, and I believed you.

You *controlled* who I saw, what I said, what I wore and, in the end, who I was. You wouldn't allow me to be myself. You constantly hounded me if you didn't know where I was and who I was with every second of the day. If I dared to not answer your phone calls, you would leave threatening messages on my voicemail telling me to call you now and demanding an explanation as to why I hadn't answered your call. This meant that eventually I would ask permission before doing anything.

You destroyed me and reduced me to a shadow of the person I once had been.

You threatened to kill me if I ever left you. I believed you and still do. I live in fear.

You have beaten me, you have thrown me across a room, you have shaken me and you have threatened me. I believe that there is nothing that you will stop at. Please please please stop and think about how it feels to be me. I don't want conflict. I don't want to hate you. I want to be able to move on with my life, and I want to not feel fear. Feeling fear has become so normal that I don't remember what it was like not to wake up in the morning feeling apprehensive and worried about what the day and the future holds, but I want to be able to focus on a happy future and not the hangover of our horrific relationship.

Eventually I found the strength to leave you. This was, without doubt, the hardest and most terrifying thing that I have ever done. The strength to do this came from my fear for the only good that came from our relationship – our two beautiful little girls. When I left, they were only 25 months and four months – neither of them knew you other than to fear you. Our eldest wouldn't go anywhere near you unless I asked her to, and this used to make you mad. Our youngest was an irrelevant inconvenience to you.

I am so desperate for them to be safe and happy and to know that they don't face a life of feeling like I do. Before I left, you didn't care for them, you didn't show any interest in them and you certainly were not involved in their care. You hated the fact that they were girls. You hated the fact that they interrupted my undivided focus on you. You hated the fact that I put them first and you hated the fact that occasionally they caused you disturbance of some kind – be it a noise in the night because I wasn't quick enough to wake and tend to them, or a little bit of mess in the house, or that I didn't have your dinner ready on time because I was caring for one or both of our babies.

You dislocated our eldest's shoulder when she was five months old – she hadn't done anything wrong. I had. I asked you to help her roll because I was still eating and you had finished. I was tired, I was so so so tired and I just needed help for that split second. I never asked you for help, and I shouldn't have done at that moment. You were so cross that I'd asked you to do it that you yanked her hard and fast over and her little arm got stuck. That scream she let out made me feel a physical pain. I should have been the one to get up. I was so wrong to ask you to do it, and I will never forgive myself for putting our baby in the position that she suffered as a result of your temper. There are so many other examples where you have mishandled our babies or lost your temper with them, but I was always there to step in and pacify the situation.

Even to this day, when I am out and I hear your ring tone, smell your aftershave, see a blue sports car, see your name on my phone or hear your name, I freeze, I panic, my palms go clammy, my mouth goes dry, my heart races, I actually feel physically sick. I am so afraid that I don't know what to do with myself. Once this passes, I feel like I must be a crazy person. I feel there must be something wrong with me and I must be over-reacting. I try so hard to tell myself to get over it and pull myself together, but in that moment of panic, I can't. I am strong, I don't do mental weakness, but I've been told that it's called post-traumatic stress disorder. I don't know if a label is a good thing or a bad thing, but at least I now know that I'm not mad and I can get better from it. But I need you to leave us alone in order for me to stand a chance of getting better. Please leave us alone. Please find someone else. You only want to control me, you don't want me – you couldn't possibly want me – I was never good enough. And you only want our girls because you know it is the only way to really hurt me – they are all I care about and you never cared about them before we left.

You send me daily messages, occasionally photos of yourself. You seem to know where I am all of the time, what I'm doing, and you say things to make it very clear that you know. Until I unplugged my landline, you called me every night – especially during the girls' bedtime, to cause havoc. I feel watched and constantly under scrutiny. Twice now, at night, I know you have been to where I live. The second time you opened the back door and let the dog out. I've no proof it was you, but I know it was; nothing was taken and no one else would want to do this. You want me to be mad, you want to send me crazy. You are doing a good job of it, but I will not let you do it. Our girls need someone to protect them, and that person is me. For that reason alone, I will stay strong.

When I lived with you, the biggest trigger for my fear was your key in the door in the evening – I would hear it go into the lock, my tummy would turn as the key turned, I would be terrified about what was about to come through the door. Four or five days out of seven, normally it would be the smell of alcohol and a fury about anything and everything – all of which would be my fault. I'm not suggesting you had a drinking problem. You didn't, but you did drink too much, and when you had, your temper would be even worse. But the drink was not the cause – your temper was there, whether you had been drinking or not, but you were quicker to see red when you had drink inside you.

I knew that you were drinking after work with work colleagues, but more often with other women. Did you do it on purpose? Leave receipts out showing where you had been, how many people eating and drinking at the swanky restaurant or bar – places we once went but now you took your new women? Often, I would be in bed when you came in, and that was a godsend. Even if I wasn't tired, if it got late and I thought you wouldn't be angry that I hadn't waited up to hear about your day, I would go to bed – I would lie there, waiting to hear you come in, to make sure you were not in a massive rage. If you were, I would pick up our eldest from her cot and take her into bed with me in the spare room. After we had our youngest, I would make sure we were all together so that I could protect our babies in case you lost it – that's when I started sleeping with them both. I was nearly always up before you in the morning, and I used to find the receipts – were they carefully placed for me to find, or did you just not care enough to hide them?

Do you know what I felt when I realised you had other women? I was relieved – I was relieved that your focus was on someone else. But it didn't seem to change your temper or your controlling behaviour towards me. You continued to hound me and want to know where I was every second of the day. How did you have the time or energy?

Towards the end, I didn't used to tell you when I'd seen my sister or one of my best friends, because I knew that you would go mental that I'd seen someone.

You used to even go mad about me talking to your family. I couldn't win.

Since I left, you have done everything you possibly can to control me, ruin my life, know about my life and get inside my head. We have been through the most horrific child contact proceedings – they are not quite over, but I know the outcome already and it breaks my heart. Why are you doing this? You went on a witness training course before the hearing so that you could come across how you wanted to. I know this because one of your oldest friends told me.

You are going to have long periods, possibly overnight, of time with our beautiful girls who are not only hugely reliant on me because I am their primary and only caregiver but also will be at huge risk of your foul temper, and they will be both physically and emotionally at risk. Our eldest is scared of you – she remembers how you treated me. Until recently she would re-enact with her dolls from her dolls' house scenes of Daddy being angry at Mummy and her. She is three years old – what have you done to my baby? Our youngest, at 22 months, doesn't really know you, and you told me on more than one occasion that you didn't want her because she was 'another girl'. You told me you felt no love for her – yet this little innocent being is going to be subjected to your wrath because you want to hurt me.

The judge put all this down to a toxic relationship between us as warring parents – apparently, it's our difference in background and none of this could be true, because I am from a privileged background and I'm educated and had a job with a blue-chip company – as if that has got anything to do with it. How could he get it so wrong? Do you know what swayed him? It was your ability to lie, fool and charm, combined with the text messages you produced from the few months after I left you. I was nice and kind and I genuinely wanted reconciliation – but only if you genuinely accepted your behavior and changed.

Remember – I believed this was all my fault; I believed I couldn't go on without you;. I really did want you back – I only left to protect our babies. The judge interpreted that to mean I wasn't scared of you and that you didn't do the things I said you did. The judge refused to look at written evidence from ex-girlfriends and friends of yours – all of whom were willing to come to court to be a witness. You paid so much to your legal team, while I represented myself or had friends helping me out, so I stood no chance – you wiped the board and money won.

That judgment destroyed me – only temporarily, but it did destroy me. I will go down fighting for our girls because I know it's not 'if'' but 'when' you hurt one of them, if you have them unsupervised once these proceedings are done. Everyone believes you and not me. How can the court system be this backward and so oblivious to domestic violence and abuse? Apparently, the constant messages and being in touch are you being concerned and caring. You are so clever about the way you do it that you make it look like you just want to be part of our girls' lives. I know the truth, I live it, I know you – you are using them to hound me. It will not work, Dan. I may be down now, and I may be down for a while, but I will get strong; I have to, in order to help these girls through the hell that you will inevitably put them through – emotionally and, at some point, physically.

Do you know what the final proof was that this is about me and not the girls – not that I needed any proof? The financial proceedings… You earn a fortune, you own a fortune, and you want to screw me and your girls on lump sum and maintenance. A genuinely caring father who wanted the best for their children would want to support them and their Mummy so their Mummy could be there for them. But you want me to go back to work. Believe you me, I don't want a penny from you; every penny I ever get from you will be poison and another penny of control, but I want to do what's best for our girls, and so I will take that control, to be there for them. I am looking for work and something that I can fit around the girls, in the hope that, one day, I can tell you to keep your money. I don't believe you will relinquish control until that day and so I am trying so hard to bring that day forward.

Just you wait and see, me and the girls will be OK, I will make sure of it. You will be a sad and lonely old man and me and the girls will make it through this. I just wish you would stop fighting, stop hurting the girls and me, and find someone else.

Please, Dan, let us go; please let me be free and let us be happy.

12

Personality, not nationality

I am a woman, a solicitor, a mother, a daughter, a sister, a friend, and I have been stalked. I still struggle to make sense of the concepts of victim, survivor or service user, or to identify with any of them, as they don't really reflect my experiences of stalking. Furthermore, I refuse to be labelled or defined by what has happened to me. I try to reflect and work on what I have done with what has happened to me.

I grew up in a supporting and loving family (flaws and all) in Latin America. I enjoyed the privileges that are less common in developing countries than in the UK, but with the misguided, or perhaps naïve belief that domestic abuse, coercive control and stalking do not happen to people like me, or, in fact, to many people at all. I was later to painfully realise that those crimes are in fact perpetrated by anyone and against anyone, regardless of origin or background, and mainly by men against the women they say they love, and in epidemic proportions.

I had my fair share of inane, intense, romantic and short-lived relationships, all of which ended on fairly amicable terms. Some of those men I would still call friends, but the whirlwind romance that turned my life upside down was like nothing else I had experienced before. With hindsight, I can now see that these were not necessarily romantic gestures:

- obtaining my address and contact details by breaking into an office

- showing up at my place unannounced

- booking a surprise weekend break a couple of weeks after first meeting

- deciding to leave his life in the UK behind and move to Latin America with me after just eight weeks of seeing each other.

However, they clouded my judgment. I would say that his constant demonstrations of affection left me with no breathing or thinking space, and, despite my own instincts occasionally making me feel that something was not right, I dismissed my doubts and those of the people close to me, arguing that it could all be down to a cultural clash (maybe that is how people behave in England?). It took me years to accept that his obnoxious behaviour was not a matter of nationality but of personality.

After eight years of marriage, I would say that the relationship was not a happy one, but it wasn't physically abusive, so there was still nothing that I could fit into a definition (perhaps definitions are not as useful or clear as they are made out be). There were, however, seemingly small comments and attitudes that slowly but surely dented my confidence and self-esteem and even made me doubt my sanity at times. There were comments about my looks, my 'low' IQ, my undesirable and toxic friends and family. He succeeded in isolating me from everyone I cared about.

He convinced me to move to the UK in the early days of the marriage, arguing that we could build our own family, away from the overwhelming intrusions from those around me, away from my long working hours, but, crucially, away from my support network, away from all those who really cared about me and to a place where he would have all the knowledge, the power, the control, where he would be the centre of my world. I went along with all of it because, like most women I know, I still wanted to make it work.

However incredible it may sound now, I did not know that this was coercive control and the making of a stalking nightmare to come. I don't blame myself, but I wish that discussions around the many means abusive men use to entrap women were more commonplace, because the current discourses do not make it simple for women to identify and report abuse. That is how, after becoming a mother, and nearly 10 long years of conflicting messages and feelings, I made the decision to leave, hoping that I would get my life back, determined to start again. But I soon learned that, just as he threatened, he was not going to let me go that easily. In fact, the stalking had just begun.

Trying to make sense of the nonsense my life had become, I can only describe it as the feeling of being asleep, knowing that it is a nightmare and desperately hoping to wake up, but then realising I have been awake for about three months. The fear, the sleep deprivation, him wanting me back with intensity, 75 phone calls in a day, showing up at my work demanding to see me, following me to and back from work, threatening to take our child away from me, reminding me of our wedding vows 'til death do us part', and slowly accepting that there was no safe haven, nowhere to run after the Family Court determined that he was allowed to know where I lived and worked, to ensure the father–child relationship would continue.

I would say with some confidence that standing up to the stalker was in some ways simpler than engaging with the police, the support services and the courts, and the rampant culture of victim blaming and minimisation of the abuse that I didn't expect. I realised that the law systematically ignores and even forces women to live with abuse.

Telling my story to countless officials was highly traumatic, especially as the police and the courts didn't seem to understand the complex dynamics of my situation, so they didn't do anything to stop him, and so he didn't stop. It was made official: he can do what he wants, stalk me every day with no consequence. The message was clear: it is acceptable to terrorise me and even use my daughter and the court to remain in my life. He is obsessed with revenge and I have been left to live in fear.

The stalker wins because it is all about him controlling me. It is about me having to worry every moment I'm awake that he may do something. It is emotional and psychological warfare, the wondering of when and where he is watching and what he will do next.

I refuse to let him be a factor in my life, so I have to fight back the best I can. I have had to reinvent myself and am determined to challenge stalking head on. Perhaps my new career, supporting stalking victims, found me, not only to help others but to help myself, even when I have to fight back the tears when seeing or dealing with the devastating effects of stalking, not only in my life but in that of my nine-year-old daughter. I still struggle to talk about her in relation to this ordeal, other than to say that I find my strength in her.

My story is not particularly remarkable as far as crime stories go, but it is nevertheless shocking, in so far as it seems to be so similar to the many other stories I hear from the people I now support and who have, like me, been stalked. Some of them have, sadly, lost their lives. They also keep us going.

13

The big green van with a ladder

They had just decided, as usual, to pick up a few beers from 'Asda's' after she had watched him play cricket with her daughter. They had joked about people saying 'Asda's' rather than Asda, or 'thee-ay-ter' rather than theatre, or 'off of' instead 'of', or 's'later' rather than see you later. This was the kind of thing that made them so compatible – a mutual enjoyment of others' linguistic inadequacies, along with a shared past – 28 years of past to be precise.

They had been work colleagues back in 1988, socialising with their respective partners, getting drunk together, laughing uproariously at nothing and seeing the black humour of an utterly inane workplace. He fancied her like crazy but, by the time he had plucked up the courage to make his move, he discovered she was dating a posh Para.

With 28 years of bumping in to each other at regularly irregular intervals, usually in Asda car park, the latest bump had resulted in an exchange of numbers, a few lunchtime drinks and the most wonderful, passionate, life-changing relationship. This time, it was Asda car park that was the scene of the latest episode of her turbulent last eight years.

She screamed, 'That's his van, that's his van! It's You Know Who's van!'

This came completely out of the blue, at full volume, and jolted him out of his beer-soaked mulling over of the day's play.

'Where?'

He knew instantly that she was referring to her former partner and father of her two children. This was You Know Who, the man who had stalked her for four years continuously, the man who had camped in the shed in her garden after she had had the locks to the house changed after he assaulted her with a knife, who had camped in the allotments to the rear of her house, resulting in a 15-foot high fence being erected so he couldn't access her garden. The man who had threatened to kill her, threatened to kill himself, groomed her friends and neighbours, made calls to her parents in the small hours and who, she had since found out, had committed a string of criminal offences before they had met.

It was this revelation that had brought to a head their relationship – a relationship that was overflowing with You Know Who's lies, mental and verbal abuse, alcoholism and multiple accusations of harassment from women country-wide.

All thoughts of cricket having vanished, he tried to remain calm. He had played over and over in his mind hundreds of times what he would do in the event of crossing paths with You Know Who. One of his bats leant against the wall just inside the door of her house; there was a short, sturdy stick he had picked up in the park a while back, which was in among the wood for the fire, and his golf clubs were swiftly accessible too. He also worried about the security of the home. He made sure that all the doors were locked and bolted and windows shut every night and before they went out to work or school. He felt that she had become a little blasé about the security issue, but hadn't mentioned it, because he didn't want to reopen old wounds without good reason. He supposed that she felt safe; after all, she had tackled the whole thing head on, telling everyone one she knew about what had happened to her, and going on to set up her own charity helping others to deal with the devastating consequences of being stalked and helping to change related laws along the way.

Her nine-year-old daughter was hysterical by now – she and her brother had been told what they needed to know about the past to satisfy the inevitable questions they had had. 'He was a dangerous man, who'd spent time in prison.' They'd been instructed what to do if You Know Who turned up at their school. These were what they needed to know. Direct contact in Asda hadn't been on the curriculum.

She pulled into a parking space some distance away from the Big Green Van with a Ladder and he asked her if she was sure it was 'his' van.

'It's definitely the same van,' a little calmer now. 'He's not allowed within seven miles of my house.' But the worry in her voice was still palpable, however.

He knew this, and Asda was only half a mile from her house. It was eight years since this restriction had been ordered by the court and it hadn't been broken, as far as she knew, in the last four years. Was You Know Who becoming more daring? Had he been shopping in Asda without a care for his court order for the last four years, and this was the first time their paths had crossed? Was it all starting again, with him roaming around her neighbourhood once more?

He knew that You Know Who lived in a town about 15 miles away, where, coincidentally, her aunt lived. The aunt had invited her to her hen night in the town recently, taking in a few pubs. She had declined the invite, pointing out to her: 'We might bump into him, don't you think?' Clearly not in this case! When she accompanied him to a cricket match just the other side of You Know Who's town, they had to go a different way, not the quickest route, for fear of seeing him or being seen. The trauma he had wrought on her was still deep inside her, and seemingly small, inconsequential actions were still hugely significant for her, four years on.

'Do you remember the number plate of the van?' he asked.

'Yes, I'm sure that's the one.' Her daughter was now curled up in a ball in the footwell of the rear passenger seat.

'I'll just take a photo of it,' he said and went up to the van, trying to look discreet while snapping the front and back of it with his camera phone. He had never seen a van like it in his life. It was like a cross between a Land Rover and the A-Team van, in a bright grass-green colour, with a ladder vertically fixed to the rear. It looked 'cool' and he glanced furtively around to see if anyone had seen him taking the pictures.

He went back to the car, where the love of his life was on the phone to her mother, who had been so supportive at the height of her tribulations. Panic had seemed to set in again – her mother didn't know the registration so they couldn't confirm if it was the same vehicle. He decided to go into the supermarket to see if he could see You Know Who. What he was going to do if he saw him, he had absolutely no idea. He had thought many times about the scenario that might bring the two men face to face. He knew roughly what he looked like, having asked to see a picture of him. This was in case You Know Who ever came to her house, so he would know it was him. Tall, about 6'6", with black hair and a grin so unbelievably creepy it almost made his blood turn to stone. He would have been no match for You Know Who (he was ex-army and trained in unarmed combat) if it had come to it 10 years ago, but now her former stalker was in his 60s and he was 49 and fitter than he had ever been, due to recent take-up of regular sport and exercise, enjoyed with renewed enthusiasm since they had met again and fallen in love.

He had visualised rugby tackling him if the occasion arose, taking the bigger man to the ground with ease with a finely executed head-on tackle – what he proposed to do after that hadn't even entered his head. He scoped the entrance to Asda and crept furtively inside. He inspected every aisle in turn, popping his head around the corner very slowly to try and catch sight of the stalker: he was stalking the stalker! He must have looked extremely suspicious to anyone who might have seen him on the store CCTV. He checked every aisle, but he didn't see anyone answering the description he was looking for. He felt very self-conscious, as if, when he came across You Know Who, he would have had a sign above his head saying 'I'm the partner of the girl whose life you tried to control and ruin but she was too smart and strong to succumb to you, you bastard!' He really felt as though he would be recognised. After the last aisle, he inspected every aisle again on the way back to the entrance, but nothing.

When he got back to the car, his girlfriend was overwhelmed to see him. 'Why don't we just wait in the car and see if it's him who drives the van away?' he asked. 'Then we'd know once and for all.'

'No, I want to go now,' said the voice from the footwell, 'please, please, please, please!'

So, they drove the half a mile home. When they arrived, her daughter ran to the bedroom and hid under the bedclothes. Her mum phoned the police to ask if the van was still under You Know Who's ownership and they didn't know. They would try to find out and call back. Half an hour later, still no news, so she called again.

'We can't give that information out, I'm afraid,' mumbled the officer, not sounding very convincing. Had they even bothered to find out? Was the incompetence in the force regarding stalking still in the dark ages?

She rifled through her dozens of folders of case notes and court documents and found what she was looking for. The registration was the same! It WAS You Know Who's van!

'Oh my god! Oh my god! He's back.'

She phoned her mother, a formidable woman who had supported her daughter through the years of torment, giving the police what-for when they tried to minimise her daughter's experience.

'Phone the head honcho,' she said, 'He's got things done before. Tell him to find out now!' Her livid voice clearly audible without being on speakerphone.

'Can you do it, Mum? The kids are going ballistic here.'

She hung up and he checked the house security – the back door was unlocked, the bathroom window was open –he heard her daughter telling her brother at full tilt all about the Big Green Van with the Ladder. He locked everything in sight and drew the curtains. It was pandemonium.

'Will the police chief be able to find out?' he asked.

'My mother can squeeze blood from a stone!' she replied.

Her mother had reprimanded the chief superintendent several times in her front room over various police ineptitudes, so he owed her. He had heard the accounts of never-ending police cock-ups. The time when six officers lost You Know Who in an almost empty pub with the help of the zip-lipped regulars; the time when they couldn't find him for five weeks, when he was staying with his own mother; the time when the police said he wasn't answering his phone when he hadn't turned up for trial; the time when blah, blah, blah – incompetents!

He was just thinking about what he would do if You Know Who turned up now with a gun and started firing at everyone – he was ex-army after all. Get everyone in the front room, squat down, call the police while he locked everything, and keep low, get the golf club and cricket bat ready. Then her mum rang.

'The Big Green Van is registered to a different owner now? Address many miles away? Nothing to do with You Know Who?' Everyone hugged.

The head honcho had come up trumps. Now there's an expression that may lose its appeal!

14

My friend Jo

Hetti Barkworth-Nanton

Jo's husband, BA captain Robert Brown, held a knife to her throat in 2007 when his resentment of her overflowed. She pleaded: 'What about the children? Think of the children.' His answer was: 'I'll be in prison and you'll be dead.'

She didn't report it to the police for fear that the children would find out about their father. She fled to her mother in the Isle of Man, who overheard a telephone conversation where he ensured she would never report it to the police: 'If you tell the police it will be the worse for you.'

Jo was a nurturer and home-maker, dedicated to creating a happy family home and environment for her two young children, and giving them the best start in life. School was an important part of that, and their school bags were always around – she knew how important their homework was.

Jo married Robert Brown in 1999, and he moved into her treasured house, which she had lovingly restored, and it became their family home. But her marriage to Brown was not a happy one. It was characterised by isolation, intimidation, contempt and silence…

Days – without a word.

But an ever-present cold, intimidating stare.

'Why did you do that?'

'You were pathetic at that meeting with the teacher.'

'He doesn't want to do his homework so I've told him not to bother.'

'I'm not eating that rubbish, I'll cook for myself later.'

Silent tears would fall down her face.

But she would wipe away the tears and have nothing but warm love and smiles as she called the children for supper, desperate to protect them from the reality.

But the reality wasn't far away.

Being told by him he had checked the house alarm records to track her movements. Concern.

Discovering receipts for surveillance equipment in his office. Fear.

Being told by him he had dreamt of killing the children with an axe. Terror.

When he held the knife at her throat, she said his eyes were cold and terrifying. Jo never stayed alone with him again.

Then started three years of increasingly sinister divorce battles.

'If I can't have the house, neither will you.' He knew she loved it, and he was determined she wouldn't keep it.

Meanwhile, smiles, love, warmth, for her children, day in day out. Off to school. Home from school. Homework. Play. Cuddles. She would never put him down in front of the children. She knew he was their father and it wasn't her job to destroy their belief in him.

For him, they were his vehicle for control. The chance to get close to Jo and put his foot inside the door – despite agreeing to a voluntary undertaking not to enter the house.

Tricking the children into divulging Jo's security codes – twice.

'They don't need to go to that school.'

'They don't need to do their homework – they didn't want to so I didn't make them' – ever.

The divorce continues – 'parity is the road to happiness'.

Regularly seen parked at the top of her drive… watching.

Seen in the garden by neighbours. And breaking into the house.

She called the police. They told her the majority of murders are committed by family members, but unless she is physically harmed, they can't do anything.

At the top of the gate again… watching.

Security lights stop working – cables cut.

CCTV stops working – cables cut.

The divorce isn't going his way, and he's slowly losing control of her. It's looking likely she will be able to stay in her home. His object of obsession.

Her mother, Diana Parkes, begs her to never be alone in the house and to keep the curtains closed at night, as she knew he was watching her.

One week before the final court hearing. Halloween. It's the last time he will see her before facing her in court. She's my best friend and we're talking. She's despondent. The realisation that none of it would be over once a decision was made. The realisation that he would continue to use the children to hurt her. To intimidate her. To control her.

We talked about his behaviour. Decided he was just weird. I tried to make her feel better. To underplay his behaviour. To will her to believe it was going to be fine.

At 4pm, Jo lets Robert Brown in through the gate in his car. She welcomes her young children, aged nine and 10, with a loving smile and open arms, and they run through the hallway to the family room, to wait for mummy to come in and give them the chicken curry she had been preparing – their favourite.

He carries their homework bags to the door – a part of the children, an extension of her love.

But this time, it wasn't as it seemed. Because this symbol of love was filled with evil.

Robert Brown had put a claw hammer in a homework bag, and used it to batter her to death with at least 14 blows to her head.

The children were put in the car to travel with their dead mother to his pregnant girlfriend's house, where he left them, before driving into the night to dispose of the body in a grave he had prepared months before, in dense woodland.

Robert Brown had the last word, continuing his control at his trial, where he was given free rein to destroy Jo's character, resulting in his acquittal of murder. He is serving a prison sentence for manslaughter and will be released in 2023. The court psychiatrist confirmed he is a psychopath. We knew that. Her children, her mother and family are terrified of him. We are all terrified of him. The nightmare will never end.

Jo was my best friend. Why didn't I know the escalating risk she was in? Why didn't I convince her to protect herself? Why didn't I know she was a victim of escalating domestic abuse? Why didn't she?

15

Letter to the CPS

Crown Prosecution Service
Newcastle upon Tyne

To whom it may concern,

My Name is Joni and I have been victimised by the relentless pursuit of Matthew Derby since 2007, after our brief relationship came to an end. Mr Derby and I had a daughter together.

For eight long years I have been subjected to a devastating stalking and harassment campaign at the hands of Mr Derby. He has devoted eight years of his life to torturing me and my daughter, invading every aspect of my life, and I am in no doubt that Mr Derby means harm to me.

I live a life of constant fear for my safety and the wellbeing of my daughter and my now elderly parents. I have had to face the devastating reality and tell my friends and family to prepare themselves for the possibility that Mr Derby could eventually harm or even murder me.

My daily routine is filled with the apprehension, fear and terror that Mr Derby will continue to:

- monitor my daily activities

- wait outside my house

- track my vehicle

- slash my tyres, as he has done on at least 15 occasions over the last two years

- slash my friends' tyres, as he has done on two occasions, and my parents' on another occasion.

And so the question is not if but when Mr Derby will seize the opportunity to cause me very serious harm. I know from my own experience that stalking takes lives. It has already taken mine in the sense that I have lost my confidence, my self-esteem, and my ability to trust others, impacting on my current and future relationships and friendships.

I am devastated at seeing my daughter affected by the limits and isolation that Mr Derby imposes on us with his obsession, the impact of which is evident in my daughter's behavioural and educational development, for which she requires additional support from school as a consequence of the atmosphere of fear we have been forced to live with.

I wonder how much longer Mr Derby will be permitted to continue victimising us and how much more I will have to modify our lives before we get the help and support we so desperately need. I am devastated by the news that the CPS does not feel ready to charge Mr Derby with the crimes he has committed against me, and I am deeply anxious and concerned about the outcome of this case and the impact it would have on Mr Derby's possible future behaviour if he is given the clear message that his actions carry no consequences.

I don't actually know what to do with myself and I am losing confidence that the terrible nightmare my daughter and I have endured for nearly a decade will ever end.

Yours sincerely,

Joni

16

The nightmare netherworld and the sheer necessity of DIY

Only a few weeks ago, a senior social worker sat in the kitchen of my new home and sympathetically told me with quite some conviction that indeed, 'When you become a victim of this sort of crime, you stop being a local authority executive. I've seen this sort of thing happen so many times... it's like they hang you out to dry.'

Fifteen years ago, I had a fascinating, fulfilling career. I felt privileged to work on the public's behalf, and especially for people who are most disadvantaged. I was hard-working and in demand, here and abroad. My income wasn't my satisfaction, nor an assured public services position and pension prospects. My gratification came in hearing from service users about their progress, the doors that had opened for them, and the barriers we'd helped to clear away.

Out of the blue, I became a target of 'persistent crime': stalking, which evidently forces one over an invisible but real 'them-vs-us' line. It slowly dawned on me that I'd been cast out, tacitly thrust into a dank, parallel universe comprised of people who look just like you and me. But, once consigned to this netherworld, we are definitely 'other'.

We 'others' become hopelessly 'less than'. Hidden in plain sight, we exist in a dysfunctional netherworld. The myriad problems with which we struggle daily are often implicitly recast as somehow our fault, our characters are doubted, the importance of our quality of life and of our human rights is downgraded, our pleas for

Stalking is a crime of terror

'It is one part threat and one part waiting for the threat to be carried out. The victim of stalking has no way to resolve the threat and the terror she feels.'

Miller M (2001). *Stalking Laws and Implementation Practice: a national review for policymakers & practitioners*. Virginia: Institute for Law and Justice. doi: 10.2139/ssrn.322283

Netherworld (noun)

1. the world of the dead
2. underworld: 'the nether-world of deceit... and espionage' – Richard M Nixon
3. no-man's land: 'lost in a bureaucratic netherworld'.
www.merriam-webster.com

appropriate, timely interventions go unanswered.

Looking back over these nightmare years, two phrases sum up my experiences and existence as the target of an obsessive, deranged stalker: 'No one is listening', and 'You're on your own with it all.'

You're on your own...

Actually, the second phrase comes from an empathic and experienced Victim Support care manager. When I was fleeing the stalker, physically disabled, traumatised, about to become homeless and in deep hiding after 13+ years of relentless stalking, once more I'd contacted Victim Support.

Victim Support believes that

• Victims of crime have a wide range of needs. Most of them are not recognised, let alone met.
• Society has a duty to alleviate the effects of crime whatever they may be.
• Reducing the effects of crime in the community is a priority requiring co-ordinated action by government.

Victim Support (2002). Criminal Neglect: no justice beyond criminal justice. London: Victim Support. www.victimsupport.org.uk/sites/default/files/Criminal%20neglect%20report.pdf (accessed June 2017)

I'd exhausted my savings, which I'd set aside for my daughter's higher education costs and my retirement; my benefits income was and is below the poverty line. My only remaining asset was our family home, which, as I built my career, I'd struggled as a lone parent to provide for my children, and to which I could no longer return. This exemplary care manager and I met in a charming, out-of-the-way café, and I described my situation.

Here it may be helpful to underline a key feature of unstopped stalking and its distinctive injuries. And please note that only the authorities call it 'persistent crime': everything in action is 'persistent' until it winds down or is stopped. Stopping something in action requires conscious decision and practical effort. All authorities and experts agree that the most effective way to deal with stalking/harassment is to intervene at the earliest stage, before the offender's obsession becomes entrenched and dangerous. This agreement does not reflect the reality for the vast majority of stalking targets.

After half an hour or so, the care manager said she was surprised at my low expectations of help and that I had no sense of entitlement. In all the years of stalking, I'd been bounced back and forth countless times like a tuppenny shuttlecock between every agency imaginable, to no avail. To no avail, I've repeated the history to a vast spectrum of 'helpers' – around, I estimate, 1,200 times now. I discovered that one can indeed be signposted out of existence.

Too often, I'd ended up being sent back to the first agency I'd been

Stalking's stealthy attrition is a key, and ignored, continuous criminal injury

This crime exponentially and destructively impacts every single area of your life – and even elements of your life you didn't know were there because you always took your commonplace freedoms and rights for granted. The damage continues for years after.

You live with constant anxiety and terror. Your health and functionality decline. Your income stops when you can't carry on working. The non-stop offending; daily damage checking and evidence preservation; trying to get police to be active; chasing repair people; viewing hundreds of hours of scary CCTV footage to find the offender in action (all evidence-gathering is a DIY job); keeping requested incident journals that are ignored or even derided; monitoring/collating endless router intrusion records; chasing the phone/internet service's anti-nuisance unit, which refers you back to the police who refer you to ActionFraud, which confirms offending and refers you back to the police - all these and much more take over your life, which becomes chaotically centred around the stalker's onslaughts.

You're continually paying for repairs; expensively shopping online because going out inflames the stalker to more monitoring, more offences; negotiating with the phone company to avoid exorbitant fees for repeated TSP/ISP vandalism; paying for healthcare and other support; beefing up security; buying/fitting new CCTV kit because amateurish retail systems are sold for their illusion of security, not for court-standard evidence production...

You have to get your car resprayed, then replaced, because it's too damaged; likewise, your PC and router, because they've been hacked yet again. You have to find ways of escaping the stalker, which involves several costly, very disruptive moves, always in the utmost secrecy.

The list is long, and everything costs more because it's reactive and often urgent, rather than planned, expenditure. Not one agency or government department helps with any of your costs, or offers any understanding of your situation. You're shoe-horned into their depersonalised boxes that say 'unemployed', 'disabled' and even 'nutcase' and 'write off'. My assessment of my hard cash losses is above £500,000 to date – it must have cost the public purse at least twice that in endless signposting, denial processes, rendering me disabled, and traumatising me and my family to the point of needing medical treatment.

Then there's the devastating carnage of your family, social and work relationships, as you're continually dealing with offences and making fruitless attempts to get help from appropriate agencies, while juggling alternating terror and exhaustion.

You stop inviting friends and family over because their visits are often marked by damage to their cars or yours, and they run the gauntlet of aggressive stare-downs by the loitering offender. You're unable to enjoy dinners, walks and concerts with friends, because every time you leave home there will be punitive damage later to your property. Your friends and family begin to suffer from compassion fatigue and fear, and fall away.

Your children are always on edge, confused, angry and sad that Mum is so terrorised and distracted, stolen from them. Your frail, poorly parents lose out on your support and die prematurely because you're so fraught and preoccupied – and too scared to draw the stalker's attention to their home by visiting them often. Your marriage disintegrates. The insidious cascade of relationship damage is infinitely more costly and in far more excruciating ways than just financial.

Sooner or later, on your own with unbearable stresses and continual fear – of the police and other callous authorities and agencies, as much as the stalker – the productive, happy life you'd painstakingly and cheerfully built crumbles and degenerates into a struggle for hourly existence. 'Murder in slow motion', in the words of Baroness Jan Royall in the House of Lords [Hansard, HL Deb, 6 Feb. 2012], is indeed the most accurate description of all this creeping life destruction.

signposted from, four steps before in these costly loops of buck-passing. So far, I told the care manager, I'd not found effective interventions from any service and wasn't hopeful – but victim support law had recently been improved under an EU Directive and I'd very much welcome anything she could help me with.

Over several weeks, she worked to get the support I urgently needed. She brokered an assessment with a specialist agency, which told me that, despite the stalker's gun access and my looming homelessness, I'd helped myself enough by fleeing, so they couldn't help. At our last meeting in the charming café, with empty hands and rueful frustration, she was wonderfully honest and apologetic: '... I get it now. When you're a victim of stalking by someone who's not your ex, you're on your own.'

Police and persistent, systemic failings

At the Spring 2016 Police Federation conference, Theresa May, a long-time campaigner for victims' rights and better support, announced that she'd asked Her Majesty's Inspectorate of Constabulary (HMIC) to investigate police neglect and abuse of women and children who are targets of repeated crime. My report has been submitted in evidence to that investigation.

To detail here the neglect, negligence or abuse from some 90% of all officers I encountered would certainly trigger the traumatic stress injuries that have directly resulted. It's true, though, that a few officers kindly understood the issues as well as the terror. Some, mostly female, even apologised for their colleagues' failings.

While some individuals have been sympathetic, most agencies have been little better than the police. Early on, my local Victim Support told me that, as I'd had support when an offender was minimally convicted, then I'd had more than my quota of attention. They said that homicide victims' families only got about three visits. It made no difference that the stalking was carrying on mercilessly after this offender's cursory conviction, and would continue until I fled my home some 11+ years later. Refusing to recognise course-of-conduct crime, Victim Support seemed to write me off scornfully as a 'persistent non-victim'.

Even worse, the hate crime agency to which I was much later signposted affirmed this disdain of persistent crime victims: in the last of three conversations with a support worker, we touched on the recent murder of a local, disabled person by her persistent persecutors. 'She was my client', the worker told me. 'She was so difficult to work with; she really brought the murder on herself.'

How to convey the vitriolic irritation behind these words? How could anyone in their right mind ever claim that a chronically terrorised, painfully disabled homicide victim is to blame for their own murder? I felt profoundly disturbed, chilled to the bone, at this worker's appalling, mind-bending attitude, and at her insistence on talking about her client. So I politely ended the call. Clearly, I'd be blamed for the stalking; obviously, there was no hope of any help from the worker and her agency.

'Police are "decriminalising crime" by getting the public to turn detective and look for CCTV and fingerprints themselves... a police watchdog warned amid fears police are giving up on investigating some crimes...

'Inspector of Constabulary Roger Baker said: "It's more a mindset, that we no longer deal with these things. And effectively what's happened is a number of crimes are on the verge of being decriminalised."'

Carter C & agencies (2014). Crime victims forced to turn into 'DIY detectives'. *Daily Telegraph*; 4 September. http://www.telegraph.co.uk/news/uknews/crime/11073394/Crime-victims-forced-to-turn-into-DIY-detectives.html (accessed June 2017)

In my opinion, these widespread, habitual netherworld attitudes constitute what psychologists call 'gaslighting', which, according to Wikipedia, is '... a form of psychological abuse in which a victim is manipulated into doubting his or her own memory, perception and sanity'. It's used both consciously and unconsciously in order to discredit us and make us go away.

Jennifer Freyd, Professor of Psychology at the University of Oregon, is a pioneering expert in betrayal trauma and institutional betrayal, which is defined as 'wrongdoings perpetrated by an institution upon individuals dependent on that institution, including failure to prevent or respond supportively to wrongdoings by individuals (eg. sexual assault) committed within the context of the institution' (Freyd, undated a).

Courageously, Professor Freyd is shining a bright light into the dank, dysfunctional netherworld to which most of us would prefer to turn a blind eye or simply can't believe really exists. Freyd is unpacking what the UK's Equalities and Human Rights Commission coyly identifies as 'the culture of disbelief'.

Freyd and colleagues coined the acronym DARVO, which stands for 'deny, attack, reverse victim and offender' (Freyd, undated b). It's invaluable in recognising abuse and in spotting the mind-bending modus operandi of institutional betrayal. Unmistakably, the hate crime agency's worker was in full DARVO-mode when talking to me.

DARVO goes hand-in-hand with secondary victimisation. Here's a selection of what DARVO-mode, secondary-victimiser officers have said to me or concerning my case over 14+ years.

'Tell her that if she makes a complaint or reports any more, things may not go well for her.' Police inspector 1, to my local councillor who had tried to advocate for me.

'Move on! Ignore it! We've dealt with it, it's all over!' Police sergeant, angrily, soon after an offender had been convicted early on. The offending immediately carried on and on for many years after that conviction.

'The Protection from Harassment Act is only for people who are being stalked by ex-partners. I've done all the training on this legislation. So we can't help.' Police inspector 1, misrepresenting legislation and dismissing course-of-conduct crime.

'You have to feel pity for the offender; the offending is obviously due to mental illness.' Police superintendent.

'It's just random offences, it's not anyone stalking you... have you seen your GP?' Police inspector 1.

'Using our CCTV is a sledgehammer to crack a walnut here.' Police sergeant to police constable when refusing police CCTV use a year or so into the stalking.

'Only Russian gangs with thousands of pounds' worth of equipment can hack into people's internet. There are no Russian gangs around here. No one's hacking your internet.' Police inspector 2, having received many pages of router records showing intrusion attempts.

'Tell us your ex-partner's name! It'll prove your integrity.' Police constable bullying me to divulge the details of a person who couldn't possibly be the stalker but whom she wanted to easily arrest on suspicion with no evidence.

'We are trained to deal with root causes... the root cause here is that you keep on making reports.' Police inspector 3.

[Laughing] 'Yeah, they'd certainly laugh at you telling them that!' Police psychologist, who treats officers for traumatic stress, when I told her about the unwanted and embarrassingly offensive sexual 'gifts' I'd received from the stalker.

'It's the CPS's fault, they don't take this crime seriously and they always need more evidence.' Superintendent.

'If you keep telling us about [the offender], we might have to talk about warning you against harassment.' Police sergeant, after about the fifth time I'd identified the stalker on CCTV.

'You have to consider whatever you did to attract the stalking.' Police constable responding to yet another incident of shocking criminal damage.

'I was sure I wouldn't actually find anything before I came over!' Police constable telling me he'd already no-crimed my report of criminal damage and was surprised to find it.

'We all have to live with this sort of thing, don't we?' Police inspector to my daughter, in my presence, erroneously expecting her to agree that I was 'too sensitive'.

'I'm going to feel embarrassed reporting this to District and sending these stills out.' Police constable with reference to a deeply frightening, bizarre offence captured on CCTV, showing the stalker I'd identified for years.

'You're on a witch-hunt. I'm not giving you your street's Neighbourhood Watch contact details.' Police Neighbourhood Watch co-ordinator when I asked for support from the local Neighbourhood Watch early on.

'Why haven't your local team had CCTV in all along? This is my job. We do this for far lesser offences!' Police technical support unit officer fitting a TSU CCTV after 11 years – too little, too late.

Initially, it took a whole year to get a police officer to visit. I'd been reporting property damage and noting bizarre incidents throughout that first year. This young officer was smart, keen and humane; he understood that something sinister was going on. He was soon taken off the case.

Before that, though, he'd told me of his sergeant's derisive minimisation of the serial offending. While doing his best to investigate as well as argue my case to superiors and the CPS, he was also subject to a false complaint from an arrested offender. He emphatically advised me to make complaints to my MP, local councillor, MEP, the newspapers... and any relevant body.

Afterwards, there was increasing neglect, negligence or abuse as the local police team bent over backwards to ignore or deter my reports. Their 'instructions', 'advice' and failures in operational co-ordination throughout were gob-smackingly irrational and mind bending. Their only effective co-ordination was in their terrifying denial/intimidation strategy. It's certainly an understatement that I was often profoundly shocked.

With a family tree including police officers, lawyers, teachers, priests, medical professionals, public servants and MPs, my whole experience and sense of our seemingly 'good-enough' world was being shattered.

'I am clear that... the actions of the police and the IPPC together have done me more harm psychologically than Richard Jan [the stalker] ever did... police forces need to learn to think about... what happens to victims when they experience crime again and again and again.'

Shauna Bailey, social worker and stalking target, quoted in the *Guardian* (2010). Woman forced into hiding by Britain's worst stalker attacks police failures. *The Guardian*; 31 January. www.theguardian.com/uk/2010/feb/01/britains-worst-stalker-police-failings (accessed June 2017).

Many stalking/harassment targets will know just the feelings I'm describing.

In 2016, Lily Allen, the singer, actress and TV presenter, went public about her seven years' experience of being stalked. The Observer, on 16 April 2016, reported Allen's criticisms of the way the police responded (or failed to respond adequately) to her reports of the stalker's activities.

Unless you are royalty or the target of your ex-partner (when you've a chance of getting some support from Women's Aid), it doesn't matter who you are, what your job is or how famous you are. In practice, most of us become persona non grata to the criminal justice system, as well as the NHS, social services, Victim Support and all the smaller silo agencies, most of which do little more than post us back to the authorities or to other silos.

In the year to 2016, nearly five per cent of women and nearly 2.5% of men in the UK experienced stalking crime. That's some 1,136,000 people. In the same period, police recorded only 4,156 cases, and less than a quarter of these ended in a conviction (National Stalking Consortium, 2016). How much clearer could it be that the criminal justice system and allied agencies are, in practice, staggeringly uninterested in this dreadful crime?

Blaming the victim – the 'culture of disbelief' and the myth of 'victim mentality'

In 2011, the UK's Equalities and Human Rights Commission published research into the treatment of disabled people who experience persistent crime. *Hidden in Plain Sight* (Equalities and Human Rights

Commission, 2011) concluded that a 'culture of disbelief' extends to those who become the target of crimes that our authorities are, in practice, deeply reluctant to deal with.

Stalking/harassment targets soon become disabled in some way or other and increasingly vulnerable to predation from secondary victimisers, as well as their primary persecutors.

Over the years, I've listened to so many of my fellow 'others' as they've told me about very confusing and confused reactions from authorities and agencies, endless run-arounds, deceitful service denials, and harrowing secondary victimisation from the professions and services that should be helping.

Anti-victimism and secondary victimisation abound: property and cash thefts, emotional and physical abuse, breaches of victims' safety and security, bureaucratic negligence and abuse, misrepresentation of facts in official records, character assassination by staff hiding their own malpractice, intimidation, snooping and stalking, abuse of power, including quid pro quos, coerced seduction and rape (even by police officers and NHS doctors). No authority or agency comes out clean in a long litany of mind-bending horrors.

'You've got so much to offer... and we're terrified of your intelligence.' NHS psychiatrist negating my trauma and refusing treatment for traumatic stress injuries.

'Help us write our strategy and funding bid, then we'll help you.' National mental health support organisation.

'You own a house/the police are dealing with your case/it's your choice to be scared to go out/you don't need support because you're not in any of our target groups.' Countless agencies and authorities.

'You can shop online, you don't need support. Are you sure this offending is even happening?' Social Services.

'You know how services should be run properly, and they aren't... so we're scared of you.' Manager, local support organisation for vulnerable/disabled people.

'Our practice doesn't take on patients with your sort of disabilities.' Practice manager, GP surgery, when I outlined my traumatic stress injuries and physical disabilities.

'This practice is acting unlawfully. We may be able to help you take legal action.' Legal department of national mental health organisation.

'We can't play with your mind: the stalking's really happening so we can't help you.' Community mental health team leader, during my consultation about traumatic stress injuries.

'You shouldn't buy a new house; you should buy a motorhome and move from place to place to avoid your stalker. Then you wouldn't be hiding your assets and costing the country anything in benefits.' Conveyancing solicitor's serious, blame-the-victim opinion when asked how to make sure my name doesn't appear on public databases, to protect my safety and security.

'You have to grow a pair.' Local support service worker, refusing support.

'Hmm... victim mentality.' GP, sotto voce and contributing to an already high load of secondary victimisation, after my asking again for treatment for traumatic stress injuries in the context of ongoing stalking.

On top of terrifying stalking, these nightmarish, behind-closed-doors systemic attitudes are plainly deeply traumatising. Yet making complaints or even just raising issues can be dangerous: you seem to be automatically red-flagged as 'difficult', a 'troublemaker' or a 'mental case', and further services are often tacitly withdrawn.

Undoubtedly, reaching out and listening to other victims helped keep me sane. Stalking is profoundly isolating, especially when the police tell you that you must suspect everyone in your life... after which they leave you on your own with it. So, I learned from others that it wasn't just me: this is happening to thousands of women, many of whom are driven to suicidal despair or madness by this hidden, lawless and practically unaccountable netherworld culture.

'First, let me repeat the premise that victim mentality is a myth. People do not choose to be abused. They adapt to it and learn to exist in and around it in order to survive. Depending on their age and level of brain development, they initially go into shock and then their brains adapt. This adaptation is now being studied as part of a new field of brain research called Interpersonal Neurobiology.'

Pamela Raphael MA, LMCH, US psychologist and psychotherapist. Raphael P (undated). *The Myth of Victim Mentality*. http://helpwithinreach.org/the-myth-of-victim-mentality/ (accessed June 2017).

Healthcare – who cares?

A few years after the stalking began, I was invited to a Westminster meeting, which included top politicians, elite police, prominent targets and one of the UK's leading trauma specialists. After my verbal report to the august group on stalking's shattering impact, the considerate doctor made her way over to me, suggested that I could be suffering from traumatic stress injuries, wrote down her details and kindly encouraged me to ask my GP for referral to her clinic. My GP simply disregarded both the eminent specialist's invitation and me.

All the GPs at my surgery just carried on minimising or ignoring me in an apparent frolic of sexist victim-shaming and blaming.

Meanwhile, the stalking was escalating, the police carried on no-criming reports and misdirecting, and the signposting horror-go-round was whirling apace. My life was fast falling apart. Inevitably, alone with it all, I crashed. I simply became physically and mentally paralysed with terror – not just of the stalker but also, in equal measure, of all the authorities, agencies and silo people who disingenuously kept me spinning round their signposting circus. If there wasn't a service gap I could be shunted through, then it seemed like they'd just invent new ones.

Corporately, the NHS, police and allied agencies were in effect working in sync to aid and abet the stalker to achieve his goal of destroying my life. After five more mind-bending years of unstopped stalking, dismissal and signposting, I was profoundly traumatised. Only after a shocking battle for proper treatment, the NHS finally assigned me a psychologist. This doctor immediately set about seriously abusing me. It was beyond terrifyingly undermining.

Though not as absolutely, petrifyingly mind-crushing as the experience of the woman I met whose stalker attempted murder and who was then raped by the psychiatrist who should have been treating her for trauma after her recovery from serious, life-threatening physical injuries. The NHS denied her complaint and closed ranks. For many years, whenever she went to an NHS facility to ask for treatment, the staff had standing orders to call the police on her. Eventually, her lawyers won an eye-watering sum in damages. But no amount of cash could ever make up for her lost, very successful former life and her severely, irreparably crushed psyche. Good-enough attitudes and treatment from the start would have easily averted the excruciating physical, emotional and financial costs.

It wasn't quite so bad for me. Of course, my NHS complaint was very distressingly negated: I was told I'd 'misunderstood' things. Then I couldn't access GP services. When I managed to get an appointment, I gathered that my records had been transformed so as to entirely misrepresent the facts and discredit me. There was sotto voce disparagement, explicit verbal abuse and no treatment or compassion.

Evidently, a bona fide, honest complaint about a dangerous NHS employee who's also exploiting other patients can lead to severe, extensive retribution. Extremely reluctantly, I was forced to go to law to protect myself and others. It took three years while the now £56 billion-a-year

'Alleging that a target has a "victim mentality" can be used as part of a bullying strategy to undermine and discredit a target, with the logic that the target complains about everything; bullying is just the latest in a long list of complaints, so the complaint has no basis.'

BullyOnline. http://bullyonline.org/index.php/bullying/134-myths-and-stereotypes-about-workplace-bullying) (accessed June 2017)

'Co-dependents attack those fostering healthy emotional and interpersonal practices instead of the abusers. They push promoters of healthy interactions to the margins or try to bully them out of the group, protecting the abuser instead of the abused.'

'Louise' (undated). *Co-dependency and Church Ministry*. [Online.] GoodPeople 2 GoodPriests. https://drnickmazza.wordpress.com/2011/08/27/codependency-and-church-ministry/ (accessed June 2017).

'Victim studies consistently demonstrate the adverse impact of being stalked... stalking is not a single, circumscribed offence, a crime characterised by repetition, persistence and unpredictability. The behaviours evoke fear, hypervigilance and distrust, which have a destructive impact on the victim's interpersonal relationships and support network. These may be reinforced by ineffectual or unsympathetic responses from the criminal justice system and helping agencies, usually born out of the ignorance that continues to surround stalking, even in professional circles.'

Royal College of Psychiatrists' advice to psychiatrists who become targets of stalkers. Mullen P, Whyte S, McIvor R (2009). *Information Guide for Psychiatrists on Stalking. Psychiatrists' Support Service.* London: RCPsych. www.rcpsych. ac.uk/PDF/11%20on%20stalkiing_final%20proof%20(2).pdf (accessed June 2017).

NHS legal empire and associates cavilled and machinated. The evidence against the NHS psychologist was abundant, witnessed and entirely damning. I won. Sadly, financial damages were given, not apologies.

The stalking was relentless throughout what I learned was a dreadfully stressful legal action in which complainants are generally treated like criminal suspects or vexatious ne'er-do-wells. In an apparent effort to undermine my credibility, the purportedly impartial Court Service Expert Witness who interrogated me at length initially wrote a court report in which I was portrayed as a 'community activist', rather than employed by major local authorities at director-level.

No one in the plethora of agencies, services and so-called watchdog and regulatory bodies cared. They all just wanted to close ranks, cover their backs, dismiss and discredit me, and even to defend the abusive doctor in any way possible. All I wanted was an honest, genuine apology, to protect others from abuse, and timely, respectful, appropriate treatment as a disabled target of terrifying stalking and mind-bending secondary victimisation.

Is it symptomatic of the systemic malaise and antipathy towards tax-paying customers that no NHS webpage gives stalking/harassment as a cause of mental and physical harm or affords a word of support for the one million+ women a year who are stalked, while the Royal Society of Psychiatrists' website has a whole section of advice for psychiatrists who are stalked, but none for their customers?

Likewise, the NHS has set up a 'stalking centre of excellence'. It focuses on stalkers. We targets are discreetly sidelined. The centre seems to make a tidy sum by assessing offenders for the courts. In the nightmare netherworld, crime really does seem to pay.

If not for some helpful community workers and superb local hospital healthcare professionals, who've done everything possible to ameliorate my painful disability, I'd have no healthcare at all in my new location. I'm still struggling to register with a GP. I still struggle daily with exhausting pain and often paralysing traumatic stress injuries.

What have I learned?

Shocking and incredible as they may seem, all the examples in this chapter truthfully record typical netherworld attitudes to targets of unstopped crime. But this reportage isn't a blaming-and-shaming project. Rather, it's an attempt to prise the lid off this netherworld of 'institutional anti-victimism', which harms every one of us in some way or other, and to prompt an honest, constructive conversation about how we can genuinely help each other when so many of us become terrified and vulnerable targets of stalking/harassment.

What have I learned in all these years of unstopped stalking and institutional betrayal? Essentially, that the systemic big picture echoes that of amateur CCTV, which offers only an illusion of security and safety. Many of us live comfortably, thanks to our over-confidence that, when we are seriously troubled, there will be services and professionals ready, willing and able to help. Sadly, I've learned that very few want to know. I've learned that 'multi-agency working' is mostly a sotto voce synonym for 'we'll work together only when it means that we can cover for each other's failures': in effect, 'us vs them'.

During the chronic infliction of this netherworld reality, every scrap of one's faith in our society and our fellow humans is called into question. For example, one is drawn to ask what sort of people now lead the NHS and why they now allocate nearly half the NHS budget to their legal department (approximately 46.6% in 2016, according to the Taxpayers' Alliance (Jones, 2016)).

Similarly, we've learned that one must protect oneself from the NHS's corporate callousnesses: 'It's all too big now. They only concentrate on their forms and they've lost the human touch', as a kindly and sympathetic Patient Advice and Liaison Service (PALS) officer put it to me last week.

The same goes for the police and allied agencies. While there are many genuinely caring public services staff, dysfunctional, co-dependent systems and leaders deeply frustrate and sadden them, and don't allow them to do their jobs humanely or adequately. Inevitably, all this creates even more problems for service users, avoidably and expensively prolonging their agony.

Plainly, money is not the problem, otherwise the NHS could not fritter away some £56 billion annually on legal frolicking, and the police could not afford their institutional denial culture, with its self-serving, labyrinthine complaints procedures. And just about all the very costly silo agencies would not exist, if these two leading institutions actually

'If you are "troubled" and you seek help from the state, you can guarantee that the interventions from the state are most likely to make you worse off. The many "helping" arms of the state are fragmented, only look at the "troubled" through their own "specialist" lens, focus their efforts on administrative reporting and meeting activity targets over doing anything useful and, if they do anything, they tend to commission services that don't meet needs...

'It is not putting it too strongly to say that the best advice to anyone who is "troubled" is to avoid seeking help from the state.

'Just think of the billions being spent to no avail. Central to the "troubled system" is the top-down nature of the fragmented services. Whitehall thinks it is pulling levers. A better metaphor would be "throwing spanners in the works".'

Professor John Seddon, occupational psychologist and managing director, Vanguard Consulting. https://vanguard-method.net/september-2012/# (accessed June 2017)

did a good-enough job first time, every time.

Unaccountability, self-serving duplicity and soulless, empire-building spin certainly appear to be major problems. So too are service leaders' absence of care and concern for their many abused, injured and struggling fellow citizens who are merely 'units' to be processed, not humans like them who bleed when cut. Crucially, it very much seems that our governments have simply lost control of some of our institutions, which often appear to behave anarchically and destructively.

What the hell happens to everyone else...?

One of my beloved children has been so dreadfully affected by the stalking, compounded by the authorities' deeply alienating attitudes, that she's emigrated to a new life in a healthier, more humanely functional country. She doesn't feel part of the UK now. As a human resources professional, she likens this netherworld pathology to 'constructive dismissal', where employers slyly make life so difficult for employees that they are forced to leave the company.

This chronic nightmare has not only split our whole family apart, but it's also disempowered, disengaged and consigned us to endless netherworld fallout, constructed by DARVO-mode leaders who callously quash challenges, complaints and whistleblowing, and are intent on masking their fiefdoms' shortcomings. As a direct result of this culture, many targeted women are irreparably injured or take their own lives, instead of leaving the company or the country.

Another of my children, explicitly because he knows he can do much better for victims than the customary netherworld dismissiveness and secondary victimisation, and perhaps in a realistic move to ensure his safety on the 'right' side of the all-too real 'them vs us' line, left a successful, lucrative career to become a police officer. It makes me very proud of him. With all his painful netherworld knowledge, he'll make a very fine, honest, victim-friendly senior officer.

By the grace of God, I've so far survived the profound shock of unfettered abuse by a stalker and equally chronic betrayal by institutions that carelessly crushed me into a paralysed fugue. Like many others, I've been forced to adapt to an impoverished, twilight existence, which entails me accommodating both hiding from the stalker and, equally terrified, minimising my public services contacts, and doing everything legal, decent and honest to protect myself from all.

Like countless others, I wouldn't have been left traumatised, disabled and constructively dismissed if all the taxpayer-funded silos had not persisted in kicking the can down the road, and if staff had not routinely ignored the reality that none of their agencies actually do much of what they advertise. Their responses certainly clarify that, as a victim of persistent crime, you are simply worthless.

Like many otherwise resourceful, resilient and rational targets, I could have handled the stalking if services and silo agencies had fulfilled just half their service contract, website and leaflet claims. Proper use of the Protection from Harassment Act 1997 would have nabbed the offender well within, I reckon, a year. As it is, in the absence of police resolution, I, like many others, must live the rest of my life in hiding, always careful about sharing personal details and forever looking over my shoulder. Meanwhile, the hurdles that our services mindlessly persist in throwing up guarantee that rebuilding one's life is ever a slow battle.

In the turmoil around the Catholic Church's confession of widespread clergy abuse of children, some have bravely critiqued the profound institutional malaise that enabled such horror. In her book, *The Codependent Church*, Professor Emerita Virginia Curran Hoffman writes: 'To the extent that a church... a closed system... assigns its members roles to play and expects them to live by rules that rob them of their inner selves, it is dysfunctional and teaches co-dependency' (Hoffman, 1991).

'Often, it's not being heard by the people who matter that becomes more traumatic than the trauma itself. The person is devalued. They feel demeaned and trivialised. Either what happened to them doesn't matter or it didn't happen at all. The person and their experience have become invisible to society, obstructed by the very people whose task it is to help and protect as well as to bring order and retribution to that experience.'

Simeon Brody, commenting in *Community Care* magazine on the stalking of Shauna Bailey. Brody S (2010). Lack of protection for Shauna Bailey sends woeful message to social workers. *Community Care*; 2 February. www.communitycare.co.uk/blogs/social-work-front-line-focus/2010/02/lack-of-protection-for-shauna-bailey-sends-woeful-message-to-social-workers/ (accessed June 2017).

One could easily substitute 'public services' for 'church'. Both sectors are primarily self-referential, closed systems that can be turned to depersonalising both staff and supplicants with misguided, politicised, rigid rules and overly zealous, unassailable beliefs and practices.

Sadly, because jobs and pensions are so often co-dependent on the favour of state institutions, the distinct parallel between the Church's dysfunctions and those of other public institutions hasn't been explored. However, it leaves the field open for people like me to posit that, co-dependently, the UK's 'helping' industry thrives on the back of others' suffering – suffering that only worsens because of depersonalised, rule-bound, impotent neglect, and even abuse. Thus, more work is generated, if only in tick-box and signposting terms. Similarly, it's tempting to speculate that the publicly funded plethora of 'helplines' and 'helping' staff exist mainly to reduce dole queues. Ticking boxes and producing statistics and glossy literature to impress state funders appears to be a career path in itself these days. Cognitive behavioural therapy (CBT) is often recommended for trauma sufferers; it's predicated on a notion of the patient's 'faulty' thinking. It occurs to me that this industry might be far more effective if it were to undertake CBT itself.

One in four professional women is stalked. Like them, I'm an educated, accomplished and articulate woman; I'd earned a senior public services position. Yet I've been disabled by the same services I'd trusted and worked with for years. Even now, I'm ashamed that I'd no idea how poor we are in practice, behind the scenes, under the glossy spin.

Being disabled and dependent on this dysfunctional state is loathsome. Like every stalking target, I just want to get back to normal. We need support to get our lives and health back. We don't want what's actually on offer: relentless pressure to become a compliant, co-dependent, chronic victim that can be kicked to the kerb and alienated. Harmed by public services' innumerable neglects and abuses, nowadays I'm often overwhelmingly, wet-myself, paralytically terrified at the prospect of having to interact with them. Now, I'm rarely without a voice recorder to ensure that I'm not waylaid by more mind-bending duplicities or abuse.

As Lily Allen asked: 'I want answers from the police. If they treat me like this, how the hell are they going to treat everyone else?' (Lyons, 2016).

Official pipe dreams vs nightmare DIY reality

Mostly, if we are to stand any chance of survival, we stalking targets are forced to do it ourselves. We try hard to live around and in spite of the incessant, frightening intrusions of an obsessed stalker – criminologists call this 'accommodating the offender' – and the spanner-chucking de facto neglect of the state. When all around are failing us and the world has become a living nightmare, we cling desperately to the prospect of getting back to normal, back to our lives, families, work, sanity and peace of mind.

The problem is, though, that one can't stop persistent crimes just by thinking positive thoughts and singlehandedly exercising one's very best efforts. Despite Professor Seddon's best advice, policing and medicine are jobs for professionals; they're not viable, sustainable DIY projects.

Unsurprisingly, we chronically, highly stressed 'others' often fail and succumb to the system's dysfunctional, spanner-clogged co-dependency. Very reluctantly, and not without a fight, we sink into needing even more help from the services that already let us down so often. That's our only option: there are no other, more functional crime-fighting and support services in the UK, unless you're ultra-rich. We develop costly, life-sapping, stress-induced diseases and disabilities; we become very unwillingly dependent on the state, and often grossly impoverished in every area of our immensely disrupted, stolen lives.

Under great duress, we either accept that we are hostage to the state's implicit and co-dependent demand that we are somehow liable for the crimes against us... or we end our own lives. Whichever, it is murder in slow motion.

These experiences are all too commonplace. In this nightmare nether-world, there's an ignored tsunami of

'Victims of stalking can have their lives ruined, causing psychological damage such as anxiety, fear and depression. The stalker is often unknown or merely an acquaintance, rendering the victim defenceless against a faceless enemy...

'In effect, stalking curtails a victim's freedom, leaving them feeling they constantly have to watch out.'

Mbubaegbu C (2010). UB Dead: torment by a faceless enemy. Eye Witness; October: 9.

'Stalkers steal lives... too many times the [offending] pattern goes unrecognised... and often continues for years until it is too late. By fully understanding this crime and through early intervention, CPS prosecutors could help put a stop to years of stalking and a victim's life being completely destroyed.'

Eye Witness (2010). CPS publishes groundbreaking Stalking and Harassment guidance. *Eye Witness*; October: 10–11. http://webarchive. nationalarchives.gov. uk/20110118193512/http://www. cps.gov.uk/news/assets/uploads/ files/October%202010%20Eye%20 Witness.pdf (accessed July 2017)

repeated crime against vulnerable people, or those who soon become vulnerable: epidemics of stalking, domestic violence, organised sexual abuse, institutional betrayal... and, when the chips are really down, the most frequent, shoulder-shrugging silo advice is to sue errant, negligent services. What does all this say about our nation's real concern and our fellow citizens' care for victims of unstopped crime and abuse?

One in five women and one in 10 men will be stalked in the UK during their lifetimes, so various government bodies like the CPS tell us (James et al, 2016). It's a massive yet silent and silenced epidemic. When it comes to stalking, there is no 'them vs us': over a third of us are equally prey to some devious but deranged stalker. And when it happens to you, you're devastatingly likely to become a buried statistic, demeaned, crushed and shunted away.

Despite the commendable EU Victims Directive 2012/29, which set minimum standards on the rights, support and protection of victims of crime, nothing much has changed in practice for victims. We now have Police and Crime Commissioners, whose responsibility for the care of victims has more often than not resulted in huge regional aggregate signposting websites and an outbreak of Police and Crime Commissioner-dependent local silo agencies, which are underfunded and so highly specialist that they exclude even more victims.

The Directive's implementation handbook (Victim Support Europe, 2013) emphasises that the legislation renders it unlawful not to believe a crime victim's reports, imposes a duty to treat victims with respect and dignity, criminalises acts that are aimed at impairing a person's physical or psychological integrity, and compels services to uphold victims' rights and to give them swift access to individually tailored, integrated support to aid their recovery and restitution.

Deplorably and very regrettably, as Lily Allen highlighted in 2016, little of this law, enacted in the UK in 2015, has found its way into practice. What's transpired instead is a significant expansion of the netherworld's unimpressive helping industry and even more silo signposting.

Yet, as far back as 15 years ago, Victim Support was strongly advocating for what's actually needed: co-ordinated government action. In practice, this means a professional, victim-centred, victim-driven National Crime Victims Service, run not as a pseudo-charity to which supplicants must make their case for help but as a statutory, Home Office, single-point-of-contact service provider. Teeth and accountability for ensuring practical service delivery focused exclusively on crime victims' rights and needs would be sine qua non operating components, of course.

Baroness Helen Newlove, UK Victims' Commissioner and herself the victim of devastating crime, continues to highlight the dire lack of adequate help, that agencies still work in silos, that legislation is needed to ensure that victims get their rights honoured and easy access to willing services. She calls for legislators to address this imbalance of justice now (see, for example, Newlove, 2016).

Having questioned and challenged services and government departments to no avail over the years, I persist unapologetically in asking who else really cares enough, who has the courage and the authority to do anything about this DARVO nightmare netherworld with its systemic 'culture of disbelief', its innumerable signposting silo agencies and the immense, impoverishing DIY burden it all inflicts on stalking targets and their families?

Currently, the unsatisfactory and inadequate answer is that, even though we're exhausted and traumatised, we stalking targets, close family and stalwart friends voluntarily form the core of:

- all genuine and effective support efforts for stalking/harassment targets
- all campaigns to raise the profile of a horrific crime that injures some 25% of British women and 10% of British men, and negatively impacts their families, friends and co-workers
- all activism and training to persuade legislators to enact – and frontline staff to implement – legislation for stronger laws and the provision for much better help for targets and all those close to them.

In other words, regardless of existing legislation, a crime that the CPS tells us 'steals lives', 'ruins lives', 'completely destroys lives' (*Eye Witness*, 2010), and directly, chronically adversely affects a significant proportion of the UK in some way or other, is left to the DIY skills of victims, their families and friends.

Apart from the short-term benefits to those individuals, authorities, silo agencies and companies that directly profit from the nightmarish 'culture of disbelief' and the vast, unexplored chasms of suffering it inflicts and perpetuates, the longer-term economics of this hidden-in-plain-sight netherworld pathology simply do not add up.

In the long run, whether the problem is ill-informed, wishful thinking about service performance or systemic, sly, deliberate dismissiveness, this netherworld is unsustainable; it's impoverishing everyone in more important ways than simply financial. Quite rationally, for victims of unstopped crime and all close to them, this 'culture of disbelief' netherworld engenders profound distrust of our public services. It doesn't seem to matter to our services that this often increases their workload and fundamentally degrades and fragments our society further.

Clearly though, for now, our nation has plenty of money to fritter away in its covertly anti-victim, laissez faire attitudes towards unstopped crime, apparently disposable vulnerable targets, dreadful service delivery and even worse accountability standards.

In a wealthy, first-world nation that holds itself out as a 21st century global leader in policing, healthcare, social services and a wide spectrum of humanitarian, human rights causes, is any of this fair or just? Is any of this good-enough?

> 'Stalking is a deeply disturbing crime with many victims living in fear for years. This has to stop. This is why tackling stalking forms a key part of our action plan to end violence against women and girls.'
>
> The Rt Hon Theresa May MP, when Home Secretary, speaking at the launch of National Stalking Awareness Week, 11 April 2011. www.gov.uk/government/news/theresa-may-backs-stalking-awareness-week (accessed June 2017).

References

Equalities and Human Rights Commission (2011). *Hidden in Plain Sight: inquiry into disability-related harassment*. London: EHRC. www.equalityhumanrights.com/sites/default/files/ehrc_hidden_in_plain_sight_3.pdf (accessed June 2017).

Eye Witness (2010). CPS publishes groundbreaking Stalking and Harassment guidance. *Eye Witness* October: 10–11. http://webarchive.nationalarchives.gov.uk/20110118193512/http://www.cps.gov.uk/news/assets/uploads/files/October%202010%20Eye%20Witness.pdf (accessed July 2017).

Freyd JJ (undated a). *Institutional Betrayal and Betrayal Blindness*. [Online.] http://dynamic.uoregon.edu/jjf/institutionalbetrayal/index.html (accessed June 2017).

Freyd JJ (undated b). What is DARVO? [Online.] http://dynamic.uoregon.edu/jjf/defineDARVO.html (accessed June 2017).

Hoffman VC (1991). The Codependent Church. New York, NY: Crossroad Publishing Company.

James D, Persaud R, Suzy Lamplugh Trust, YouGov (2016). *The Stalker in Your Pocket*. London: Suzy Lamplugh Trust. www.suzylamplugh.org/2016/04/stalker-pocket/ (accessed June 2016).

Jones C (2016). *Medical Blunder Pot Doubles to £56bn*. [Online.] London: Taxpayers Alliance. www.taxpayersalliance.com/nhs_medical_blunder_pot_doubes_56bn (accessed June 2017).

Lyons K (2016). Tiny proportion of stalking cases recorded by police, data suggests. [Online.] *The Guardian*; 18 April. www.theguardian.com/uk-news/2016/apr/18/stalking-cases-recorded-police-data-lilly-allen-charity (accessed July 2017).

National Stalking Consortium (2016). *National Stalking Consortium Calls for Commitment to Stalking*. [Online.] London: Suzy Lamplugh Trust. www. suzylamplugh.org/news/call-for-commitment-to-stalking (accessed June 2017).

Newlove H (2016). *Victim's Law: the government has a responsibility to get this right*. [Online.] London: Victim's Commissioner. http:// victimscommissioner.org.uk/victims-law-the-government-has-a-responsibility-to-get-this-right/ (accessed June 2017).

Victim Support Europe (2013). *Handbook for Implementation of Legislation and Best Practice for Victims of Crime in Europe*. Brussels: Victim Support Europe. http://ec.europa.eu/justice/events/assises-justice-2013/files/s/51.1.13 74573250handbookforimplementationandbestpracticeforvictimsofcrimeineur ope_23713_en.pdf (accessed June 2017).

17

A counsellor's experience

I met my stalker when I was working in a counselling service. The service was used by a high percentage of clients with mental health issues, so it was usual for counsellors to encounter all sorts of complex boundary challenges. He was a client and came to me for counselling.

This client was very pushy. He had a particular sense of entitlement, and pushed my boundaries with behaviours that I found quite challenging, but he also presented as vulnerable and anxious. He fitted into what the person-centred model calls fragile process: sometimes he saw me as the perfect counsellor and sometimes I was this awful person, and he'd tell me that he hated me. He had this very polarised view of me, which I found quite unsettling. So, there were ruptures in the alliance right from the start.

But, in the context of the organisation where I worked, that was quite common. So I didn't think about him as in any way different from other clients. I just noticed, when I was working with him, that maybe he was pushing me a bit too much. I was quite inexperienced as a therapist, and, looking back, I can see I was a bit naïve. Also, my manager wasn't at all helpful or supportive. In fact, they tried to pressurise me to see more fragile clients than I thought was ethical. I tried to talk to them about my concerns, but they didn't listen. I asked for additional training but was told that the budget could not cover this.

In this service, clients could book themselves in for sessions. So, a client could book in, have a session, disappear, and then book in with another therapist, see them, and disappear. This is what this client was doing. The managers knew what was going on but didn't try to prevent it.

The client was sometimes very accusatory, but if I suggested that maybe this was not the right service or I wasn't the right counsellor for him, he would almost beg me to see him. So, there was a history of in-and-out with the service with this client. But he sometimes seemed very angry, and he directed his process onto me. On one occasion, I was counselling another client, and he stormed into the organisation and was shouting, 'You care more about your other clients than about me', and was enraged. He told me that he was jealous of others in my life.

At one point, he was saying he wanted to look after me, and then he came out with the ideas of hating me again. It was almost as if he fantasised that there was a kind of special intimacy between us that was at times also loaded with hate, but it was in fact just a standard therapy relationship. Sometimes it was almost as if he was trying to take care of me. It was like he was trying to get into my head, saying things about the kind of person I was and what he thought I was capable of, as if he was trying to hurt my feelings and insult me. He admitted this to some degree.

He'd send me messages, analysing my character and behaviour. He was basically pulling my personality to bits and saying I was a bad, evil person. I had a lot of therapy at that time, and I think, deep down, there was a slight doubt in my mind that maybe he was right. He sent me emails and notes. I've kept them, locked away, in case of any problems, because they were really angry; they really showed the level of rage in him. He seemed to be blaming his whole life on me. I was his saviour and the devil. I felt he wanted something from me, as though I owed him something, and sometimes I thought, maybe I do, maybe I have done something wrong and this is my fault.

He'd make all sorts of little observations about me and my mannerisms, as if we were going out, and make occasional statements as if he was in love with me. It was affectionate in some ways, but poisonous in others. I felt stupid because I didn't feel he was necessarily going to attack me, but I felt very uncomfortable when he was hanging around outside the buildings where I worked. I felt he was trying to get into my psyche, and, because he was outside the building, he was controlling me, but there was no physical threat. It feels ridiculous but I just had this sense that he was there, waiting. I didn't know what he was capable of. Compared with some people's experience, it was a fairly low level of activity, in a way, but it made me feel really unsafe and stressed.

He'd say he hated women and that I was symbolic of all women. I started taking different routes to work, different modes of transport. There would be periods when he got on with his life, then we'd bump into each other and it would start again.

Then he made an official complaint about me and I had to go through an internal complaints procedure. I thought there were some things I could have done differently, such as more explicit contracting, things like that, but going through the complaints process was very difficult and, even though he had made complaints about other therapists, the organisation didn't support me. They just told me to bring in my indemnity insurance certificate and basically the message was, 'You're on your own.'

Looking back, I think one of the problems was that it was someone else in the organisation who abruptly terminated the relationship with the client. They sent him a letter saying that, while the complaint was being investigated, he shouldn't continue seeing me – and this seemed to fire him up. He wanted something from the process that wasn't what we were there to provide, and he wanted immediate answers.

I wish the organisation had provided some mediation early on, because the procedure was not helpful to me or the client. I surrendered myself to it. It became an organisational thing, a legal issue, not an interpersonal one, so the client was left feeling even more injured when the organisation found there wasn't a case to answer, and he reframed all sorts of things and made up all sorts of stuff. I don't think anything would have stopped it happening, because that was his process, but I think the legal process prevented a more mediated response, and that could have mitigated against it. Maybe he felt he hadn't been heard. He probably felt he didn't have much control and was trying to exert control.

I knew he'd done this with other people in that same organisation, and the view was that he was ill and needed support. But once I left the organisation where it happened, it became between him and me.

I did genuinely care about his wellbeing but, as time went on, I also became scared of him.

When he was starting to push me more and more, and having this love and hate relationship, just when I thought I would need to close it down, he said he had sexual fantasies about hurting me. It was not a direct threat. It was always couched in terms of his fantasies. That was very unsettling; there was no actual threat or risk you could put your finger on. He seemed to be getting more and more angry because he wasn't getting what he wanted. He also rang my professional body and made accusations to them as well.

I contacted them and they said, as long as there is an internal complaints process that's ongoing, we might not need to get involved, which I felt was a reasonable response, but the organisation was unsupportive and I became more ill with stress. Without the support of my supervisor and counsellor, I dread to think how I would have survived. I became withdrawn for a while and avoided going out much.

I felt let down and injured by the organisation; I felt I had been scapegoated. The way they said, 'You are on your own.' I didn't want to stay there. So, I got a better-paid job where I was happier and I went through a process of healing from it. I changed my practice, changed my boundaries, had more training, so it actually helped me to develop professionally. I had this post-traumatic growth period. However, this client kept coming back into my life periodically.

I remember walking through a local area, a few years later, and I bumped into him, and he started shouting and waving his arms at me. A lot of time had passed; I thought I should try to talk to him but he started coming out with accusations. After that, he would appear at bus stops and wait outside the place where I was working, so there was a period when I was scared to leave the office on my own in the evenings after work. I know he had looked up details about other therapists, tried to find out where their cars were parked and tried to find out where they lived.

In the daytime, I just got on with it, but I did worry about getting home in the evening after work. Sometimes I asked people to walk me to the bus stop. Colleagues and friends were generally supportive. I'd just say, 'There's someone who keeps following me', and people would ask, 'Do you want to contact the police?' But I felt he had serious mental health problems, and when I worked with him, he was very clear he didn't want to use mental health services, so I didn't feel I should be doing anything that might mean he ended up in psychiatric care. Also, he never actually directly threatened me – it was always couched in terms of his fantasies – so he wasn't doing anything illegal. I suppose it was frustrating for other people that I didn't report him, but I thought it would fire him up even more – that if the police had gone round to his house and cautioned him, it would have made it worse. I thought I would be better off lying low. I think if he had ever come round to where I lived, I would have rung the police. But it's always felt to me like low-level activity. I think he was just wanting me to know he was there; he perhaps wanted to scare me.

I moved jobs a few times and each time there'd be a lull, and then something would fire him up and he would seek me out again, all across the county. He would travel to find me at whatever service I was working. I would see him waiting outside, or he'd appear at bus stops saying he would ruin my career – on one occasion, after he'd shouted at me at the bus stop, I actually passed out on the bus. I got on the bus, leaving him at the stop, and there were no seats, and I ended up collapsing on the floor.

I felt like he had some power over me because of our history. He would ring up places where I worked and rant angrily to my colleagues. I just told them they'd have to make their own mind up.

It's still happening now, 15 years later. Every so often I bump into him, and there'll be a flurry of activity. One time, after seeing him, my emails were flooded with porn. I had a feeling that it was him.

I was once stalked by someone who did that thing of hiding in the bushes and following me home, and I reported him to the police, and they got him in the end. That was easier to handle, and this person was very disturbed. I thought he probably could become dangerous, and it turned out he had been following other women.

I haven't told many people about it because I feel, in some way, it's quite trivial, and it wasn't a huge level of activity. Sometimes I'd go for months without seeing him, and then I would see him, or think it was him, and often it was. He would appear and disappear. I think he was very uneven in his mental health. I stopped going places where I thought I'd meet him. There was one particular spot where I really liked going and he turned up there, so I stopped going. But then I went one day, very early in the morning, and he wasn't there, but I remember feeling really anxious and having the sense that the anxiety would follow me for the rest of my life: that if I went there, and he was there, I would have all this following again, and I didn't want it.

I have had a lot of therapy over the years. When I went through the complaint, I was in therapy with a really good therapist and I was able to unpick in therapy the things he was tweaking about me. It was lucky I had a really good therapist and could do that. You know how people say perpetrators are able to pick up certain vulnerabilities in their victims, and I was able to unpick this in therapy and work out what was my part in this, what I could do differently. I was blaming myself.

There was this other layer to what was happening – there was the direct activity and its effects, and beneath that there were these unresolved issues that I had, that made me feel I was in some way responsible, and made me less able to report him to the police. I think I was already vulnerable and he knew that, he could almost sniff it out on me.

There was a point when I thought I would never practise again and I had a break, and I felt I returned with a healthier perspective on the work. So, the experience was beneficial in a way; I learned from it. I am now more boundaried, more aware than I was. I would be much faster now to flag up these issues with forensic services, with the multidisciplinary team, and to refer the client on. I think I was naïve to think I could handle it myself, which was reinforced by poor management of someone who was an inexperienced counsellor. I now have a better understanding of the importance of working in teams and would now stand up to a manager if given poor advice or support. With clients with complex process, this kind of situation is quite common – the way he was determined to forge a special link with me, and reluctant to engage with other services, or didn't feel able to.

Now, I would ask myself, should I be working with this client? I am now much more confident with clients with difficult processes. I don't ask if the client's reality is right or wrong; I listen to their stories. It's made me more open-minded and less quick to judge what is going on. But I only work in services where I am fully supported by experienced managers.

In retrospect, there were some warning bells, which I reported to my managers, but they ignored them, and so I then normalised them. These days, I listen to my instincts and withdraw. So, as well as being more open to the client's process, I am more private, less in the public domain, more explicit about boundaries, more careful, without being over-defensive. If I hear warning bells, I ask myself, 'Why is this happening?' and I am much more likely to act. This experience was low level, but it consumed a huge amount of my energy and worried other people who cared about me. For a low-level activity, I spent a huge amount of time worrying about it and changing my routines and public presence to reduce any potential risk.

When I look back at my story I feel sad both for me and for my client. I was unsupported and he was unwell. We both needed a wider team to advise us and hold us through this, or to take over his care, instead of directing blame on to us. I feel that we were both blamed and let down. I know my learning curve has cost me a lot of tears, but it has improved my practice and resilience – I now know to demand full support from my employer when I'm working with vulnerable clients.

18

Escaping control

Sitting here, reminiscing about my past, knowing that it almost killed me, I still can't help but find humour in this crazy state of affairs called my life. It's an attitude I adopted as a survival mechanism. It all started when, as a young girl, I met a boy in America. I didn't get a very good vibe off him in the beginning, but after knowing him for about two years through mutual friends, I warmed up to him. I should've stuck with my initial instinct. He was very charming and constantly tried to impress me, so I eventually fell for him and we developed into an item. The more time that went on, the more attentive I thought he became. I was a teenage girl in love, naïve, rebellious, and was not willing to listen to anyone's advice. Everyone I knew pretty much hated him, but I was in complete denial. How could an extremely intelligent, talented, handsome leader, who always helps people, be seen as controlling and manipulating?

After dating for just over a year, Jake became quite disrespectful and dismissive. The more I pulled him up on it, the angrier he would get. He became jealous of me seeing my friends, would lie about his whereabouts constantly, disappear for days at a time, and started talking down to me in front of people. When he introduced me to men, he would refer to me as his wife. When he introduced me to women, however, unless they were family members, he would introduce me by my first name. He always had to know where I was, and would show up to places to cause an argument. Even after all of that, I believed that I could help him and change him to be a better person. Soon after, I became pregnant and he was over the moon about the news, as he had always told me that he wanted a son, and so did I. His behaviour deteriorated rapidly however, and he became verbally abusive towards me and made me feel very useless. I was a young woman of 21 by this point, and was already going through a stage of insecurity, without his contributions. Amazing what love can do in terms of tolerance.

When I was seven months pregnant, Jake wanted to borrow my car as always, but I refused. He had been gone for days and I was not in a position to be without a vehicle again, especially in the States, where public transport is practically non-existent. He took my keys and got in the car anyway, so I sat on the top of the hood of my car, heavily pregnant and refused to let him take it. He then drove off full speed to back out of the spot at a right angle, throwing me off the bonnet of the car. His friend intervened, but Jake was too much feared for anyone to speak up to him too much. My neighbour called the police, but nothing ever came of that. The next incident happened shortly after, at our house, when he angrily requested $100 and I refused to give it to him. He threw me across the bed (at this point I was eight months pregnant), took the money and disappeared. Obviously, I was drifting away from him, but I was about to have his child, so I reluctantly stayed with him.

Two weeks after the birth of our son, Jake had to leave the USA and resume his life in Britain, where he is a citizen. During the two weeks in which he was present, he would still take my car and I would be left without nappies or any means of obtaining them. In a way, it was easier when he left the USA. I did promise, however, to reunite with him in the UK if he left, and for us to have a fresh start with our family, which I fulfilled six months later and moved to Britain with my son. Yes, I know I should've left and, ashamedly, I took him back many more times for the sake of my son, and obviously because I was naïvely in love with him at first. The move to the UK was definitely an adventure of a lifetime that has tested my strength through and through, but, as they say, 'what doesn't kill you makes you stronger'.

My son and I arrived at the airport and could not find anyone for about an hour, until Jake finally showed up. I don't know why, but from the moment I arrived, I knew that I had made a massive mistake coming to live with him. Once again, my intuition was right. We moved into a small studio flat, and I managed to get a job at a nearby shop. It was quite strange, being completely isolated in a foreign country and only knowing Jake and a few of his relatives. I did have a few laughs at work with customers, but this quickly led to Jake not only intimidating male customers who smiled at me, but also accusing me of having an affair with my boss's son. This was comical as by then, in his opinion, I was having an affair with just about every male I came into contact with, including young lads and men older than my dad.

This control caused me to lose my job, my freedom and my funding options, which led to more isolation. Jake used to stalk me while I was at work and confront people about speaking to me, and went to the extremes of shouting words such as 'I'm going to chop you into pieces' at me for smiling and talking to customers. My boss called the police on one occasion, for which Jake repaid me by nearly breaking my back by body-slamming me with his arm across my back. He knew so many people, just as he did in the States, if not more, who would report back to him if they saw me. Jake would literally know my every move. This stalking behavior became much more severe after I moved to the UK, as my only networks at that point were local friends and he was fully aware and resourceful of this fact.

Jake's aggression became progressively worse, and it turned from verbal intimidation, humiliation, suppression and control to physical hostility. Initially this was by punching through and damaging walls, closets, doors and various other objects. Later on, let's just say, I became skilled at playing dodge ball with the TV. I ran away with my son and managed to hide out for four days before his friend spotted me and called Jake. Jake showed up, grabbed the buggy and was not letting go. I had to go back and play nice for my son's sake. This is when I was introduced to flying against walls and doors with force, repeatedly.

My next experience involved dribbling sessions with my head against a tiled wall with my then one-year-old in my arms. Jake was smart, I have long hair, so no one would question or notice bruises and bumps on my head. When I physically ran out of the house with my son in my arms, he grabbed me by my hair when I got to the bottom of the stairs, being much faster and stronger than me, and pulled me back up the stairs by my hair while punching the back of my head, with my son still crying in my arms, until I temporarily lost consciousness. He then locked me in the flat with himself there to keep me from escaping. He took the rest of my money out of my purse, and took my phone and my son's and my passports and birth certificates. 'You chose to have my child, so you are mine forever', were his words to try to justify his actions. The most core-destroying incident was when Jake broke my son's toys because I refused to have sex with him. This emotional blackmail worked, but at the expense of my soul.

I knew that the only way to escape from him was timing. On this occasion, I found a slot of a few hours where Jake would definitely be out of the house. I made no plans, other than the fact that my son and I were leaving. The time came; if I stayed, he'd kill me. Jake had a gig he was performing at and I knew that he would be gone for at least a few hours.

I packed whatever I could think of in about 30 minutes and ran to a near restaurant to call for a cab, as Jake had taken my phone. This would later have an impact on Jake's stalking, because when they asked me where I was going, I frantically said, 'I don't know, just get a cab.' The person who rang the cab company then randomly said the name of a local town to complete the request. This area he mentioned is where Jake was looking for me thoroughly for over a year after my son and I finally escaped.

So, my son and I got into this cab with a couple of suitcases at about 10pm and I told him to drive. 'Where to?' he asks. 'I don't know, just drive,' I respond. I had hidden £100 from Jake and planned to use what was left from this after paying for the cab ride on a hotel room of sorts. When we got to the hotel, the cab driver kindly offered to help me with my bags, seeing I was distressed and had my hands full with my son – and then he shut the door behind him in my room after a friendly conversation with the hotel manager in their language. Needless to say, he mistook my fear of my ex-partner for vulnerability.

Long story short, I was so terrified of Jake finding me that the cab driver did not intimidate me at all when he called in to report going off duty for the rest of the night. He then proceeded to attempt to move on me, with my son sleeping next to me. Baffled by my reaction of laughter and lack of fear at his foul attempts while continuing to watch Dave Chappelle, he decided to masturbate while watching me instead of listening to my request for him to leave. While he was there with me, he couldn't tell Jake my whereabouts, so I felt safe, as no one else knew where I was. He then became fearful of the consequences of his actions and offered a ride in the morning and to let me use his phone for as long as I needed, in exchange for my silence. Given the circumstances and the lack of money and communication devices, he was a safer choice than Jake. If Jake caught me, I'd be dead. The cabbie at this point was more scared of me than I was of him.

The cab driver came back in the morning to let me use the phone as promised and, after hours of calling, I was told that I would be unlikely to find a place to stay within the next 48 hours. Plan B: go to the police, as I couldn't go to the housing office, which was around the corner from where we lived. I explained to a lady cop that my son and I had just had to flee from domestic violence and we could not return. Her response to that was, 'What do you expect me to do about that?' Plan C: Social Services – I have my one-and-a-half-year-old son with me, with nowhere to sleep, in the middle of winter. After being at their office and not leaving from about 8am and threatening to sleep on their doorstep until they found somewhere, they eventually found me a place by 9pm.

Social Services gave me the money for a ticket to this discrete location, which I could not know until I arrived. Another adventure begins.

'When you get to this location, call us and someone will meet you,' they said. At this point, I'm assuming that this is somewhere near a phone, as they knew I didn't have one. We finally arrived, with a buggy and two suitcases, at 11pm, at a train station where the exit was across a bridge via many stairs, in the middle of nowhere in the dark night – no phones, no taxis, no civilization. Luckily, a couple of business guys were confused by my demeanor and situation and offered a lift to my next destination. I don't condone hitch-hiking, particularly with a young child, but desperate times call for desperate measures, and I was not turning back. The next location was a few miles up country lanes; I had no clue where I was going. The lads let me use their phone before dropping me off in the middle of a huge field with no lighting. Joy. After a few minutes, someone appeared out of the darkness and escorted us to the refuge. We finally made it, but the fear was lingering for months to come. Every time I saw a blue Honda Civic, I would freeze in fear, even though I knew that Jake had sold that car. The fear was irrational but instinctive, like some sort of a survival mechanism developed through instilled fear, perpetrated by Jake.

Jake's mistake was to take my phone. Now he had no way of contacting me. Brilliant! Of course, my inbox was bombarded with long, threatening emails, but these were easier to ignore as I didn't have internet access or a computer. He started appearing at friends' houses, driving everywhere he could think of, contacting anyone I knew; no one had heard from me. I told no one that I even left, never mind where to. His threats turned brutal and he started threatening my parents in the States. Luckily, he didn't know their exact address, so I felt relatively safe, as he had never been to their house, although it did trigger me. He then got arrested for a crime that he still claims he did not commit. He received a five-year sentence and served half. He came out and got his life together, got a job and appeared to be behaving himself for years after.

After being at the refuge with my son for two months, we were moved to another refuge and stayed there for seven months. Eventually, we were offered a flat and lived there for a total of five years. I remained in contact throughout with Jake's family, since I was always close to them and they are my son's family. They have always morally supported my escape, as the environment was unbearable, and have never condoned his behaviour towards me. A person's mistakes should not reflect on another through mere association. After being out of prison, Jake had reinvented himself and was positively engaging with society, household obligations and work commitments for many years.

His family were begging me to let him see his son as he was missing him lots and had a breakdown when we left. I did eventually meet with him, not for me and him, but for my son's sake, who was at that age where he was frequently asking questions about his father. This was five years later, and I know he was a complete 'you know what', but he was still my son's biological father, who was in fact always loved by children, including his own son. I eventually let him see our son, after initially only doing so in the presence of his family. He was great with him for many months and really did seem like a reformed man who had his act together.

At first, he was brilliant. After a few months, his true colours came out and he became verbally threatening towards me. Then he decided to throw an X-box controller at my head, which I luckily dodged, as it went through the wall. This was followed by him throwing a half-full vodka bottle from across the hallway at my mirror. I had never seen so many minute pieces of glass spread throughout my front room. My friend, her two-year-old and I were in the kitchen. The mirror was between the kitchen and the front room. If the bottle had gone towards the left rather than right, we would have all been covered in glass. My son was at his friend's house at this point, but finally said, 'I don't want Dad here anymore', and I wholeheartedly agreed. However, it's Jake; it's not exactly like I can ask him to leave and he will politely walk out.

Long story short, I told him we were done and he decided that he wouldn't give me my house keys back until I signed over my car registration to him, which involved the upper part of my body bending backwards out of the window with him over top of me, preventing me from manoeuvring out of this position. At this point I thought I'd do what everyone who hasn't been in a situation like this suggests to do; call the police. The result was similar to my expectations, he took the phone off me and squashed it until the screen went black. Do people really think that a psychopath like him will wait around for me to dial 999 and talk to the police? Eventually, I got bored with this acrobatic height experiment and signed the papers. He then took back the touch-screen computer he gave to his son as a present, so he could sell it. Some father, eh? My son still remembers this. I then also found out that he took my debit card while I was not aware and used it to open loans in my name, with irreversibly damaging effects to my credit rating.

He left for the night; we left for good! I stayed with a friend for a night and then at a couple more friends' houses for two weeks, until we were accepted into yet another refuge. On the night we fled, I stayed up all night completing my final course project from scratch until the morning, when I sent it off with minutes to spare; somehow, I managed to get over 80% on it. It was lucky we left when we did, as Jake sent two men to break into my flat late in the evening, but they were eventually deterred by people's presence. Can you imagine if we hadn't left? What would they have done to me in front of my son, or worse yet, to my son? On this occasion, I reported it to the police, and they were a lot more responsive. I had a phone this time, so many threats of violence and death were presented in evidence. Jake then managed to skip the country while being in violation of probation and recall to prison. He further appeared in numerous newspapers in relation to his crimes.

Of course, no mention of stalking, domestic violence, death threats and intimidation; those things are not significant enough for the police to investigate. Even so, I have a Prohibited Steps, Residence and Specific Issue Order against him from ever removing my son from me or from anyone's care I entrust him to. He then created a Facebook account with a slang name implying that he will murder me, just to post a picture of me for the world to see with the caption, 'If you see this bitch, slice her face!' It has now been four years since we fled from him.

If the police choose to bring this up now and require me to attend court to testify against all of those crimes committed by him towards me years ago, it would re-arouse his animosity towards me and would increase the probability of him actually catching me. Whether or when the police actually decide to prosecute him for those crimes, they will make the situation really dangerous, because they waited too long to act. I also had a non-molestation order, which expired after two years of receipt, as though the threat would actually vanish at this point.

I don't understand why this wasn't dealt with at the time of his capture. 'Whether it takes me five, 10 or 15 years, I will execute you' was just one of hundreds of his threatening texts to me. He is extremely dangerous, yet cunning and charming, and I had one of the highest risk ratings in the refuge, with 23 out of 25. Yes, it was my fault that I gave him another chance, but people do that sometimes for their children's sake without adopting a crazy, possessive stalker who is out to destroy you by any means necessary. I asked him once, 'Why are you being so horrible?' and his response was, 'You took him (our son) for five years. It has only been one (year). You have four years (of abuse) to go!' Nothing that Jake has done towards us has he ever been punished for; only the monetary crimes he has committed.

After returning to the UK years later, while still on the run from the police, Jake decided to turn to burglary. This is when the police took him down in a 'man-hunt operation', as reported by various newspapers, for nearly 20 burglaries in a space of a few months, but only charged him for a fifth of these. He is currently serving his sentence for the burglaries and is about to be released in the summer of 2017, after serving only a couple of years, disregarding the violation of probation and recall, never mind domestic incidents.

There has never been any mention of any of the crimes committed towards me or my son. Yes, I found out later that he picked up my son by his throat for not eating baked beans, and blackmailed him not to tell me by threatening to do it again. My son still refuses to eat lunch if there is a mere presence of baked beans on his plate. He suffers from occasional nightmares about his dad and fears him profoundly. Our house did get flagged by the police for emergency response due to the obvious threat that Jake poses. My son has had to become very mature, very quick through our random migration acts and through witnessing other women in the refuge, bruised and terrified. However, due to resonating issues, my son then became extremely rebellious to the point of violence. This lasted for a few years. I didn't know what to do with him. Thankfully, he has now become a morally strong and respectful young boy. He will not harm anyone younger than him, even if they hit him, and categorically will not put his hands on girls. This rollercoaster ride has made us both strong people who got our life back together from scratch – again.

I finished my BSc with a 2.1 while living in the refuge and never missed a single assignment. I have since been working. My son is on a very competitive sports squad and is prospering rapidly. The fact that Jake never got punished for any of the 'domestic' crimes means that he will be released soon again, to persevere with his stalking attempts, threats and attempts to destroy what we have built up. Although I believe he would be much calmer and less likely to hunt if he wasn't triggered by the statements I made. I wish they were never made in the first place as nothing at all has been done about any of it and, in exchange, I may now have to awaken a sleeping bear whenever they do decide to give him a slap on the wrist about his past. He will at most get a two-week sentence, based on the many cases I have observed, and my son and I have the rest of our lives to be frightened of him again. Disappointingly, it does appear that the police prefer quantitative research of counting murder victim statistics over qualitative, which would involve the engagement in actual preventative measures.

19

Life after Clare

Tricia Bernal

In the early hours of 14 September 2005, there was a loud knock on the door and two police officers were standing there. 'It's Clare, she has been shot,' and I knew from their faces she was gone. 'It's Michael, isn't it?' I said.

Clare was a beauty consultant in Harvey Nichols. In the January of that year, she had dated Michael Pech, a security guard working in the store, for just three weeks. During this short time, he showed extreme signs of jealousy, possessiveness and controlling behaviour. He talked about them being together for ever and resented the time she spent with others. Clare decided to end the relationship after he refused to leave her one day and go home. He sat outside her flat for two hours and only finally left when Clare's flatmates got angry with him.

The next day Clare ended the relationship and that was when the stalking began. There was an intense period of only a few weeks when he tried everything to win Clare back, talking to work colleagues and manipulating them to feel sorry for him, that somehow Clare was responsible. She felt everyone was talking about her. He used mirrors to watch her for hours on end at work, followed her home, texted her over 50 times a day and found any excuse to speak to her. Pech was in complete denial that the relationship was over. At this point he got angry, and sent her threatening messages like, 'If I can't have you, no one else will,' and, 'I will kill myself if we are not together.' It was making Clare ill, and finally she said to him that she would have to report him if he didn't leave her alone. With that he said, 'If you report me I will kill you.'

Early evening on 13 September, 10 minutes before the store was due to close, he crept up behind Clare as she was working on the beauty counter and shot her four times in the head, before turning the gun on himself.

The first emotion after hearing the news was denial: Clare had gone on a long holiday and will be coming home one day. This lasted for almost three years, with intermittent waves of grief spilling over me when I least expected it. I see the back of a young girl – is it Clare? Mum and daughter linking arms, laughing, a marriage, a silly movie, anything can still trigger that raw emotion 10 years on… How angry I get when I hear of families falling out over petty arguments; what a waste of precious time. One day their loved one may no longer be there.

The first weeks were a blur, a frenzy of media interest and intrusion, the funeral and the inquest. I asked for the inquest to be widened to find out if more could have been done to protect Clare on the grounds of the Human Rights Article 2, the Right to Life.

All the family asked for was the truth, to question whether a similar tragedy could be prevented, an opportunity for the coroner to question whether the system had failed Clare.

The coroner was not best pleased and made comments – quote: 'I deal with 12 murders a day, why should your daughter be any different? Who will pay for this? I am overworked and underpaid… it is not my job… With no enthusiasm whatsoever, I have no other choice but to continue this inquest.'

Because of these comments, we felt the coroner could not command our confidence and we obtained a Judicial Review to try to prevent him from continuing to act in this case. We were unsuccessful and the coroner stayed in position. Our initial representations to the coroner had been about broadening the scope of his investigations. The eventual inquest was still not scoped as we had expected, but, after the Judicial Review, the coroner could be in no doubt as to the seriousness of our representations. It seemed that the inquest included a little more scrutiny that might not have been there had we not brought the Judicial Review.

We wanted the Judicial Review to prevent the existing coroner from continuing with the inquest, as, with his clear reluctance to continue, we would never get the truth. However, coroners had a greater power at this time. A Judicial Review can rarely be overruled, but between the coroner, the Metropolitan Police and their barristers, they achieved this, securing a court room at the High Court of Justice. Needless to say, we did not stand a chance, so the inquest did go ahead over the next two days. As anticipated, the inquest was a whitewash, there was no real scrutiny and the coroner concluded nothing could have been done to protect Clare, and no one could have predicted what was to happen.

Many families have gone through similar secondary trauma after being abused by the system, just when they think it cannot get any worse. If they challenge or seek answers they can pay dearly, not only financially but emotionally too (see Casey, 2011).

Since then I have learnt that Clare was a high-risk victim of stalking and all the danger signs were there but not understood.

My guilt in underestimating the danger Clare was in was, and still is, overwhelming. How could I believe anyone could harm her? She was beautiful inside as well as out, and there was not a nasty bone in her body. She was shy, gentle and sweet. She did not want to get Pech into trouble. She only wanted the stalking to stop.

The police also did not consider Clare high risk and a formal risk assessment was never carried out, in spite of the threat to kill. No one at that time really took stalking seriously.

We all thought Pech would get over it, that he didn't really mean his threat to kill her. It was only when he was arrested for breaking bail conditions and he grinned at Clare as the handcuffs were put on that Clare and I realised he was capable of carrying out his threat. This man had no fear of the consequences of his actions.

Clare never saw him again, believing the 'professionals' had dealt with it, that the stalking had stopped and that life could go back to normal. Little did we know that, after serving eight days in Belmarsh Prison for breaking bail conditions, he was let out with the same bail conditions, to return for a court hearing in August. During this time, he went back to Slovakia for four months. He was an ex-military man and retrained in arms over there, legally buying a gun and smuggling it back on a coach.

The inquest now over, where now? I felt a real injustice had been done to Clare by the system but knew it would be almost impossible to challenge it further, financially and emotionally. I began to research how stalking was dealt with in other countries, the groundbreaking work being done in Australia and America. Clearly stalking was prevalent, often seen at the point of separation and all too frequently leading to homicide.

It became crucial to raise awareness of the high-risk factor of stalking among statutory agencies and to make victims and their families take it more seriously.

I started campaigning with two other mothers who also lost their daughters, and with Tracey Morgan, a victim of stalking who has been campaigning for years. She introduced me to Frank Mullane, who had been through the judicial system and could advise me. Frank had lost his sister and nephew two years before Clare's death, and he supported me through those first difficult years.

Campaigning took the form of attending, networking and eventually speaking at conferences, and on television and radio, on domestic abuse and stalking. We wrote letters, had meetings with many influential people, became involved in the training of frontline workers, and met some wonderful people along the way. who gave us strength and encouragement.

Frank has since set up a charity called AAFDA (Advocacy after Fatal Domestic Abuse), which is a centre of excellence for reviews after domestic homicide and for specialist peer support. AAFDA offers families bereaved by homicide (particularly domestic homicide) practical and emotional support, including advocacy with a number of statutory reviews – domestic homicide reviews (DHR), mental health inquiries, Independent Police Complaints Commission (IPCC) enquiries and inquests.

It has now become law that a local community safety partnership must commission a DHR after a domestic homicide and fatal domestic abuse. I am privileged to have worked for AAFDA for about four years now. I often wish there could have been a requirement for a DHR in Clare's case.

Over the last 10 years, since Clare's death, we continue to campaign. One of the mothers is Carol Faruqui. Carol, whose daughter Rana was stabbed 16 times by her ex-boyfriend, has become a very special friend and truly knows how it feels to lose a daughter in such horrific circumstances. Like Clare, her daughter was stalked after she ended their relationship and her stalker killed her when she wouldn't go back to him.

Carol and I founded the charity Protection against Stalking (www.protectionagainststalking.org), along with some other very committed individuals. One of our first aims was to get a stalking helpline for victims of stalking. In collaboration with Suzy Lamplugh Trust and the Network for Surviving Stalking, we achieved this aim in 2010. Then, in 2012, along with fellow campaigners, we got the stalking law passed and were awarded Dod's Charity of the Year (an award scheme run by the Dods Parliamentary Companion, which publishes parliamentary briefings on the people who work in the Palace of Westminster), and The Charity Times Campaigning Charity of the Year award.

There is much work still to be done to make the lives of victims of stalking safe, and now many people are making a difference and we no longer feel we are on our own. As a charity, we know the importance of sharing information and working collaboratively.

I think about my daughter every day and miss her so much. To make something positive out of such a tragedy has certainly helped with my loss.

Clare's death has made a difference to the views of many people and stalking is seen as the terrifying crime it is. Police, the Crown Prosecution Service and other frontline workers are still being trained using Clare's case as a classic example of a high-risk victim of stalking, with all the danger signs being present but not recognised. This training, I know, has helped to save lives.

References

Casey L (2011). *Review into the Needs of Families Bereaved by Homicide.* London: Ministry of Justice. www.justice.gov.uk/downloads/news/press-releases/victims-com/review-needs-of-families-bereaved-by-homicide.pdf (accessed 23 May 2016).

20

Call it what it is – stalking!

Naomi Stanley

Stalking to the end of the road

He is a killer and it's three days since he appeared.
He is a killer and I'm on a list.
I'm on a 'High risk of Homicide' list.
I know it and I'm fighting for my life.
Three days pass and I know he is stalking me again.
I see him walking towards me, on the same side of the
same road.
As he gets closer, I shrivel in the tightness of fear.
As we become parallel, I turn my head away.
Three days later, I am running up my front steps, keys
in hand.
As always, my heart is racing with the scramble to
get indoors.
The race I must win if he is to appear again.
But, as I get my keys close to the lock, I stop.
All the fear drains and instead I am tired.
So so tired. So very very tired.
Of All This.
And right then, there is a sudden rush, a rising of pure anger.
Three days later and I know he is stalking me.
I see him on the same side of the same road.
The same road we are at the end of.
And as he gets closer, my fear rises and then it dissipates.
Yes, my fear just leaves – evaporates!
Taken by a wave of absolute rage,
I am almost pole-axed by the surge.
And he is almost beside me.
This time I turn my head towards his and I look.
I am staring into his eyes and I hold the gaze.
I hold it still and steadily and as I do so,

I am thinking my words out loud.
And they are these words.
Great biblical words!
'Come here!
Just one touch of me and mine
And I will SLAY you!'
We are parallel again but not equal.
We never have nor ever shall be.
I am staring into his eyes and they are shocked.
He has never encountered this in me before.
We are frozen in that second with everything that came before.
And then he turns his head and looks away.
He looks away and I am awash with life.
I am bathed in light as I hold tall.
Three days later and I know he cannot stalk me.
I am walking towards my mother's house on the same road.
The road we reached the end of.
My mother is dying as I take the call.
It could only have ended this way.
It is three days since he hung himself.
We are frozen in that second
Along with everything that came before.
It is three days.
And yes, he was a killer.

I wrote 'Dancing Towards Freedom', below, following the time I managed to finally leave the man who abused, stalked and tried to kill me. This poem followed some months after he cut up my bicycle with an angle grinder and then threatened to kill me with it. I began dancing again, one of several strategies in order to recover my shattered self.

Dancing towards freedom

He struck her out, that shining light
Her happiness cut down to fade
And dim until she woke in shade
All sad and broken, so much might.

Where could she go, that shattered mind
But grasp the only wisp of chance?
Breathe hard and feel another kind
The friend who motioned her to dance

And dance she does but slowly till
Her wounds be soothed and let her feel
Recovering her strength and will
The bird whose wings caught in his wheel.

Naomi's story: the real meaning of plant pots

I wanted to die because I was being stalked. I believed I would most likely be killed. It was slow, mental torture, with a constant threat of death. The stress was terrible. I would sometimes want to die just to get it over with.

I remember, as a child, feeling frightened by old black-and-white movies where a woman was being stalked by a killer but nobody believed her. Or the ones where a woman's husband was plotting to kill her and no one believed her. We didn't call it stalking then. It was just 'suspense' in scary movies.

I had a career for many years as a registered psychiatric nurse. But it did not qualify me for dealing with a stalker, and my life was wrecked by the experience. I'm still recovering. I suffer with severe post-traumatic stress disorder, and I receive treatment for this. My daughter is also receiving treatment. So, the difficult consequences and effects are ongoing.

For the record, I didn't realise that what I went through qualified as stalking for a while. I'll explain why this was.

I knew that when a stranger behaved towards someone in the way my ex was treating me, it was called stalking. But I had been in a relationship with my stalker and I had come to know him well. When we separated and I began calling the police out for help, they referred to it as 'harassment'. When I questioned why, they would tell me that, in law, harassment amounts to the same thing as stalking, and it's a lot easier to get a conviction. So, they stuck with that way of dealing with my situation – harassment, criminal damage to my possessions, those kinds of words. But these terms totally minimised my daughter's and my experiences. Harassment and criminal damage are just some of the symptoms of stalking. Having a stalker is being forced to live with the knowledge that someone is obsessed and fixated with you 24 hours a day, seven days a week. One or both of you may die as a result.

I accepted the legal terminology and felt my experience was constantly downgraded – I was just being harassed. This seemed to imply I was entitled to feel harassed, whereas what my daughter and I were living with left me reeling with anguish and fear of being killed.

When my domestic violence worker finally named it as stalking, I felt a great relief. Unfortunately, although it was acknowledged as stalking on the DASH (Domestic Abuse, Stalking and Honour-based Violence) assessment form, by the MARAC (multi-agency risk assessment conference) and the police, the strategies for dealing with my situation were implemented as if stalking was not the primary and underlying offence. Stalkers are obsessed and fixated and therefore it is unrealistic to expect any rational or co-operative response. But my stalker was dealt with as if there was an expectation that he might suddenly undergo a personality change and snap out of his abusive stalking behaviour. This was so frustrating, because I knew that none of the usual approaches used for harassment would work. We were way beyond that and into a very different realm. So, I lived with the stalking and a set of policing and judicial responses that were inadequate. I began to feel like one of those women in the old suspense movies, who is given reassurances that everything will be fine when she knows otherwise.

'Oh, so he's ignored your written request to cease contact? We will go to his house this evening and explain to him.'

'We've had a word with him and he's assured us…'

'OK, Naomi, we've decided to issue a Police Information Notice...'

'I see… Well, that means he's breached the PIN...'

'Well, we aren't sure he understood because he's had a drink, so we are going to call on him again today and issue another PIN...'

'Naomi, we are going to charge him with harassment...'

'I'm afraid the Crown Prosecution Service knocked it back again...'

'No, we don't understand why either...'

'We're going to caution him...'

'Yes, he's breached that caution but unfortunately, what he's done now is a slightly different offence...'

'We can give him another caution but for criminal damage this time.'

'Yes, I know it's frustrating but that was a caution for a different charge.'

'He followed you and turned up and abused you in the street? You have any witnesses?'

'No? Yes, I understand... Yes, he deliberately chooses a place and time where you don't have any witnesses. Yes, these guys are crafty...'

'You say he tipped 10 litres of red paint over your bike? But no witnesses...You say there are red footprints from your bike to his flat? We'll try to get someone out but I can't promise you...'

'Naomi, I've worked in the police force for 18 years and I've seen hundreds of these cases. He's genuinely remorseful. We're letting him go with a different caution...'

There was a point when I found out that the hundreds of texts, photographs, emails, incidents and hours of statement writing were all irrelevant. I would have to start all over again. Return to Go. Right from scratch.

But, why?

'Naomi, we used all your historical evidence and the statements when we issued the caution. We can't use that evidence again. A caution draws a line under everything.'

That was one of the worst moments throughout my stalking ordeal. Being informed that everything I had gone through for months, everything I had reported, all the hours of time in police stations preparing statements, could not be used because once a caution is issued, the same evidence cannot be used again. A 'line' had been drawn and yet here was no line for me. There was only a continuing hell.

Here is something I wrote at the time.

He has moved my plant pots on the fire escape, the bit of the fire escape which is beside my bedroom window. I ring the police. Again.

'What? You're calling to report your plant pots have been moved?' (in a very sarcastic voice).

I explain this is a longstanding complex situation of 'harassment'. And yes, I do want the moving of my plant pots to be logged.

You see, harassment brings out ideas of bickering between neighbours, or old lovers, feuds albeit with unreasonable behaviour, but qualitatively different to stalking. It sounded as if he thought I was reporting something petty.

'So, you want me to log that your ex-boyfriend has moved your plant pots by approximately two inches?' (incredibly sarcastic voice now).

I'm sitting on the floor, slumped against the wall as I try to persuade him to take this seriously. I'm so drained of energy that I cannot stand up any more. I'm so exhausted. I've been advised by an independent domestic violence worker to report everything he does, no matter how small. These little incidents I endure every day are significant because each occurrence shows that he is still close by, watching, waiting, following, attempting to unnerve me, trying to mentally derail me in the hope of reigning me in, wanting control, planning his next attack. I know he spends every waking moment obsessing about me, trailing me, working out ways to hurt me, wanting my attention. There is nothing he hates more than the words 'no contact'.

I live in a siege situation. I don't live anything like a normal life. In fact, my life ceased a long while back. I don't socialise any more, I don't have anything left to share with friends. My life is reduced. Stripped back to basics. It's about security and survival. It's about working out the safest route, locks, curtains, hypervigilance, staring into the distance to make out whether a shape, a gait, a flash of a certain shirt colour could be his.

I don't live any more. I only exist and that's by stealth.

I explain to the police officer on the other end of the phone line that the plant pots are right next to my bedroom window, so this means he has climbed the fire escape and come to within inches of where I was sleeping.

'Oh, so you saw him?'

'No.' I explain that I didn't see him but that I know it was him.

The policeman then says that unless I have seen him or someone else has seen him do it, I don't 'know' it was him.

I hear my voice getting higher, more desperate and I try to hold myself in check.

But I snap back.

'Look, I've told you, it's a long, complicated situation of continuing harassment which you will see if you check the records. I've given you his name. He does this to frighten me, he changes things to show he's been close to where I am. He leaves signs, markers, cable ties... There is NOBODY else who would do this! It has all the hallmarks of him – he's obsessed with me!' I'm at danger point with my energy level, which is drying up rapidly like a thin stream in a drought. I've spent two years explaining this kind of shit to people who just don't get it.

'So you want me to log that your plant pots have been moved and that you THINK it was your ex?'

I begin to cry. I'm sobbing.

He reminds me to keep a 'rational, balanced view' of things. I can tell he thinks I'm being histrionic about something minor. He is saying that maybe I just 'thought' he moved the plant pots as I'm 'imagining the worst'. In the end, I become cold with rage and frustration. I ask him to just log it and hang up.

My independent domestic violence worker, Charlie, is very excited as she tells me about the conference she attended about stalking. 'My jaw nearly dropped to the floor!' she cries. 'They said that one of the most commonly reported incidents involves plant pots! Apparently, women who love their plants will often experience their stalkers moving the pots because the stalkers target them deliberately. They know that women will recognise the plant pots have been moved immediately and they will also know who has done it!'

My doorbell rings in the middle of the night. I can barely stand as I stumble into the hallway. My daughter is already standing there, her sleepy eyes instantly forced open, fear etched across her face.

'It's him, isn't it?'

'I don't know.' We are both whispering to each other.

We both know it is him but I am stating that I don't know. This is an effort on my part to retain some kind of calm in our insane life with my stalker, as suggested to me by people wanting to help us. Despite the ongoing systematic abuse and relentless stalking, I deny the swirling cortisol; instead, I pay homage to the experts who remind me how to act in a situation they have never experienced. Somehow, I am trying to convince myself and my daughter that, against all odds, it isn't him. I want to delay the inevitable. When I hear his voice, low, demonic and threatening, over the intercom, there is an automatic response. I feel my strength being sucked away and I begin retching with fear and anxiety again. He leaves before the police arrive.

No, I did not see him. Yes, I recognised his voice. And of course, he will deny it. For three days, I can only crawl and retch. I know I am sick with anxiety, but I also know there is something else wrong. I know I am ill. I am deeply sick from three years of this, but I am also ill with something physical. I know it but I just cannot deal with anything else.

(It is to be another six months before I seek help. I am diagnosed with cancer six months after he breaches bail and just two days after the court grants me a lifelong restraining order.)

I keep telling everyone in the various services that I know that this can only end in one of three ways. He will either kill me, kill himself, or kill us both. I know this.

I rehearse the obvious possibilities so I can best prepare myself.

In the first one, he jumps out at me again, only this time he knifes me to death. During the past three years he has regularly informed me that my days are numbered. He has told me he will never let go and my experiences indicate that he is utterly fixated with me, so much so that he wants me dead rather than to know I am alive and not by his side. He has repeatedly told me he does not accept us living apart because we are meant to be together forever. He will not accept it is over. His suffocating and controlling behaviour while we were together for such a short time continues through our much longer separation. He is obsessed and fixated.

During the second imaginary scene, I am informed he has hung himself. Throughout our relationship, he would use the threat of suicide as a means to manipulate and control me. When we separated, I told him I was not responsible if he chose to kill himself. I no longer feel paralysed with anxiety that he may carry out this threat. I like his parents a lot, and I used to feel eaten up with the fear of the impact his suicide might have on them. I still dread this but I can do nothing about it.

In the third scenario, he appears in my bedroom, having broken in with a sledge hammer. He bludgeons me to death and then stabs himself fatally.

I am prepared for any of these three scenarios, in as much as any human being can be. He once arrived with a cordless angle grinder, threatening to kill me, after having just cut my bicycle up. Fortunately, on that occasion the police were already on their way, having been called by neighbours. But the trauma of being threatened with death by a machine that cuts metal lives on. So, being bludgeoned to death seems a realistic possibility. My overriding terror is how my daughter would be affected by my murder.

It is the desire to protect my daughter that motivates me to survive every day. This immense need to live helps me to keep on keeping on and it is this overriding primal instinct that will help me to fight back physically if I need to.

The year following my acquiring the restraining order was spent being treated and recovering from cancer. A positive side to being so ill was that it enabled me to shelve my fear and thoughts of him. He was, during this period, busy being monitored and attending some kind of course from probation to address his domestic abuse issues. I think that domestic violence was not the fundamental problem, although it was a symptom, in the same way that harassment was only a symptom. The problem, as evidenced by his relentless stalking, was one of obsession and fixation.

During the last three months before my stalker died, I had seen the probation link worker and informed her that he was turning up wherever I went, again. She told me that it was a difficult one; if I informed the police, he would be questioned, but there wasn't enough evidence to charge, as he would just deny it. The risk was that arresting him might cause him to escalate his behaviour, she said. Although this was in contradiction to other professional advice, I agreed. I was terrified of things escalating again.

In the few days before he hung himself in my old garage, I saw him three times. My eldest daughter reported having seen him standing on the border of his exclusion zone, looking up at my windows. I knew he was stalking me again and I also knew we had reached the end of the road.

I hope that in the future, when it becomes evident that a perpetrator of stalking behaviour presents with all the typical signs of obsession and fixation, the responses from services and professionals will be more appropriate. The strategies designed for use in harassment crimes cannot be used to elicit rational responses from individuals locked into the psychology of obsession and fixation. It does not work. You may as well offer a sticking plaster to stem a haemorrhage. In terms of conviction rates, it may be easier to convict using charges of harassment and criminal damage. But in terms of dealing with the long-term issues of stalking and the prevention of murder, physical harm and the devastating psychological toll on victims, the correct charges must be made, because only then will the serious nature of stalking receive the appropriate responses and treatment.

21

Anna's story

Anna Stanley

My Mum's experience of domestic abuse and stalking was the most harrowing few years of our lives. It is for so many women in the UK. Thankfully, my Mum's experience has meant she has devoted a lot of time to improving the services available and the police's attitude surrounding myths that often help perpetrators of violence.

I was studying for my A levels at the time. The sheer terror pervades your life, affecting every aspect of your being, and in particular your mental health. I was younger then, and naïve to the real impact Jeff had on my mother. I had no idea why she kept going back to him, even after calling the police, or after his destruction of all our plants outside our house, or threatening to kill our cat, or breaking into her garage and trashing all her belongings (to name just a few). This alienated me from her for a long time, causing distrust and, worse of all, strong resentment for what I saw as keeping me in danger for such a long time.

I realise only now how debilitating it was for her. My own recent experience of anxiety has been revelatory because it has shown me how much of your strength can feel lost because of it. I know that whatever I have felt was but a taste of the magnified experience of anxiety she felt. I know now that fear of what will happen if you leave your abuser and the post-traumatic stress you feel if you do, are why so many people stay with their abusers. I am no longer the bitter, resentful teenager with as much underlying misery as misunderstanding. I'm a young adult filled with admiration and deep sympathy for what my Mum went through.

I wasn't the direct victim of stalking, my Mum was. I have no doubt her experience was more harrowing than mine. Nevertheless, to acknowledge that does not undermine the impact it had on me. Being a teenager – with all the economical, practical and emotional dependence that entails – a feeling of being trapped permeated my life. To an extent, I was trapped.

On several occasions, I was reduced to crying frantically, looking for ways to get out in secret from my Mum. My Dad forwarded various addresses of children's refuges in Brighton. He suggested I move into one. The thought of doing so scared me and I imagined having to lie about it to my friends. I decided against.

Trying to do my best in academic study was made harder. I think, for a while, my Mum hid the degree to which she was being stalked. But, as a child, you can always sense what is going on. Especially when you see your Mum devolve into a nervous wreck. I understand only now I am older the toll it was taking on her. I can appreciate only now the daily outbursts of anger towards me were a reflection of her highly anxious state of fear. Hearing her crying was a sign of how trapped she felt.

Feeling trapped is bad enough, but seeing my Mum scared made me feel all the more unsafe. It became the norm to have the phone (and internet with it) unplugged from the wall. That way her boyfriend's continual calls would go unheard. The door buzzer would be detached, so we wouldn't hear it when he was incessantly ringing our bell at night. The windows would be scrupulously locked, so he couldn't break in. We would often see him lingering outside. Every time I left our flat, I was faced with a reminder of him: a huge red splat of paint on the road outside, which went over my Mum's bike. I overheard people commenting on it and felt embarrassed. There are many examples I could give of ways he stalked and abused my mother. I don't like talking about it much, because it makes me feel very sad.

I will move onto the psychological impact of living in a highly anxious and threatening environment. It still affects me, three years on. I have post-traumatic stress disorder. I am seeking help for it. I still wake up with my heart racing if I hear sounds at night. It manifests in other negative ways too.

Unfortunately, at the time it was happening I didn't know the symptoms of anxiety, so I didn't really understand what was happening to me. Looking back now, I realise I was in a constant state of high anxiety. I had disassociation a lot. I felt quite transcended, like I wasn't really there. I had anxiety attacks and feelings of depression and panic, a lot. Feelings of being uncared for and unsafe in your own home will do that quite quickly.

If I could encourage any considerations from my experience, it would be these:

- I think it is very important that the services available for victims of stalking continue even after the stalking has finished. Both my Mum and I suffer with post-traumatic stress disorder, which means we are still suffering the effects of what we went through

- I also think more should be done for the children and teenagers who live with a parent who is victim to stalking and abuse. I know I would have benefited from any acknowledgement or psychological support.

Stalking as allowed abuse

22

Stalking. Well, it's a word, I suppose, but one that has many connotations, so much stigma, so much pain assigned to it that it makes me not want to use it, to say it, or even to write it down. I did not feel I was being stalked. I just thought he couldn't let go. I tried to help him let go and that was a mistake. That made him think that he could continue, that I was condoning what was happening, that I was happy with him doing this – following me, phoning me.

It started on 10 April 2006 and the actual stalking ended at the end of August 2011. I do not know all the times he followed me, as I did not realise what was happening and mostly have tried to block them out, so I cannot give exact dates of these events. But they were numerous, and most evenings and weekends he would be watching me. I kept a log of the phone calls for the solicitor, but I do not know all the times that I was followed. I put it out of my mind. Often, on a night out, I would wonder if he was watching me. I had a shadow, constantly. But this was a dark, evil shadow that I could not get rid of. Sorry I cannot be more specific, but I have spent years trying to forget these events and it is difficult to remember and definitely difficult to write this down. This is probably the hardest thing I have ever had to write. It is a very difficult subject to write about and really get across the horror and impact it had on my life. I think about that Police song 'Every Breath You Take'. Yes, that was what it was like: everything that I did was being watched. I do get cross when I hear that song as I do not know how anyone can take an event that is so horrible, so destructive to a person's life, and minimise it like this in song.

So yes, whatever connotation the word 'stalking' has, I have to use it. I was being stalked.

How did I get like this? How did I get into this situation where I was one of 'those' people? I am not one of 'those' people. I am strong. I am in control. Well not anymore. That control over my life had been taken away. I had been robbed of it by someone who I thought loved me. And it is about control. It is about how much he could control what I did, where I went and who I spoke to.

So here I was in a situation that I thought I would never be in. This was new territory and my instinct was to pretend it was not happening. If I buried my head in the sand, it would go away and everything would be OK.

It doesn't appear to work like that. The more you bury your head, the more you pretend it is not happening, the worse it gets, and the worse it gets, the more difficult it is to deal with it and acknowledge it, and the more difficult it is to tell people what is happening, as I know what the comments would be. I know, as I would be saying the same thing if someone told me this story: 'If it's that bad, then why have you let it go on for so long?' So, I pretended that it wasn't happening. After all, it must be my fault as I had not done something about it sooner; I had let it happen; so, this is all my fault. This is one of the main reasons that I did nothing about it for so long.

So, I pretended. I became very good at pretending. Sometimes it is easier to pretend that everything is fine than to deal with reality. But I really wanted someone to see through the pretence, to notice what was happening. But no one did. They accepted that I was fine. In reality, I do not think that I really wanted people to know the truth. To know that I am a weak person that has allowed this to happen to them. OK, that's a bit harsh, but that's what people think about women who are being abused or stalked, that they must be weak. I am not a weak person. In fact, you have to be an incredibly strong person to get through this and come out the other side with any semblance of sanity. But that is what people who have not been stalked think. They think you're weak. Also, people don't want to deal with someone who has 'issues'. And I have 'issues'. Lots of them. So, I carry on pretending.

I should probably start at the beginning, as I have realised that I am not getting to the point. As I said, I have covered up and now uncovering everything is painful. I have locked this pain away for so long. I have been strong for so long that talking about this makes me feel vulnerable and I don't want to feel vulnerable again. I don't want to have that pain back. I am close to tears thinking about all this again. Thinking about what had happened and how I felt at that time. I know that my writing is coming across very 'matter of fact', but that is the only way I can tell you what happened without causing too much trauma to me. I don't want to relive those feelings and writing this is making me relive those feelings.

Anyway, back to the beginning. Not sure where the beginning is, though; not sure where it all started. Not really sure how I got myself into a position where I allowed myself to be abused. Gosh, there, I said it. I don't ever think I have actually said that or written it down. I have never used that evil, twisted, shameful word 'abuse' before. I suppose I never thought of myself as being abused. But I was, and I allowed that to happen. Not an intentional conscious allowing, but an 'insidious creeping into my life without me even realising' allowing. But I did allow it. I allowed it and for years did little to stop it.

Admitting these things suggests a weakness that is not valued. You get pity, but also you get, 'She must have brought it on herself;' 'She must have done something to deserve this.'

So, I cover up. Covering up is good. Covering up works for me. It's my safety blanket. It feels warm and nurturing, protective, almost. Covering up is my sanctuary, and I need a sanctuary. I suppose we all need a sanctuary; well, this is mine. It's my soul.

I have developed a whole barrage of walls, barricades and obstacles to prevent anyone from penetrating my soul. There have been the lucky few who have been allowed to get near. But, inevitably, these lucky few have let me down, abused my trust and scarred me further. I am not sure if it was inevitable, or whether I expected them to do so, and in expecting this, it became a self-fulfilling prophecy. Anyway, the outcome was that I felt hurt and even more lost. So, more walls are built and more barricades block the way and the amount of obstacles doubles. Anyone who would even try to get through that would be worth knowing, yes? Actually, no. Anyone, it seems, who is brave enough to try and get through the walls, barricades and obstacles tends to be the sort of arrogant, selfish, dominant, controlling man that is exactly the kind of man that I do not want. The kind of man who would abuse my trust and scar me further. So here is the dilemma: the walls are there to protect me, but in building them, I have made it impossible for the gentle, sensitive man to even contemplate coming close.

Writing this, though, does feel like my soul has been penetrated. I have lost my safety blanket and my sanctuary in order to tell you my story. As soon as this is over, I will repatch and rebuild those walls and barricades. I will not let anyone else know anything about me. You are the lucky few.

Have I told you that I am a romantic? Well I am. I have romanticised about love so many times. The kind of love I want. It is very fairy-tale-like and so impractical and impossible. I have set myself an impossible task. I dream of a white steed and a knight in shining armour. But, as I have said before, I tend to find that these knights in shining armour may at first appear to be rescuing me, but actually they are just taking me from one ordeal and putting me into another. You see, I am not a damsel in distress, and there are no knights in shining armour. I am just me, who pretends I am fine, and the knights are just people who also pretend. Pretend to be caring, kind and genuine. So, it is all just one big game of pretence. I suppose Shakespeare was right: 'All the world's a stage and all the men and women are simply players.'

Very few people know much about me, apart from what I let them know. So, they all think I am strong, happy, confident and in control. Very few people would even guess that anything bad had happened in my life.

I am good at covering up.

I am good at concealing my feelings. In fact, if I could live in a world where I had no feelings, I would be happy. Feelings are overrated. They cause too much pain and hurt. They allow others to manipulate those feelings. I decided that I was going to have one feeling only: I was going to be happy. No one would be able to change that status, because it was my choice to be happy. My happiness was a state of mind and therefore not a result of any situation I was in or any action by anyone. So, my happiness stays intact. Well, this is the theory. I can keep this up in public, but in private, well, that's a different story. Still, as long as no one suspects, then all is fine. This way I could be in control. Because generally I am not in control. I am usually controlled. I am used to being dominated and I allow that. I don't know why I do. It seems strange to me to even think about the fact that I might allow this to happen. Writing this down makes me realise what I have accepted, and that this is not right. It has made me rationally think about why I do this and what I really should do. I need to change the cycle. Change the habits. Change my habits.

But that is the problem: my thinking is skewed. I did not allow this to happen. I did not choose this. I just chose the wrong man. The kind of man I thought was a knight in shining armour who would rescue me from my foes, but turned out to be my biggest foe.

I got married. I got married to a man I thought I was in love with. I thought he was in love with me. I was wrong on both counts.

I married a man who had a temper, and in that temper, he became violent. I became accustomed to it. I went to casualty when I needed to after the beatings, for treatment. I was becoming somewhat of a regular.

They found it surprising how 'accident prone' I was. Never suspected anything. The broken bones, the cuts that needed stitches, the new bruises, the old bruises, the constant 'accidental' walking into doors, falling downstairs. Gosh, no one ever suspected.

Why didn't I walk away? I don't really know. I thought I could fix things, I suppose. Fix him. I couldn't. But, strangely, I never felt like a victim. I had watched programmes where women would talk about such events and act like victims. It never occurred to me that I was. Perhaps I was defending my position. Perhaps it was a case of 'Well, I'm not like them.' You see, I am a successful, intelligent woman. I am respected in my job and am usually in charge, in control. So how can a woman like that be so strong in one area of her life and so weak in another? It's a paradox and therefore cannot happen. The two states cannot exist together at the same time. So, I could not possibly be a weak person, I could not possibly be a victim. So, this was not happening and I would just deal with it as I do with all the problems I deal with at work. I am a problem-solver. Also, he was my husband. I had made a commitment. Yes, he was a violent, brutish sort of man, at times, but loving and caring at other times. I put up with the brutish times and clung onto the caring times. I made excuses and this made it difficult to do anything about it, as I had 'put up' with it for so long: how could I now change that and walk away? Anyway, I did walk away, but only after 20 years.

That was not the end, though.

I wish it was.

That was when the stalking started.

He found it difficult to let go. I suppose that is a polite way to say that he became obsessive. I never predicted that could happen.

Let me spell out the events, as it might make it easier. It started with him coming round to the house and banging on the door, demanding to speak to me. Wanting to 'sort things out'. He was drunk, so it was not really conducive to a serious conversation about the state of our marriage. He kept coming, and in the end, I had to call the police.

Then I got the phone calls. I counted them once: there were 25 calls in one day. All times of the day and night. This was happening most days. It was pointless changing my number, as he would need to contact me if anything happened to our son when he had him. I must point out at this point that he had never been violent to our son. Just to me, and, I subsequently found out, his mother.

The endless calls at night were difficult. It resulted in my sleep being interrupted. I was sleep deprived, and that meant that it was difficult to function, to stay rational, to stay calm.

I spoke to the telephone company, who told me that the only thing they could do was block his number completely. They were kind and sympathetic, but blocking his number was not the answer. I spoke to the solicitor, who sent him a letter informing him that he could not call me or come round to the house, unless it was to do with our son.

This helped for a while, but only a short while. Less than two weeks, in fact. Then it all started again. But this time he was not calling me, he was texting me.

I did not realise at this point that he had been following me as well. Following me everywhere I went. There were apparently a number of occasions, but it was only afterwards that I realised that I had been stalked, when I received a text from him asking me if I had had a nice night out to such-and-such a place, or that I was looking nice in that blue dress. How did he know what I was wearing? Where had he been to have seen me? I did not notice him; where was he?

These texts did send a chill down my spine. Made me cold and numb, but not with fear at first, that came later, just with confusion and disbelief. I suppose denial is a great comfort, but it does not really help. The texts continued: 'Whose car was parked outside your house?' Now, I realised, he was watching my house. 'That car was there all night, you're a whore.' They got worse. More graphic. More insulting. 'I walked around your house, the spare bedroom curtains were not closed, he was in your bed.'

I will not insult you by recounting how offensive his texts became. I ignored them. But I did sometimes reply, which was a mistake, as then he realised he was getting to me. I was trying to justify myself. I did not need to. But I felt I had to.

I had started dating. But this new man lived in a different city. It was at least an hour's drive to his house. I went frequently, and he came to mine frequently. But when he came to mine, I asked him to park five minutes away, and I would pick him up and bring him to my house. I thought it would be easier and less visible if his car wasn't in my drive. I had allowed my ex-husband to manipulate the situation, and it made the new relationship very difficult. Very odd.

I find it difficult to write about this. I am angry that I resorted to such measures, angry that I felt I had to resort to such measures. I have eliminated my feelings from this and cannot now see why I allowed him to make me change the way I lived.

It was seeing him drive past my new partner's house that brought home to me what he was actually doing, and that this was stalking. He followed me on holiday and was in the room next to mine in the same hotel. I found out that he basically followed me everywhere I went. I was being stalked.

He would just say that he was looking out for me, and making sure I was okay. Sometimes he would say that he had a right, as we had been married for 20 years, and I was his. I belonged to him. No man was going to have his wife. We were not even married any more, and had been divorced for two years, yet, according to him, I was still his wife and I still belonged to him.

Anyway, I told my friends what was happening. Their comments were very strange. Not what I was expecting. Not supportive at all. There was a lot of joking and humour about the whole thing. As though they were brushing it off because they did not want to think about it, or to think that he could do this. They were obviously very uncomfortable with the whole thing. The best comment I remember was, 'Oh, so you're a celebrity now that you have your own personal stalker.' Mostly people did not believe me. They did not believe that I was being stalked. They just looked at me with an odd look.

I realised that people had not taken me seriously when later I would get comments such as 'You two were so good together, you should get back together,' or 'He's the right man for you, he treats you so well.' No one believed me. These were the friends I had had for years. In fact, some were childhood friends and had known me most of my life. So, I did not mention it again. I did not talk about it. I just kept it all to myself. Pretending again. I mean, if you cannot talk about this to your oldest friends, then who can you talk to? If your friends don't believe you, then no one will. This came as a bit of a shock. Not only was I being stalked, but no one believed me, and no one wanted to talk about it. So, this made me want to cover up even more. To put up even more barriers.

That made me realise that stalking is not a serious issue, not a bad thing, and quite funny, in fact, to some people. In fact, to most people I came into contact with. It was only serious if someone was killed. He had not killed me, so it was not serious, it was just a joke. It only seemed serious to those who had a similar experience. I have only just met people with a similar experience; this is four years after it all stopped.

So, there I was dating a guy, making him jump over hoops to prevent my ex-husband finding out. How bizarre that sounds. I was in his house, an hour from my house by car. I was looking out of the window, and I suddenly froze. 'What's wrong?' he said. I had just seen my ex-husband's car drive past. 'No, it can't be, there are lots of cars like that, it won't have been.' It was. He had followed me over the motorway and driven to my new partner's house. I felt as if someone had walked over my grave.

I was on edge all night. I could not settle. Could not enjoy the evening. I was in turmoil. My biggest fear was what would happen when I got back home.

I again went to the solicitor who had arranged for an injunction to stop him coming within 100 yards of my house. This did not stop him. This did not mean that he could not follow me to wherever I was going. Just that he had to be 100 yards from my house, that was all. I was followed everywhere. This was my life for five years. It was difficult doing anything. I could do nothing without him knowing about it. Nothing was secret, nothing was private. He knew everything. He followed me everywhere, even when I went on holiday. He was not violent now, made no threats, so there was nothing that could be done legally.

His texts were vile, but interspersed with declarations of undying love. How can someone who says they love you make you feel so unsafe and on edge all the time? I was on edge all the time. Found it difficult to relax. If I was talking to a man, I would always have the thought in the back of my head that he was watching, and so my conversations were short and the personal space between us was intentionally large.

I had the chance to move to a completely different part of the country. It would be impossible for him to move. He was tied to his job. I moved 250 miles away. I moved into my house and soon began to realise just what stress I had been under, as it lifted. He could not just park up around the corner and watch my every move; he could not just follow me any more. Then the phone calls started. Now that our son was at university, my ex-husband did not need to call me, so I just blocked his number. I feel lighter, less burdened. But I had to move away from my family, my friends and my job in order to feel lighter and less burdened. When my friends ask me why I moved, I tell them it was because I was being stalked. They start to look uncomfortable, and start to brush it off with a joke. It is all just a joke to those who have not encountered this.

So, the resolution was for me to move. To leave everything and move. But I am genuinely happy now. Genuinely relaxed and contented with life. I have tried to change the cycle. But, unfortunately, you cannot really know someone until it is usually too late. I am more choosey and less accepting of certain behaviours, more confident a person and happy to walk away from a relationship when it is not working. This is normal. This is what normal should be like. I still worry that I will end up in that situation again. But, these days, those worries are fewer, and some days I don't even think about it.

As I have already said, writing this has made me feel vulnerable. It has brought back the pain that I thought I had left behind. Writing this has opened up Pandora's Box. But, instead of unleashing all the evils in the world, it has unleased all the pain and suffering in me. It has been therapeutic, though, as putting all this down in black and white has made me realise what I had actually accepted and what I had endured for years. It makes quite difficult reading. Obviously, I have glossed over a number of things and minimised some events, as writing down the full details of all the events would not be therapeutic. The fact is that I found writing this glossed-over version hard enough. I never thought I would be a person that would have accepted this. The therapeutic part of it is simply that, even though I had accepted all this, I have also coped with it; I have developed very good coping and problem-solving strategies and come out the other end stronger and more resilient. I have seen my strength echoed throughout this process. So yes, it turns out that I am that strong person I pretend to be, and it is not pretence after all. I have also realised that, as with Pandora's Box, what is left behind is hope. Writing this down has shown me that I have hope for the present and the future.

So, there you have my story. It's probably not that bad in comparison with some stories. Probably worse than others. But it is my story and I am now happy to share it. There is a life out there for me, one without abuse and without being controlled.

CONCLUSIONS AND REFLECTIONS

Concluding summary

23

Alec Grant

This chapter summarises and develops the main points emerging from the contributions of the three main contributor groups to the book: academic and research psychologists, third-sector workers, and victims of stalking and their relatives, friends and partners. An emerging consensus should be apparent from these contributions – about the nature of stalking, the shortcomings in victim support provision and structures, the characteristics of stalkers, and the lived experiences of victims of stalking. This consensus is fully supported and underscored by the content of the chapters in the 'Police and the Courts' section. Confirming, and giving testimony to the overall picture emerging in the book, this section needs no summary.

In relation to the psychology of stalking, in my introduction I discuss a key, seriously under-acknowledged issue: the relationship between stalking and behaviour driven by psychopathic and narcissistic tendencies. I am not claiming that *all* stalkers, by definition, are narcissistic psychopaths; more, that I and my co-editors think that these characteristics are frequently present in stalking behaviour, without this being sufficiently and adequately recognised and dealt with by the judiciary, the police, the professions and the public at large. This, we believe, has grave consequences for the victims of stalking.

Following this, I summarise the urgent need for public, professional and public training, the inadequacies in the support services currently available for victims, and stalker and victim characteristics emerging from the first-person contributions to the book.

What can we learn from the psychology of stalking?

Stalking perpetrators

As Short and Barnes point out in chapter 1, stranger stalking, of the sort experienced by Peter James, is less likely to result in acted-out aggression, although such perpetrators may have mood problems and be delusional. Ex-partner stalkers, the subject of most of the victim stories in this book, show some different characteristics. This group is more inclined to act out aggression. They are also more likely to exhibit personality disorders, patterns of poor relationships with previous partners, drug and alcohol problems, envy, jealousy, anger, poor personal boundaries and heightened sensitivity to rejection. They are more inclined to experience ambivalence about the ending of the relationship with the victim, to believe that the relationship will or should resume, and to engage in revenge taking, which may turn into domestic violence. Stalking, for this group of perpetrators, may be a way for them to improve their feelings of low self-worth.

Psychopathic behaviour may also be prevalent in this group. Psychopaths are narcissistic, have superficial charm, are manipulative and prone to boredom, and lie constantly. They are also callous and strategically manipulative in order to get the outcome they desire. Lacking remorse or guilt, psychopaths are vindictive, emotionally shallow, unempathic and fail to accept responsibility for their actions (Cleckey, 1982; Dinwiddy, 2015; Hare, 1999).

Narcissism

It is worth spending some time considering the nature of narcissism in the context of psychopathy, since this appears to be a frequent factor in intimate partner and child abuse, as well as in abuse acted out in workplaces (Wylonis & Sadoff, 2008).

What is it like to be inside the mind of a narcissist? Whitaker (2017) describes this well. They have a deeply entrenched sense of entitlement and specialness, and are egotistical, with a firmly held sense of their own importance and superiority. They believe they deserve privileged treatment, which they expect by right from those around them. Having little or no empathy for other people, they usually regard others as objects to be manipulated, not people with their own thoughts, feelings and needs. As objects, other people are there to supply the narcissistic psychopath's need for special treatment. They act out a 'false self' – in the case of stalking, often as the victim who deserves pity and sympathy.

It should be stressed, at this point, that psychopathy and narcissism are characteristics of identity that are on a continuum, rather than discontinuous. To put it plainly, it is more appropriate and accurate to regard the behaviour and interior life of people in general – men and women – as more or less psychopathic and narcissistic rather than assuming that someone can be either psychopathic and narcissistic or not.

The response of professionals

Unfortunately, as stressed in the introduction, professionals from health and social care, and from the legal and police services, are often likely to be 'taken in' by the 'false-self' charm and strategic manipulation of many stalkers. It is doubly unfortunate that there also exists a tendency among many health and mental health professionals in practice and education to avoid acknowledging the extent to which the behaviour of stalkers is driven by psychopathic tendencies. This tendency is so firmly embedded in the professional consciousness that it is maintained even when confronted with very high-profile, internationally famous people whose substantial threats to the world are clearly driven by narcissism and psychopathy (Goodman & Grant, 2017).

This tendency prevails because of two related assumptions. First, the influence of the humanistic curricula in health and mental health training places 'labelling' in conflict with an assumption that healthcare workers need to trust and accept people unconditionally. The second assumption is that bad behaviour should not be pathologised, because doing so contributes to the public fear of people with mental health problems generally, and feeds into the stigma those people experience. However, while the need not to label on the basis of these assumptions seems generally reasonable, in the specific context of stalking, it can result in non-action and collusion with perpetrators, and the disregarding and trivialisation of victim stories.

Stalking victims

Such disregard and trivialisation is unfortunate, in the light of the descriptions in this book of the lived experience pattern of stalking victims. Supporting the points made in the introduction about the neglect for victims' concerns, Short and Barnes' chapter also describes the way that stalking victims are blamed for having brought their problems on themselves. They outline victims' responses: most commonly fear, together with understandable paranoia, distrust of others, feelings of helplessness and loss of control. Common mental health difficulties include depression and the post-traumatic stress disorder symptoms of flashbacks, avoidance, re-living trauma, sleep disturbance and startle response. Vulnerability to infection and longer-term physical health problems are also part of the picture. At existential and relational levels, if damaged reputation, broken family and interpersonal relationships, loss of work and social isolation are added to the mix, it is not surprising that victims frequently contemplate suicide.

What can we learn from third-sector experts?

In chapter 3, Wrixon describes the thousands of calls and emails to the national stalking helpline each year, where demand for the service exceeds the supply of available response resources. According to Wrixon, stalking victims who contact the service are mostly women, and perpetrators mostly men – frequently ex-partners. That said, in chapter 2, Rachel Griffin asserts that 50% of those contacting the national stalking helpline are stalked by someone other than an ex-intimate partner: these include acquaintances, neighbours, colleagues and ex-colleagues, family members, and strangers.

Wrixon asserts that, notwithstanding small pockets of good practice, the police and the judiciary are not up to speed with recent policy changes, which feeds into the picture of victims not being taken sufficiently seriously. Griffin argues that stalking is seriously misunderstood: that many who report cyberstalking to the police feel their response is unhelpful; that there exists a lack of mandatory training for police officers, despite the introduction of the stalking law in November 2012.

What training does exist for police officers is inadequate. All of this may, arguably, contribute to the attitudinal and cultural lag around the crime, reinforcing the point made in the introduction about the absence of the socially validated reality narratives and practices needed to respond appropriately and sensitively to stalking victims. This is reflected in Wrixon's description of the dearth of specialist support services, especially at a local level. The existence of Veritas-Justice in Sussex, and similar charities in other parts of the UK, does not represent a uniform provision of such services throughout the country. The call for more specialist stalking organisations to work in partnership with other organisations in the voluntary and wider public sectors is also taken up by Griffin in relation to the work of Suzy Lamplugh Trust.

It's something of a paradox that stalking is a high-incidence, high-impact crime, and yet it is minimised. Griffin suggests that this may be because the individual incidents that contribute to a pattern of stalking – for example, sending emails or text messages – are in and of themselves often legal acts. It is appalling that it is still often the case that stalking is only taken seriously when it is seen to have led to physical violence. Moreover, Griffin asserts that relatively few police and crime commissioners commissioned stalking-specific services in the three years from early 2013 to early 2016. This lack of access to refuge/ safe housing provision, the invisibility of stalking in risk management structures, and stalking falling outside the remit of independent domestic violence advocacy services means that third-sector services are heavily over-subscribed and compromised with regard to what they can provide.

What can we learn from experts by lived experience and their loved ones?

The system that should help is largely unsupportive

The victim and victim-related contributions to this book are testimony to the fact that small pockets of good practice are apparent in some statutory and legal services and professions, and from some professionals. It seems clear from the stories that sometimes police, social work and solicitor responses are helpful and sensitive to victims' needs. This happens when these professionals take victim reports seriously, and when they understand and act on the possible outcomes of escalating stalker behaviour.

However, this is not a consistent picture. At a general level, victims report that they are often treated like nuisances, disbelieved, and labelled as troublesome and manipulative. They become embroiled in ineffective, bureaucratic, vicious circles that take them nowhere. Services that should result in early preventative interventions generally don't live up to this. Service responses seem generally slow, and the advice from services and professionals is seen to lack credibility because it betrays poor knowledge of the lived experience of stalking. More worryingly, services are described as covering their backs and closing ranks to protect themselves from public criticism.

With specific regard to the police, victim stories in this book paint a picture of frequently unsympathetic, brusque and dismissive police officers, of police officers not believing victim accounts and accusing victims of histrionics and exaggeration. Police officers are described as sometimes trivialising victims' reported experiences, and reframing what they are going through as simply 'harassment'. More generally, police response and liaison work is often seen also to be slow and unresponsive to victims' requests for help, even when they report intimidation, domestic violence, or death threats.

In the UK, at any rate, this picture of a lack of stalking risk recognition may be partly explained by the current underfunding of police forces, which in turn leads to revised priorities and redefinitions of what are regarded as valid crimes. However, it may also suggest broader, more entrenched, cultural problems, despite the progress in stalking law and policy in recent years. This points to an enduring failure to recognise stalking as a socially validated reality, an issue discussed in the introduction.

The dangerous underestimation of the seriousness of stalking is illustrated in accounts that describe police attitudes towards stalkers. Police officers are described as believing stalkers' reassurances that they will behave themselves. The idea that stalkers just need a 'slap on the wrist', as if their behaviour were on the same level as naughty children stealing apples, should cause concern.

The Crown Prosecution Service (CPS) and the Crown and Family Court processes are described as, at worst, farcical, punitive and weighted in favour of perpetrators, with the CPS sometimes being unwilling to bring charges. Coroner and judicial responses can constitute a 'whitewash', with court systems described in Dickensian terms – startlingly like the interminable and ineffective Chancery process described in Dickens' novel *Bleak House*. Court systems seem often to be oblivious to domestic abuse and violence, with judges euphemistically mis-labelling serious, violent domestic stalking as feuding between 'warring parents'. Solicitors' injunctions to prevent stalkers being in the proximity of victims, or to take down defamatory websites, can be ineffective.

In the absence of visible damage to people or property, the 'system' simply doesn't seem to work for victims. Given the inadequacy and patchiness of training and education, at the very least it seems that more of this is necessary across the board. This should include more and continual training for police officers, given their 'frontline' status, and for mental/health and social care practitioners, who, in our experience and given our comments above, are not adequately prepared to deal with stalking in sufficiently hard-headed, victim-supporting ways.

Such training and education, which in our view should include this book as a primary reference, will provide clear information for the public, public and third-sector professionals and workers, and legal and judiciary services and personnel about the characteristics of stalkers and victims.

Stalker characteristics

Stalkers can be, and are, extremely abusive to victims, the families and friends of victims, and often to their own children. At worst, stalkers can be, and are, killers of victims. They sometimes take their own lives, manipulatively threaten to commit suicide, or make suicide gestures and attempts. The fact that they often tell victims that they could or will kill them functions to increase their levels of control over them.

Stalkers are obsessed with and fixated on the object of their stalking intent and behaviour. With a past history of poor relationships, many don't seem to be able to make it in life in acceptable ways. So, chameleon-like, they lie to victims about who they are in ways that will eventually erode partner trust in them, in order to inveigle themselves into relationships with them.

A typical form of manipulative abuse perpetrated by partner and ex-partner stalkers, sometimes commencing before the breakdown of their relationship with the victim and the start of stalking, is 'gaslighting' (Stern, 2007). This refers to perpetrators manipulating situations repeatedly to trick their victims into distrusting their own memories, perceptions and, sometimes, sanity. The term comes from the 1940s stage play and film *Gaslight*, which portrays a husband who tries to convince his wife and others that she is insane. He does this by manipulating small elements of their environment, then insisting that she is mistaken, remembering things incorrectly, or delusional when she points these out.

Gaslighting is a cruel and insidious form of abuse aimed at control, which is often very difficult to prove. It makes victims question the instincts they have relied on throughout life, so they feel increasingly unsure of anything, and come to believe whatever their abusers tell them, regardless of their own experience of the situation. A typical example among many is when a perpetrator repeatedly accuses a victim of forgetting things that they claim to have told the victim, when in fact they have never told them about these things in the first place. The perpetrator's goal is to make the victim question their own grasp on reality, reducing their self-confidence, and thus their ability to resist their abuser.

Some of the controlling gaslighting strategies that perpetrators may use include refusing to listen to victims' sense of reality; challenging victims' memories of events, as in the example described above; denying or pretending to forget things that have really occurred, or promises they have made; trivialising victims' thoughts and needs, to the extent that victims come to believe that these thoughts and needs aren't really important, and openly mocking victims' perceptions.

The use of gaslighting anticipates perpetrator attitudes that manifest in ex-partner stalking, where perpetrators seem to regard victims as their own property, to be dealt with as they like, imagining themselves to be the centre of their victims' universe. They are possessive of them, and often subject them to close and intrusive monitoring and surveillance. Pathologically jealous, they don't accept the need to end relationships in normal ways. Their low tolerance for rejection makes them vengeful, and they take revenge by 'upping the ante', by escalating stalking, doing their damnedest to ruin their victim's life, and sometimes enlisting the help of their friends in this. In this context, some stalkers engage in cyber defamation of victims by (as described in some of the accounts here) setting up false Facebook profiles in their victim's names and posting character-damaging material.

Stalkers are highly manipulative and plausible. They are charming and manipulate bystanders, the judiciary, the police, health and social care professionals and victims' families. Their level of manipulation is strategic, extending even to them going on witness training courses so that they can influence the outcomes of hearings, as one contributor to this book describes.

It is, therefore, an understatement to say that stalkers are generally not to be trusted.

Victim characteristics

In concluding this chapter, I believe it is important to stress that the victims of stalking are victims of prolonged terror. They report that they feel like they are under siege. The constant threat of violence, or of their own death even, results in continual anxiety, hypervigilance, and a narrow focus on survival. Life becomes mere existence. Terroristic perpetrator tactics include posting pictures of victims and their homes to them, and moving plants outside victims' homes, because the perpetrator knows they will notice.

Stalking as terrorism can result in different forms of victim death and loss: physical death, by murder or suicide; social death, by victims losing their jobs, homes, finances, social status and respect, friends and family, physical and mental health, existential security, and hope.

Moreover, in terroristic siege situations, victims lose privacy, formal and informal support structures, and the confidence to confront perpetrators through fear of their reprisals. Even their close friends can trivialise their experiences, not want to talk about them, or romanticise them, as in, 'I wish I had my own personal stalker.'

The absence of public narratives to adequately explain their lived experience can result in victims doubting themselves and those experiences. Some are not even aware that they're the victim of stalking, even after the stalking experience has ended.

The children of victims are often vulnerable, develop post-traumatic stress symptoms, and need safe houses and places of refuge, which aren't always available. Victims' friends and relatives other than their children can also be stalked, or can experience secondary trauma. Some of these friends and relatives relocate to other countries, and the friends of murdered victims can be left with survivor guilt.

This dysfunctional world can become a living hell for victims, where, to quote one contributor, they can become 'signposted out of existence'.

References

Cleckey H (1982). *The Mask of Sanity*. St Louis, MO: CV Mosby.

Dinwiddy SH (2015). Psychopathy and sociopathy: the history of a concept. *Psychiatric Annals 45*(4): 169–174.

Goodman B, Grant A (2017). The case of the Trump regime: the need for resistance in international nurse education. *Nurse Education Today 52*: 53–56.

Hare RD (1999). *Without Conscience: the disturbing world of the psychopaths among us*. New York, NY: Guilford Press.

Stern R (2007). *The Gaslight Effect: how to spot and survive the hidden manipulation others use to control your life*. New York, NY: Morgan Road Books.

Whitaker P (2017). I am special and I am worthless: inside the mind of a narcissist. *New Statesman* 17–23 February: 55.

Wylonis L, Sadoff R (2008). The psychopath in the workplace: disability, direct threat and the ADA. In: Felthous A, Saß H (eds). *The International Handbook of Psychopathic Disorders and the Law: laws and policies, volume II*. Chichester: John Wiley & Sons (pp125–135).

24

A reflection on some of our editorial conversations

Helen Leigh-Phippard

During the course of our many editorial meetings for this book, it became clear that this was a very different project from the other books in the series, for a variety of reasons. About halfway through the editorial process, we decided that, rather than simply acknowledging those differences among ourselves as editors, we ought to be reporting them somewhere in the book. This is an attempt to do just that. It is not a verbatim record of our conversations, but a brief reflection on the many and various issues with which we grappled as the book project developed.

From our very first editorial meeting, we knew that, because of the very particular character of stalking, the book would have to include a very wide range of stories. With the possible exception of *Our Encounters with Self-Harm*, the other *Our Encounters* books don't foreground 'professional' stories, but we all had a sense that this book would not feel complete without stories from professionals and third-sector workers. It was also inevitable that the book would have to include stories from family members and/or friends of people who had been murdered by their stalkers.

It is difficult to express why, precisely, it was so important to include these stories. One reason, is that we want professionals, academics, journalists and survivors to read this book. We want the book to have as wide an audience as possible, and to achieve that, we knew we needed to tell the story from as many perspectives as possible.

But equally important is that we wanted to tell an honest story of what it means to be stalked, to know someone who's being stalked, to be the parent, sibling, child, partner, friend of someone who has been stalked; what it means to try to help, whether professionally or as a volunteer, someone who is being stalked, and sometimes to be unable to help someone in that position.

We also had to grapple with whether or not to include the stories of stalkers; how to include stories from men, so we didn't end up with a book that simply reinforced stereotypes (women = victims, men = perpetrators or police officers); whether we should address the question of celebrity stalking; how much attention we should give to cyberstalking. All of these were fundamentally important questions, but the answers weren't entirely clear until the book began to take shape, because so much depended on the contributions we could get.

Recruiting contributors really was the thorniest issue, from the start. We would have liked to have a strong international dimension to the book, but it proved very difficult to recruit contributions from outside the UK, and the usual obvious channels for making these appeals (the internet and social media) were self-evidently difficult places to raise the issue of stalking and expect to successfully recruit writers in a relatively short time. So, we had to rely very much on personal contact and Sam and Claudia's networks. Fortunately, these networks are good, so the survivor stories here are not all British, although they are not as international as we would have wished.

As time went on, it was clear that it was a big ask to expect survivors of stalking to write full accounts of their stalking experiences. We were asking contributors to relive their personal traumas and, while we did succeed in soliciting some very detailed contributions, the book was beginning to look unbalanced, with professional contributions outweighing survivor stories. So we had an editorial meeting to discuss how we might address this.

We concluded that the solution might be to ask survivors and family members for a short contribution. Instead of asking for a full narrative of their stalking experience, perhaps we could ask for a short piece of prose, a poem, or 'a letter' to, for example, the police, an MP, their stalker, a support service they had used, anyone who they might want to write to. We thought that this kind of writing might be cathartic, rather than traumatic, and it might be much easier to solicit these kinds of contributions.

We were right. Sam and Claudia wrote to a number of people who had previously turned down invitations to contribute, and to some new contacts, asking if they would be willing to provide something shorter like this, and had a number of positive responses. What's more, when these pieces started coming in, we realised that their diversity and quality added enormously to the book.

One final reflection is that, when it comes to stalking, many survivors will never feel entirely safe, and this added a whole additional layer of complexity to the editorial process. There were questions of safety, anonymity and disclosure. As editors, it was our responsibility to ensure that the contributors of survivor stories in particular stayed both well and safe while writing their stories, and that what they wrote didn't contain information that might identify them, or disclose any information they might regret at a later date.

Some of these issues had arisen in the other books in the *Our Encounters* series, but there were important differences. For example, some of our writers might still have active stalkers or might find currently inactive stalkers became active again; or they might find themselves embroiled in criminal cases with their stalkers at some future point in time.

These questions of safety necessarily slowed down the whole editorial process. One prospective author had to withdraw because of concerns about future legal action. In other cases, authors wanted to be named and we, as editors, had to have lengthy discussions among ourselves and with the authors concerned about the wisdom of this, given their circumstances.

In summary, it was no easy task putting together a book that would give an honest picture of the experience of both being stalked and living with or working with someone who is being stalked, without being voyeuristic and in a way that would provide valuable learning and, hopefully, keep survivors well and safe. It has been a very valuable and deeply humbling learning experience.

June, 2017

Practical advice and contacts

Practical advice for victims

- Report stalking incidents to the police.

- Keep a diary of all incidents and how they make you feel.

- Keep text messages, emails, objects and screenshots for evidence. **DO NOT GET RID OF** your phone or devices, as this may lose relevant evidence.

- Consider carrying a personal alarm.

- Vary your daily routine and take different routes to and from work.

- Know where the nearest safe location is – for instance, a police station. If there isn't one nearby, you could use a 24-hour supermarket with security guards and CCTV cameras.

- Talk to the police about using CCTV and/or installing a panic button at your home.

- Ensure all your doors and windows are locked before you leave home or go to sleep.

- Don't engage with your stalker in any way.

- Talk to neighbours, colleagues and/or your line manager about the harassment, if you feel comfortable doing so. They may be able to help by collecting further evidence on your behalf or by putting protective measures in place.

Practical advice for all professionals

Stalking is a pattern of repeated and persistent behaviour that is intrusive and engenders fear. One person becomes fixated or obsessed with another and the attention is unwanted.

Stalking behaviour can be seen as unwanted communications, including telephone calls, messages and intrusions such as waiting for, spying on, approaching and entering a person's home. Additionally, the stalker may make complaints to legitimate bodies or use the internet and social media to continue their campaign. Occasionally, they will make threats, damage property or use violence, but even if there is no threat, **stalking is still a crime.**

If you support victims

- Believe them and take them seriously.

- Ensure you listen carefully and record everything you are told.

- Record the extent of the victim's perception of risk of harm.

- Take seriously disclosures of threats to kill.

- If the stalker and victim have previously been in a relationship, ask the victim to complete a DASH (Domestic Abuse, Stalking and Honour-Based Violence risk assessment (www.dashriskchecklist.co.uk/dash/) and the 11 stalking and harassment screening questions (www.dashriskchecklist.co.uk/stalking/).

- If there is no history of a relationship, ask the victim to complete the 11 risk screening questions.

- Ask if there is a restraining order.

- Ensure the victim keeps a diary of all stalking incidents and keeps all messages, gifts etc.

- Seek specialist advice from your local police force. Each force has a single point of contract or other specialist unit, such as a public protection department.

- Refer the victim to relevant local and national support/campaign organisations.

Contacts

Action Scotland Against Stalking
Web: www.scotlandagainststalking.com

Crown Prosecution Service
Web: www.cps.gov.uk
CPS public enquiries
Tel: 020 3357 0899
Email: enquiries@cps.gsi.gov.uk

National Stalking Clinic
Web: www.beh-mht.nhs.uk/mental-health-service/mh-services/
national-stalking-clinic.htm
Tel: 020 8702 6104

National Stalking Helpline
Web: www.stalkinghelpline.org
Tel: 0808 802 0300
Email: advice@stalkinghelpline.org

Network for Surviving Stalking
Web: www.scaredofsomeone.org
Email: scaredofsomeone@gmail.com

Paladin Service (National Stalking Advocacy Service)
Web: www.paladinservice.co.uk
Tel: 020 7840 8960
Email: info@paladinservice.co.uk

Police (England, Wales, Northern Ireland and Scotland)
Web: www.police/contact
Tel: 999 for emergency calls or 101 for non-emergencies

Protection Against Stalking
Web: www.protectionagainststalking.org
Email: info@protectionagainststalking.org

Stalking Risk Profile
This website is for anyone working with victims or perpetrators
of stalking
Web: www.stalkingriskprofile.com

Veritas Justice CIC (Training, Advocacy and Advice)
Web: www.veritas-justice.co.uk
Tel: 07736149940 or 07736149960
Email: info@veritas-justice.co.uk

Victim Support
Web: www.victimsupport.org.uk
Tel: 0808 168 9111
Email: supportlineemail@victimsupport.org.uk

Support for Victims – USA
Web: www.victimsofcrime.org
Web: www.safehorizon.org

Support for Victims – Australia
Web: www.stalkingresources.org.au/is-stalking-a-crime
Web: www.angelhands.org.au/resources/stalking-and-cyber-stalking